MIGHTY MORPHIN POWER RANGERS

HIGGINS · PRASETYA · LAM · HERMS
ORLANDO · HOWELL · LAWSON · LAFUENTE

VOLUME THREE

BOOM! STUDIOS

SPECIAL THANKS TO
BRIAN CASENTINI, MELISSA FLORES, EDGAR PASTEN, PAUL STRICKLAND, MARCY GEORGE, JASON BISCHOFF AND EVERYONE AT **SABAN BRANDS**.

Ross Richie CEO & Founder
Matt Gagnon Editor-In-Chief
Filip Sablik President of Publishing & Marketing
Stephen Christy President of Development
Lance Kreiter VP of Licensing & Merchandising
Phil Barbaro VP of Finance
Arune Singh VP of Marketing
Bryce Carlson Managing Editor
Mel Caylo Marketing Manager
Scott Newman Production Design Manager
Kate Henning Operations Manager

Sierra Hahn Senior Editor
Dafna Pleban Editor, Talent Development
Shannon Watters Editor
Eric Harburn Editor
Whitney Leopard Editor
Jasmine Amiri Editor
Chris Rosa Associate Editor
Alex Galer Assisociate Editor
Cameron Chittock Associate Editor
Matthew Levine Assistant Editor
Sophie Philips-Roberts Assistant Editor

Kelsey Dieterich Designer
Jillian Crab Production Designer
Michelle Ankley Production Designer
Grace Park Production Design Assistant
Elizabeth Loughridge Accounting Coordinator
Stephanie Hocutt Social Media Coordinator
José Meza Event Coordinator
James Arriola Mailroom Assistant
Holly Aitchison Operations Assistant
Megan Christopher Operations Assistant
Amber Parker Administrative Assistant

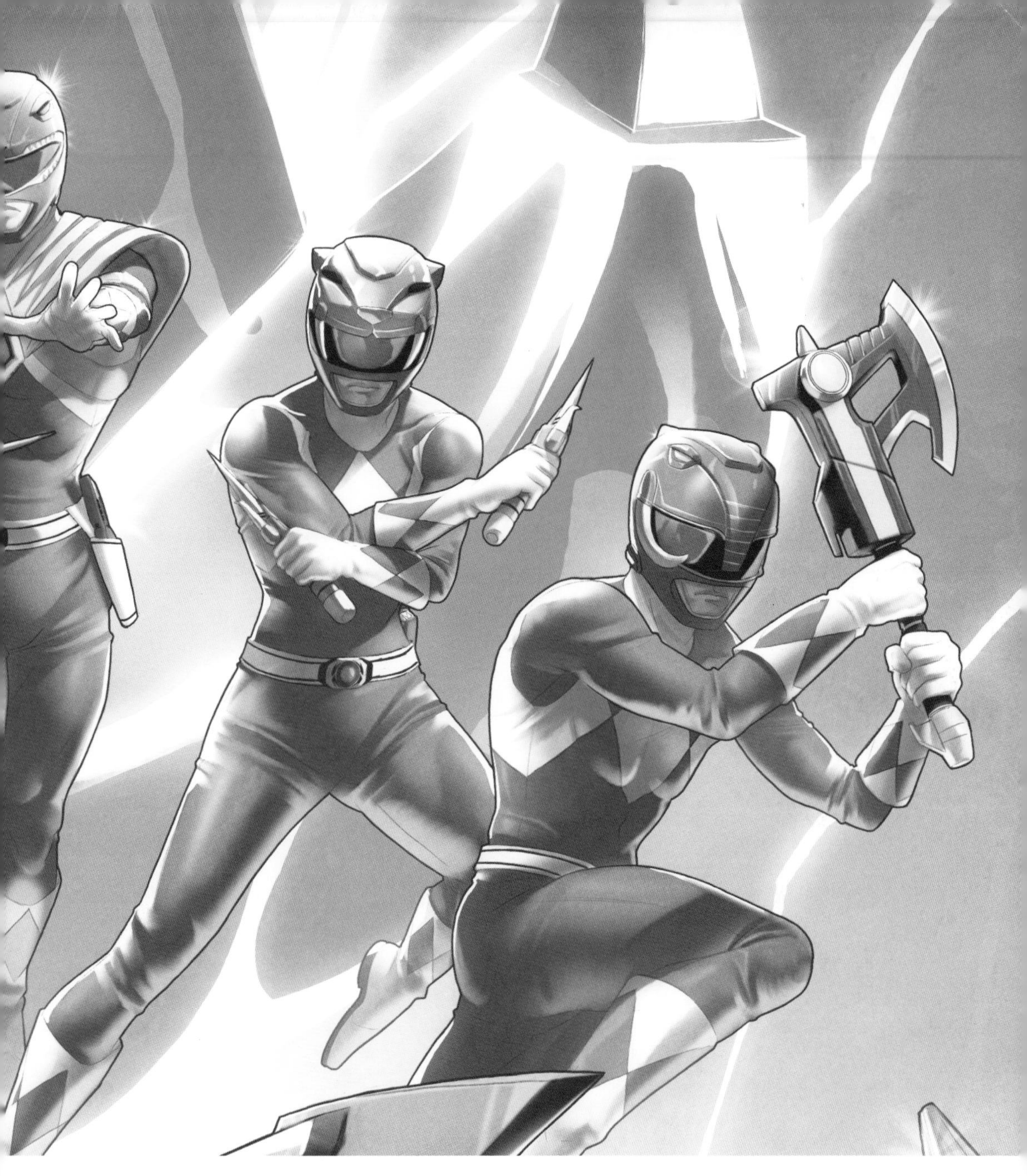

WRITTEN BY
KYLE HIGGINS

ILLUSTRATED BY
HENDRY PRASETYA CHAPTERS 9, 11-12
JONATHAN LAM CHAPTER 10

COLORS BY
MATT HERMS CHAPTERS 9, 11-12
JOANA LAFUENTE CHAPTER 10

LETTERS BY
ED DUKESHIRE

COVER BY
GOÑI MONTES

DESIGNER
JILLIAN CRAB

ASSISTANT EDITOR
MATTHEW LEVINE

ASSOCIATE EDITOR
ALEX GALER

EDITOR
DAFNA PLEBAN

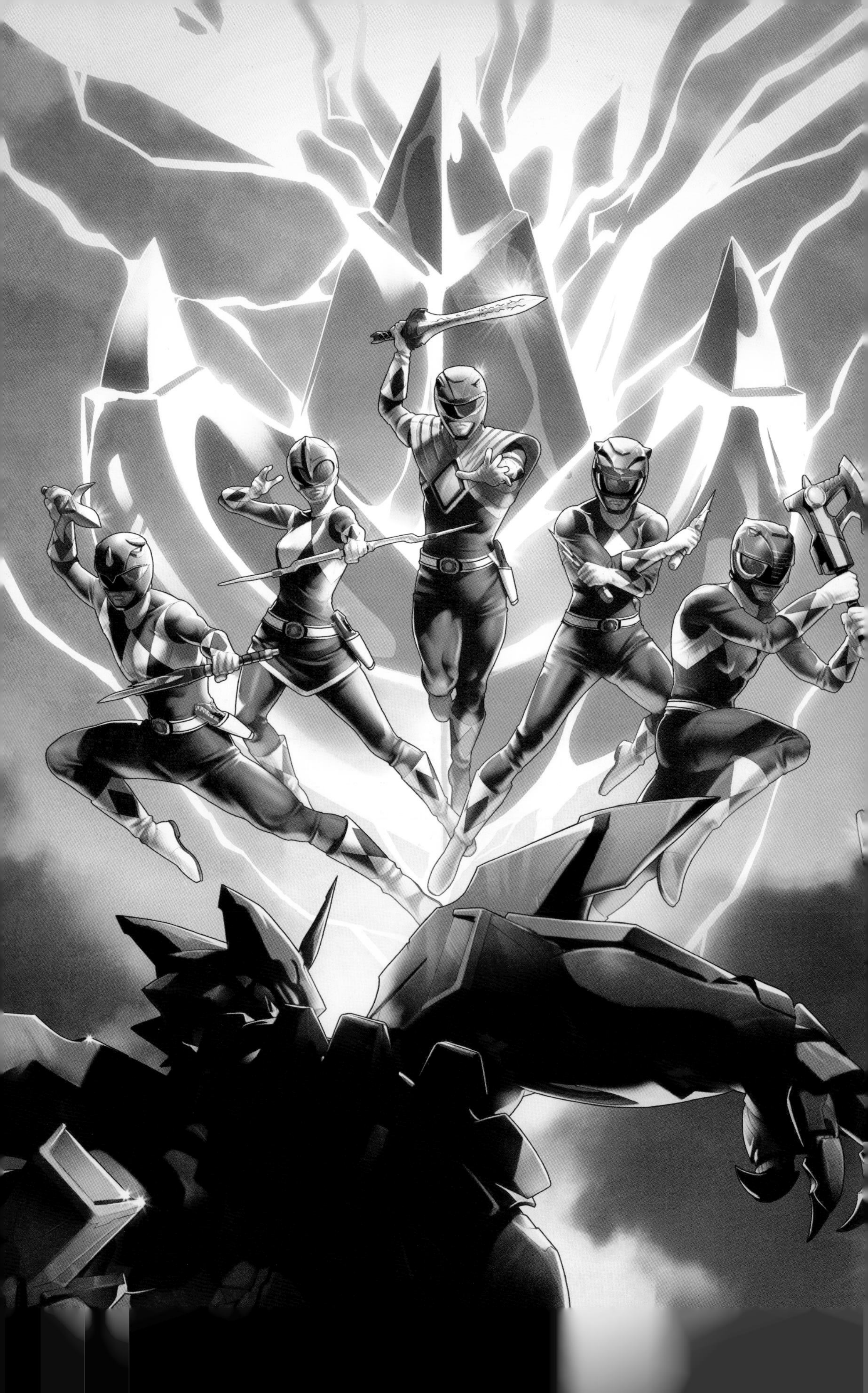

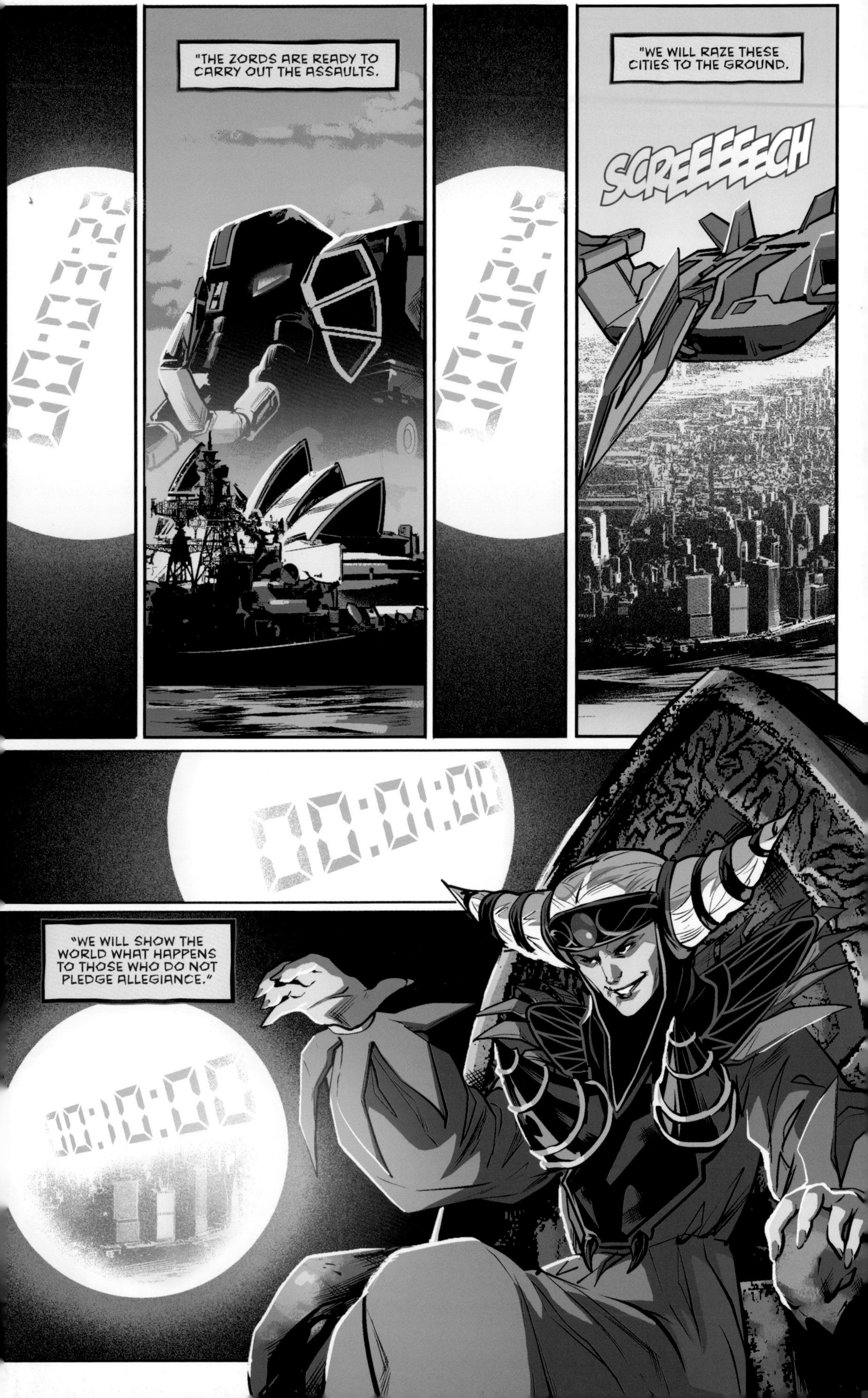
"THE ZORDS ARE READY TO CARRY OUT THE ASSAULTS.
"WE WILL RAZE THESE CITIES TO THE GROUND.
SCREEEEECH
00:01:00
"WE WILL SHOW THE WORLD WHAT HAPPENS TO THOSE WHO DO NOT PLEDGE ALLEGIANCE."

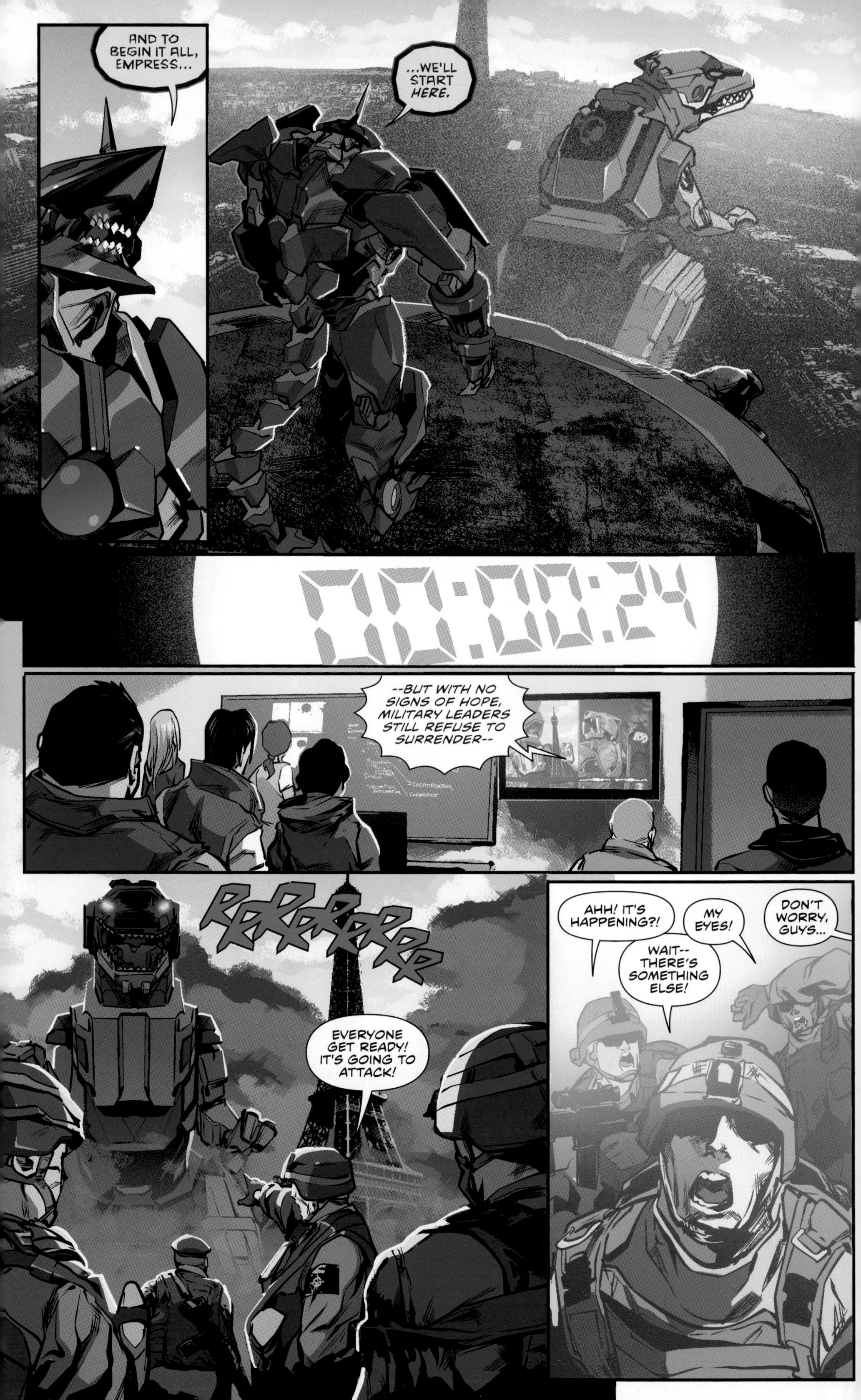
AND TO BEGIN IT ALL, EMPRESS...
...WE'LL START HERE.
00:00:24
--BUT WITH NO SIGNS OF HOPE, MILITARY LEADERS STILL REFUSE TO SURRENDER--
RRRRRRRRR
EVERYONE GET READY! IT'S GOING TO ATTACK!
AHH! IT'S HAPPENING?!
MY EYES!
DON'T WORRY, GUYS...
WAIT-- THERE'S SOMETHING ELSE!

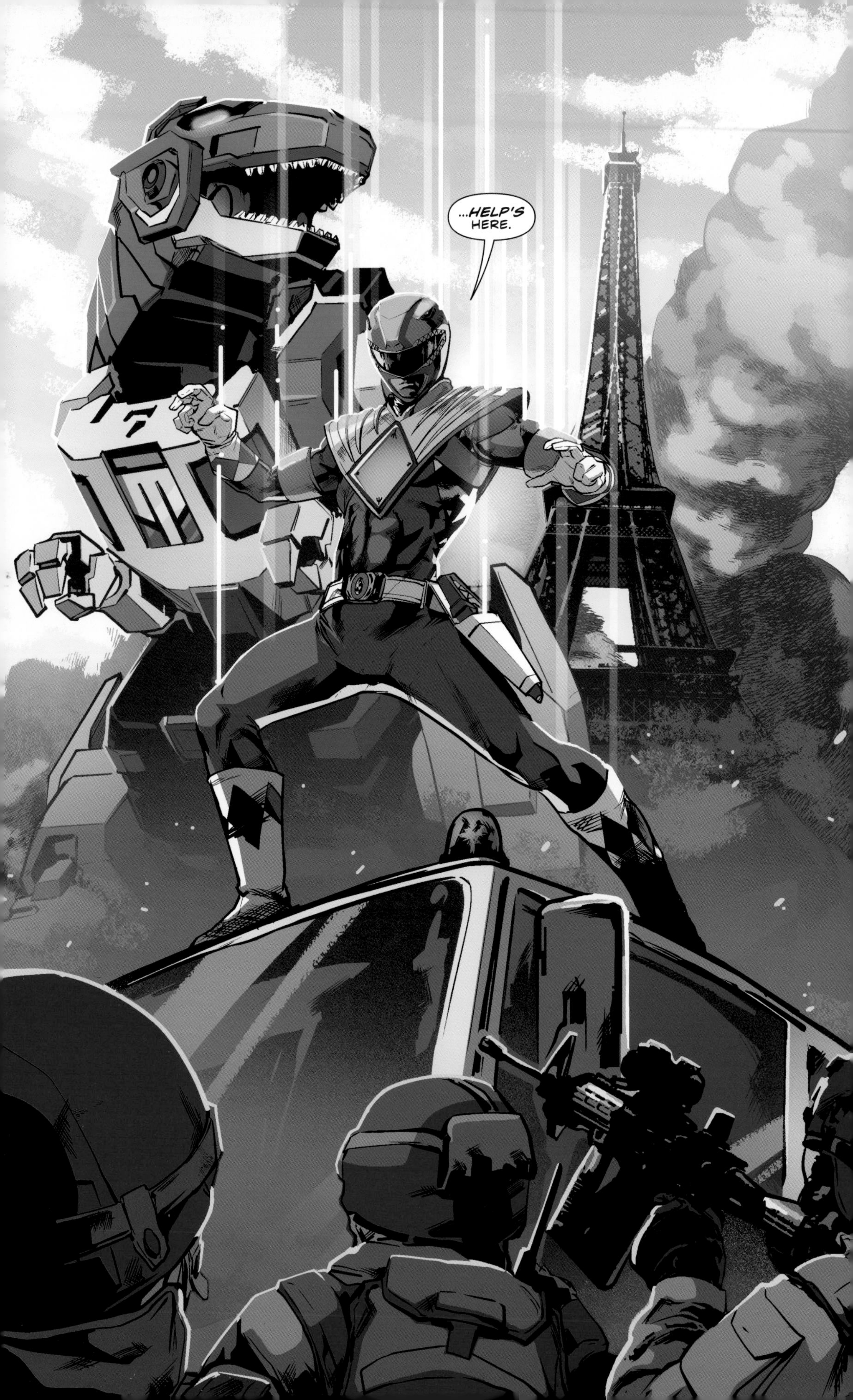
...HELP'S HERE.

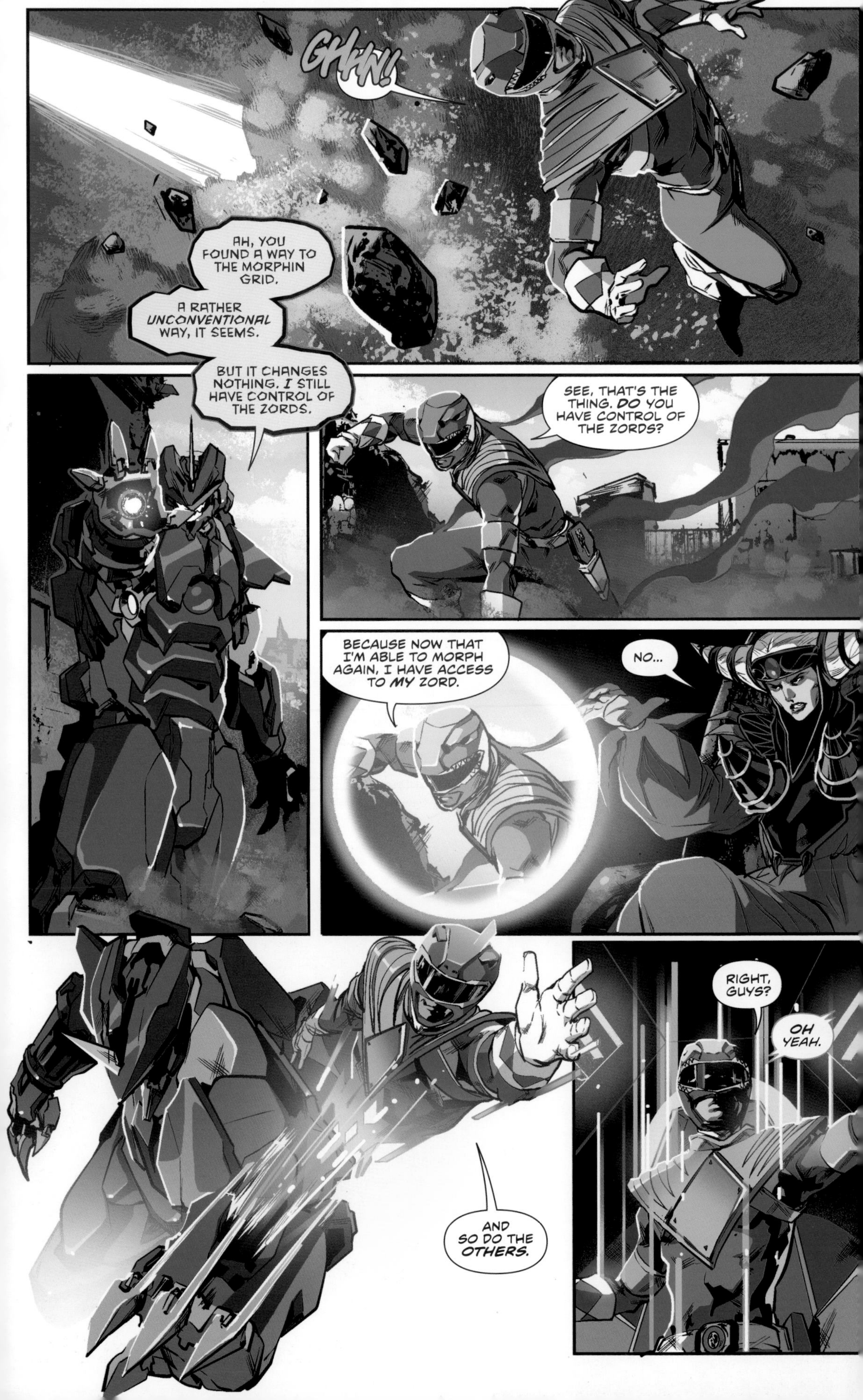
GHAA!
AH, YOU FOUND A WAY TO THE MORPHIN GRID.
A RATHER UNCONVENTIONAL WAY, IT SEEMS.
BUT IT CHANGES NOTHING. I STILL HAVE CONTROL OF THE ZORDS.
SEE, THAT'S THE THING. DO YOU HAVE CONTROL OF THE ZORDS?
BECAUSE NOW THAT I'M ABLE TO MORPH AGAIN, I HAVE ACCESS TO MY ZORD.
NO...
AND SO DO THE OTHERS.
RIGHT, GUYS?
OH YEAH.

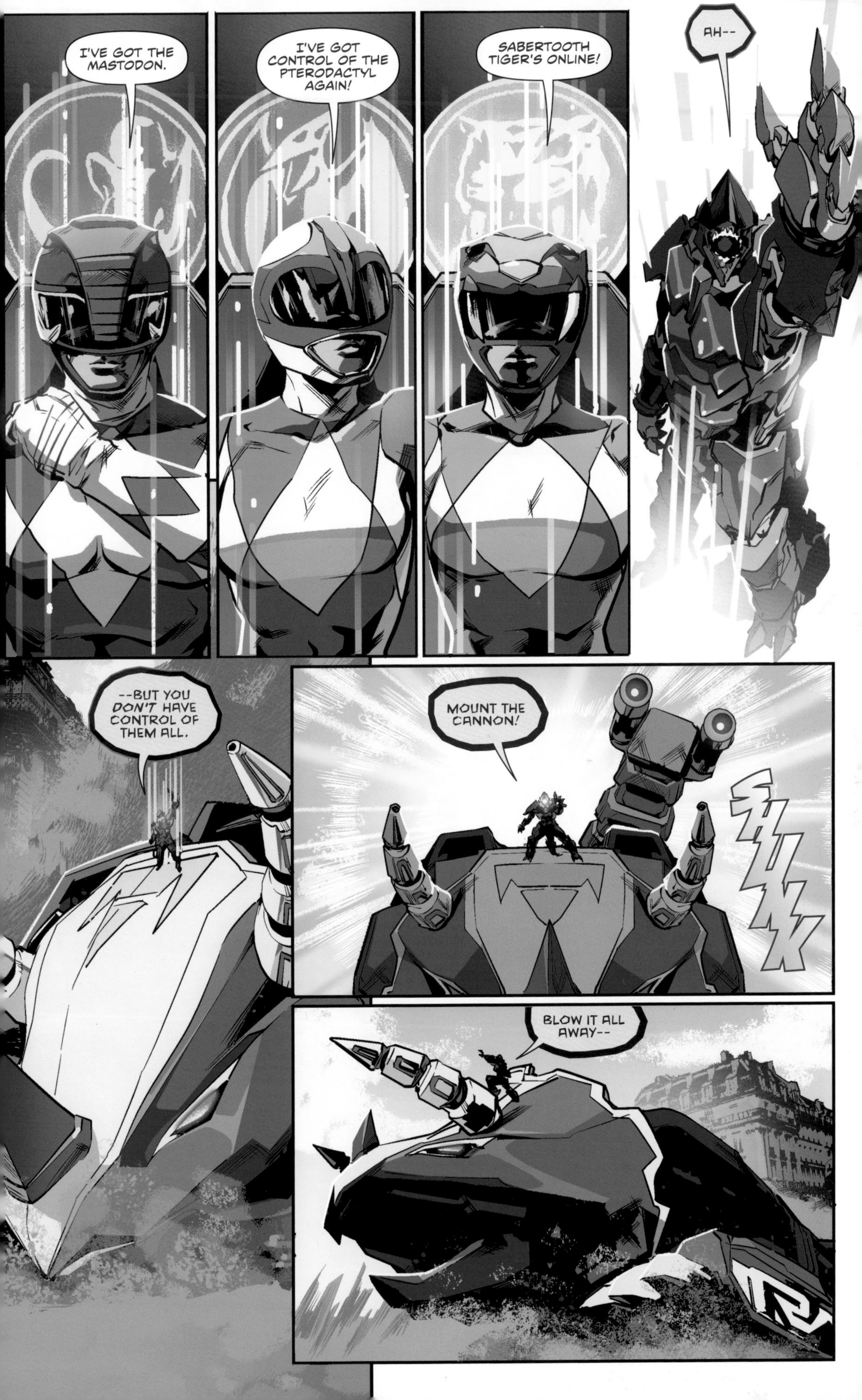
I'VE GOT THE MASTODON.
I'VE GOT CONTROL OF THE PTERODACTYL AGAIN!
SABERTOOTH TIGER'S ONLINE!
AH--
--BUT YOU *DON'T* HAVE CONTROL OF THEM ALL.
MOUNT THE CANNON!
SHUNK
BLOW IT ALL AWAY--

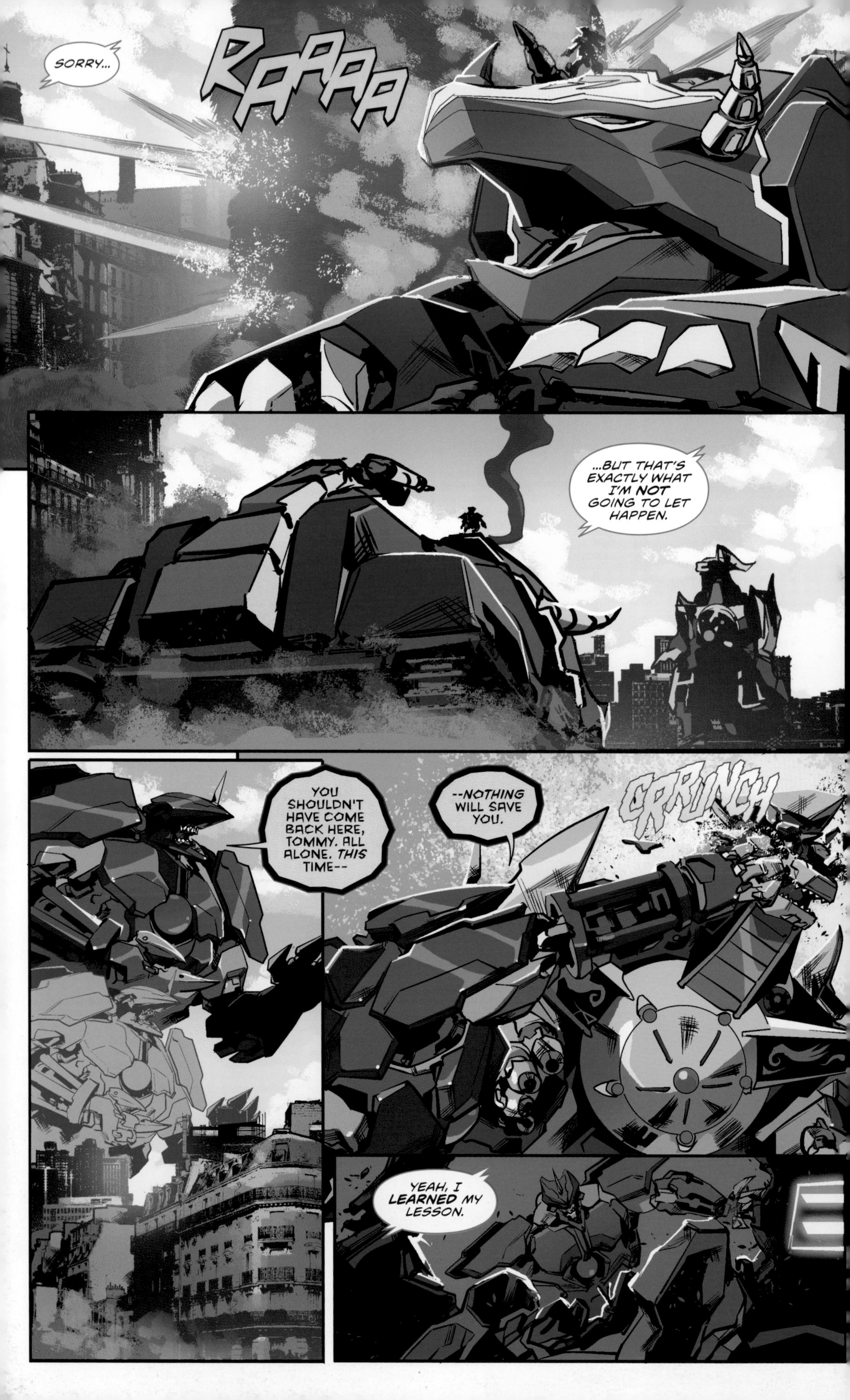
SORRY...
RAAAA
...BUT THAT'S EXACTLY WHAT I'M **NOT** GOING TO LET HAPPEN.
YOU SHOULDN'T HAVE COME BACK HERE, TOMMY. ALL ALONE. *THIS* TIME--
--NOTHING WILL SAVE YOU.
CRRUNCH
YEAH, I **LEARNED** MY LESSON.

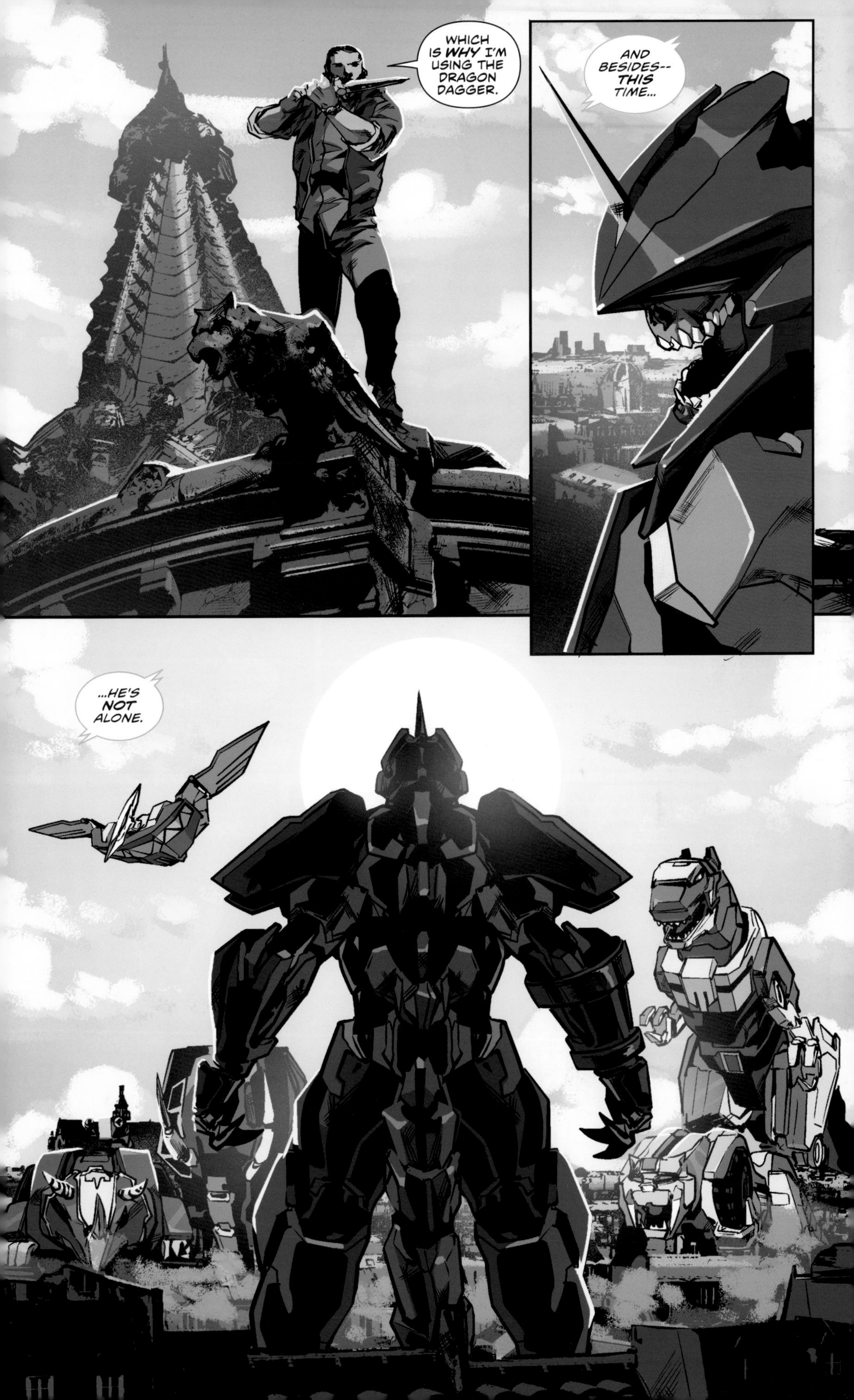
WHICH IS WHY I'M USING THE DRAGON DAGGER.
AND BESIDES-- THIS TIME...
...HE'S NOT ALONE.

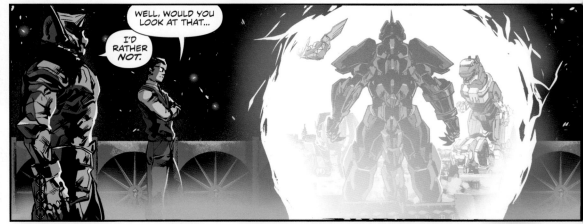

WELL, WOULD YOU LOOK AT THAT...

I'D RATHER *NOT*.

≶PFFT≶ HE SHOULD HAVE SEEN THAT BLOW COMING A MOON'S DISTANCE AWAY.

YOU, UH, REALLY DON'T *LIKE* THIS BLACK DRAGON CHARACTER, HUH?

DO *YOU?*

WELL, SEEING AS HE'S THE REASON RITA'S IN THE COMMAND CENTER, MY FRIENDS LOST THEIR POWERS, AND I'M STANDING HERE RIGHT NOW...

IT WAS A QUESTION YOU WERE NOT *SUPPOSED* TO ANSWER, BLUE RANGER.

OH, IT WAS *RHETORICAL.* GOT IT.

IT SHOULD BE *ME* LEADING THIS CHARGE. NOT...SOME *OUTSIDER.*

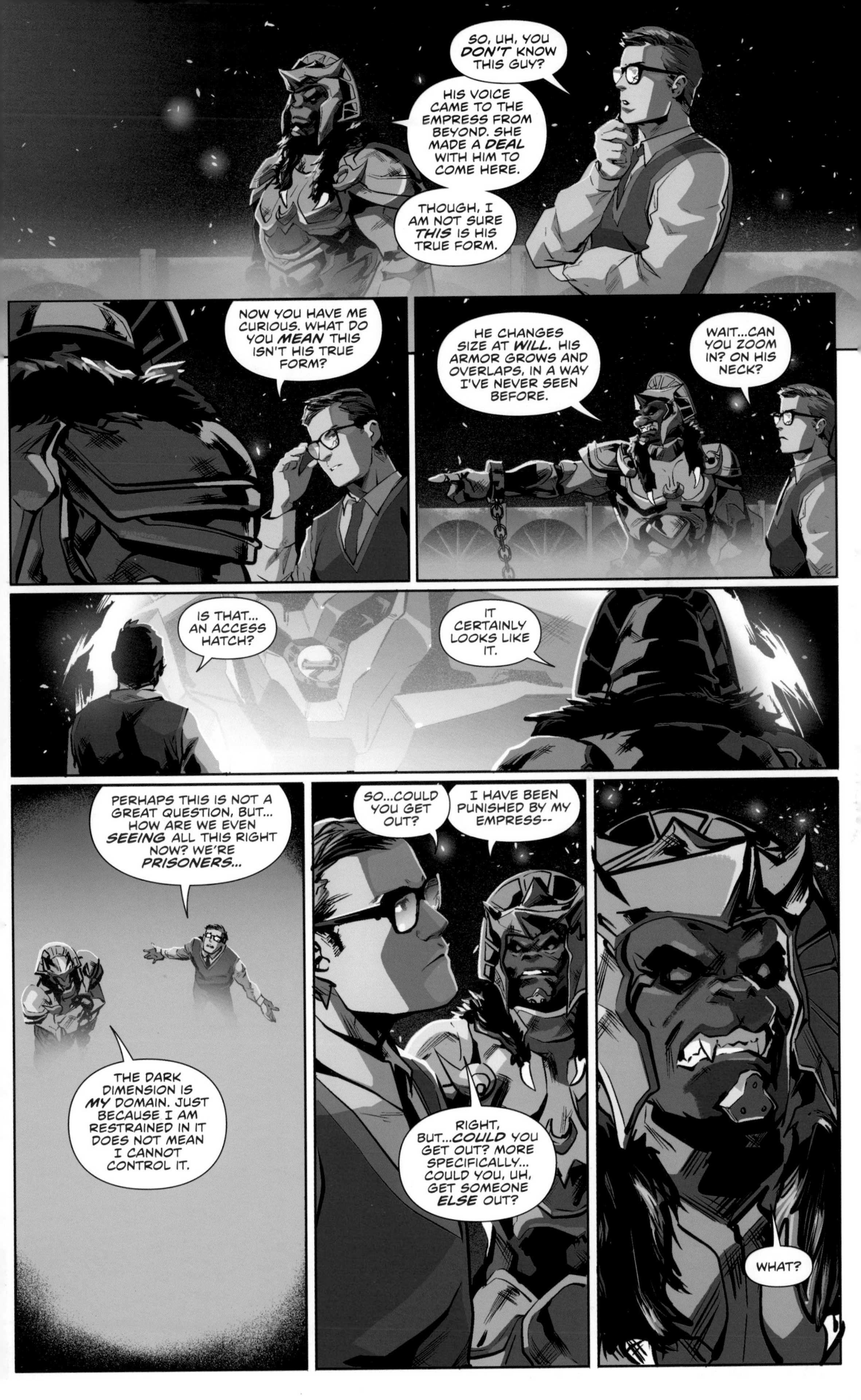
SO, UH, YOU DON'T KNOW THIS GUY?
HIS VOICE CAME TO THE EMPRESS FROM BEYOND. SHE MADE A DEAL WITH HIM TO COME HERE.
THOUGH, I AM NOT SURE THIS IS HIS TRUE FORM.
NOW YOU HAVE ME CURIOUS. WHAT DO YOU MEAN THIS ISN'T HIS TRUE FORM?
HE CHANGES SIZE AT WILL. HIS ARMOR GROWS AND OVERLAPS, IN A WAY I'VE NEVER SEEN BEFORE.
WAIT...CAN YOU ZOOM IN? ON HIS NECK?
IS THAT... AN ACCESS HATCH?
IT CERTAINLY LOOKS LIKE IT.
PERHAPS THIS IS NOT A GREAT QUESTION, BUT... HOW ARE WE EVEN SEEING ALL THIS RIGHT NOW? WE'RE PRISONERS...
THE DARK DIMENSION IS MY DOMAIN. JUST BECAUSE I AM RESTRAINED IN IT DOES NOT MEAN I CANNOT CONTROL IT.
SO...COULD YOU GET OUT?
I HAVE BEEN PUNISHED BY MY EMPRESS--
RIGHT, BUT...COULD YOU GET OUT? MORE SPECIFICALLY... COULD YOU, UH, GET SOMEONE ELSE OUT?
WHAT?

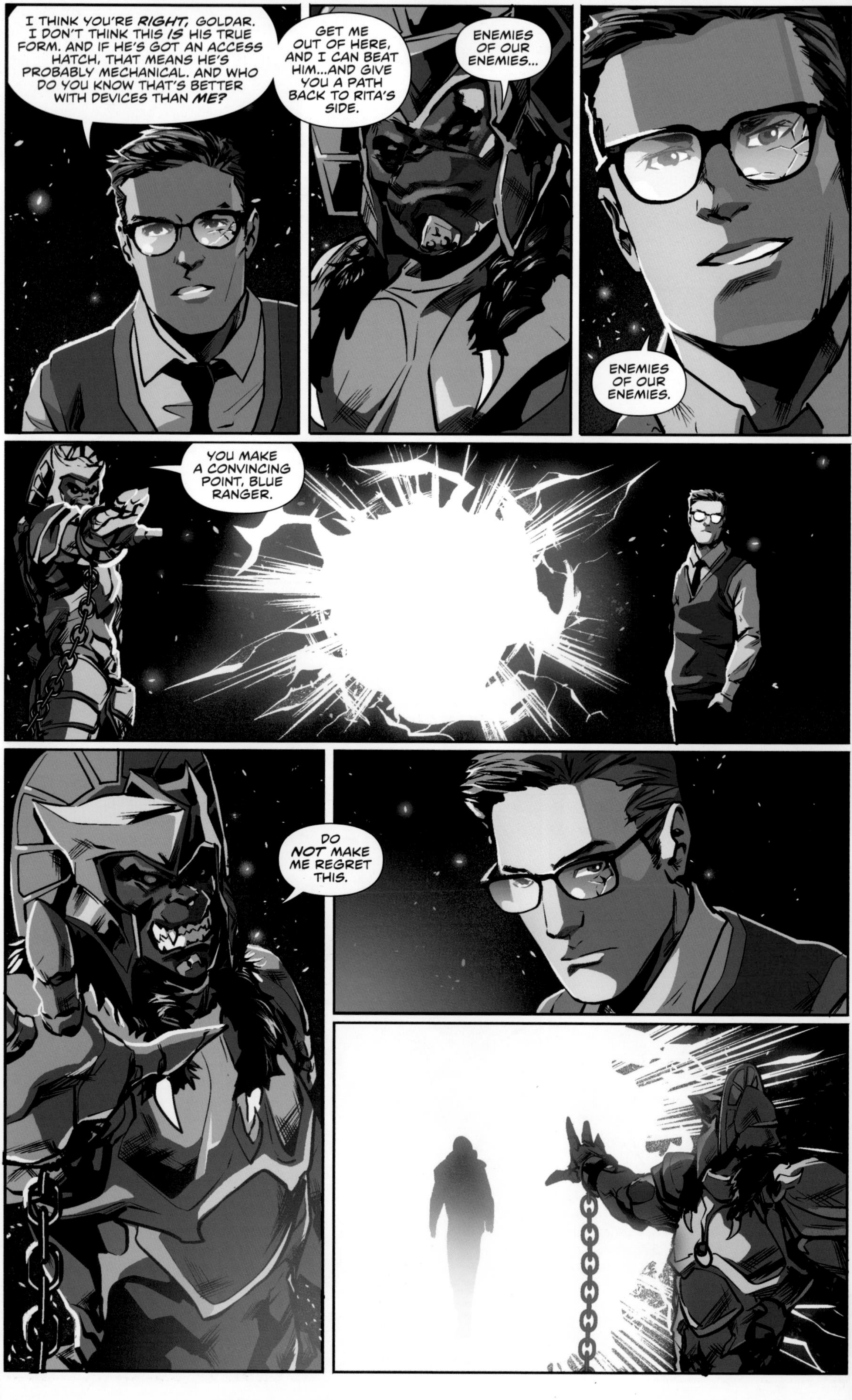
I THINK YOU'RE RIGHT, GOLDAR. I DON'T THINK THIS IS HIS TRUE FORM. AND IF HE'S GOT AN ACCESS HATCH, THAT MEANS HE'S PROBABLY MECHANICAL. AND WHO DO YOU KNOW THAT'S BETTER WITH DEVICES THAN ME?
GET ME OUT OF HERE, AND I CAN BEAT HIM...AND GIVE YOU A PATH BACK TO RITA'S SIDE.
ENEMIES OF OUR ENEMIES...
ENEMIES OF OUR ENEMIES.
YOU MAKE A CONVINCING POINT, BLUE RANGER.
DO NOT MAKE ME REGRET THIS.

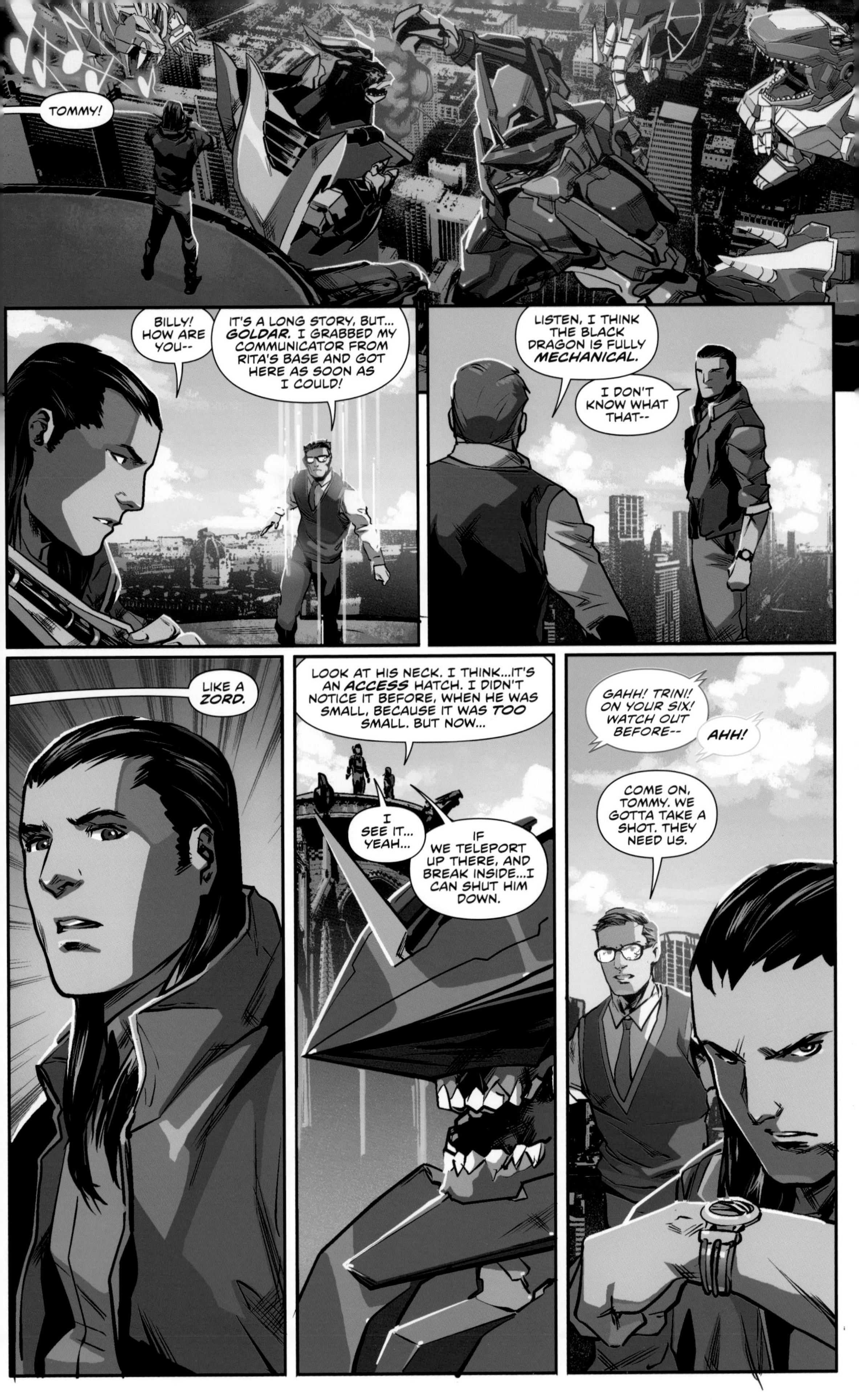
TOMMY!
BILLY! HOW ARE YOU--
IT'S A LONG STORY, BUT... GOLDAR. I GRABBED MY COMMUNICATOR FROM RITA'S BASE AND GOT HERE AS SOON AS I COULD!
LISTEN, I THINK THE BLACK DRAGON IS FULLY MECHANICAL.
I DON'T KNOW WHAT THAT--
LIKE A ZORD.
LOOK AT HIS NECK. I THINK...IT'S AN ACCESS HATCH. I DIDN'T NOTICE IT BEFORE, WHEN HE WAS SMALL, BECAUSE IT WAS TOO SMALL. BUT NOW...
I SEE IT... YEAH...
IF WE TELEPORT UP THERE, AND BREAK INSIDE...I CAN SHUT HIM DOWN.
GAHH! TRINI! ON YOUR SIX! WATCH OUT BEFORE--
AHH!
COME ON, TOMMY. WE GOTTA TAKE A SHOT. THEY NEED US.

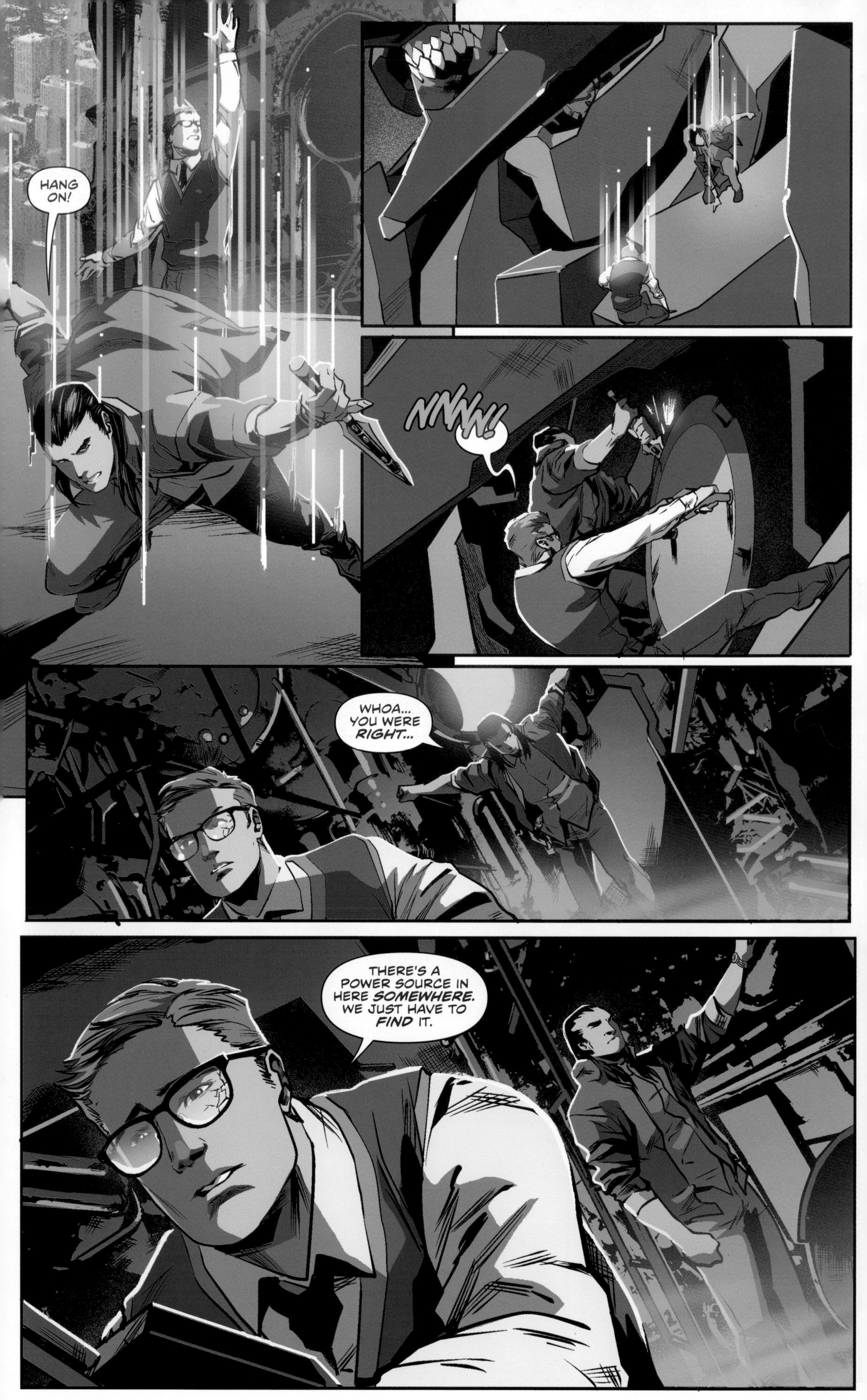
HANG ON!
NNNN!
WHOA... YOU WERE RIGHT...
THERE'S A POWER SOURCE IN HERE SOMEWHERE. WE JUST HAVE TO FIND IT.

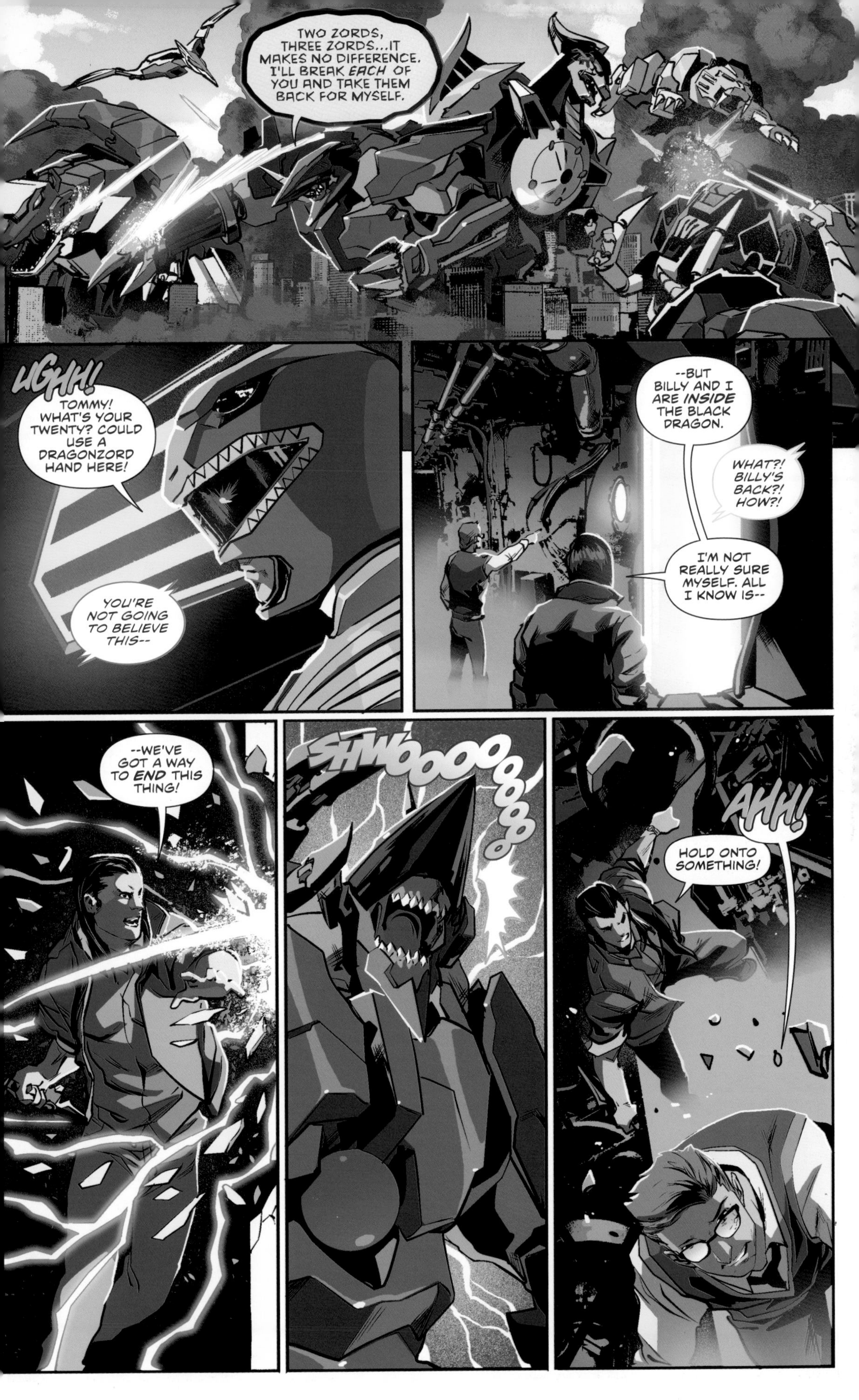
TWO ZORDS, THREE ZORDS...IT MAKES NO DIFFERENCE. I'LL BREAK EACH OF YOU AND TAKE THEM BACK FOR MYSELF.
UGHH!
TOMMY! WHAT'S YOUR TWENTY? COULD USE A DRAGONZORD HAND HERE!
YOU'RE NOT GOING TO BELIEVE THIS--
--BUT BILLY AND I ARE INSIDE THE BLACK DRAGON.
WHAT?! BILLY'S BACK?! HOW?!
I'M NOT REALLY SURE MYSELF. ALL I KNOW IS--
--WE'VE GOT A WAY TO END THIS THING!
SHWOOOOOOOOOO
AHH!
HOLD ONTO SOMETHING!

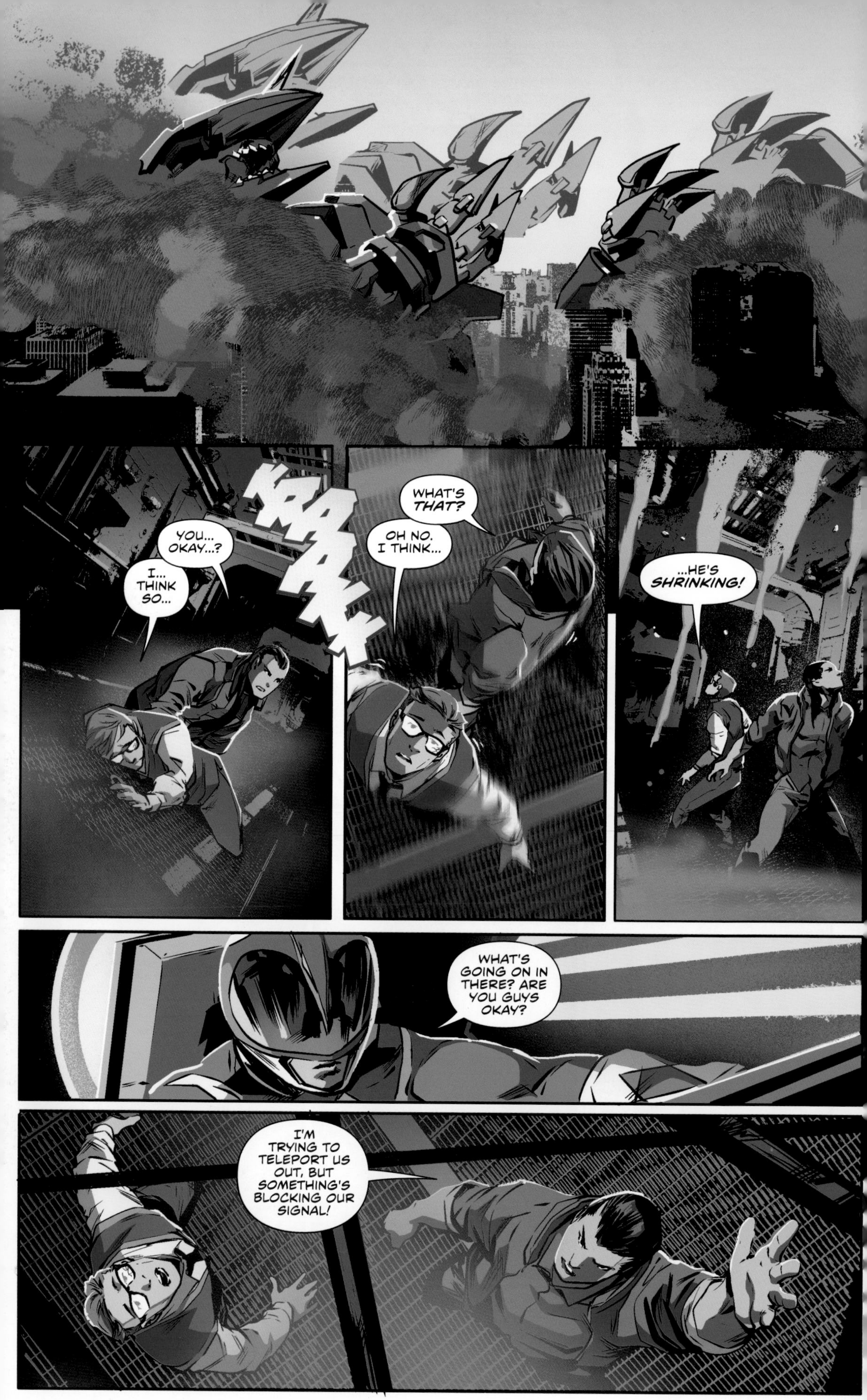
KRAKK
YOU... OKAY...?
I... THINK SO...
WHAT'S *THAT?*
OH NO. I THINK...
...HE'S *SHRINKING!*
WHAT'S GOING ON IN THERE? ARE YOU GUYS OKAY?
I'M TRYING TO TELEPORT US OUT, BUT SOMETHING'S BLOCKING OUR SIGNAL!

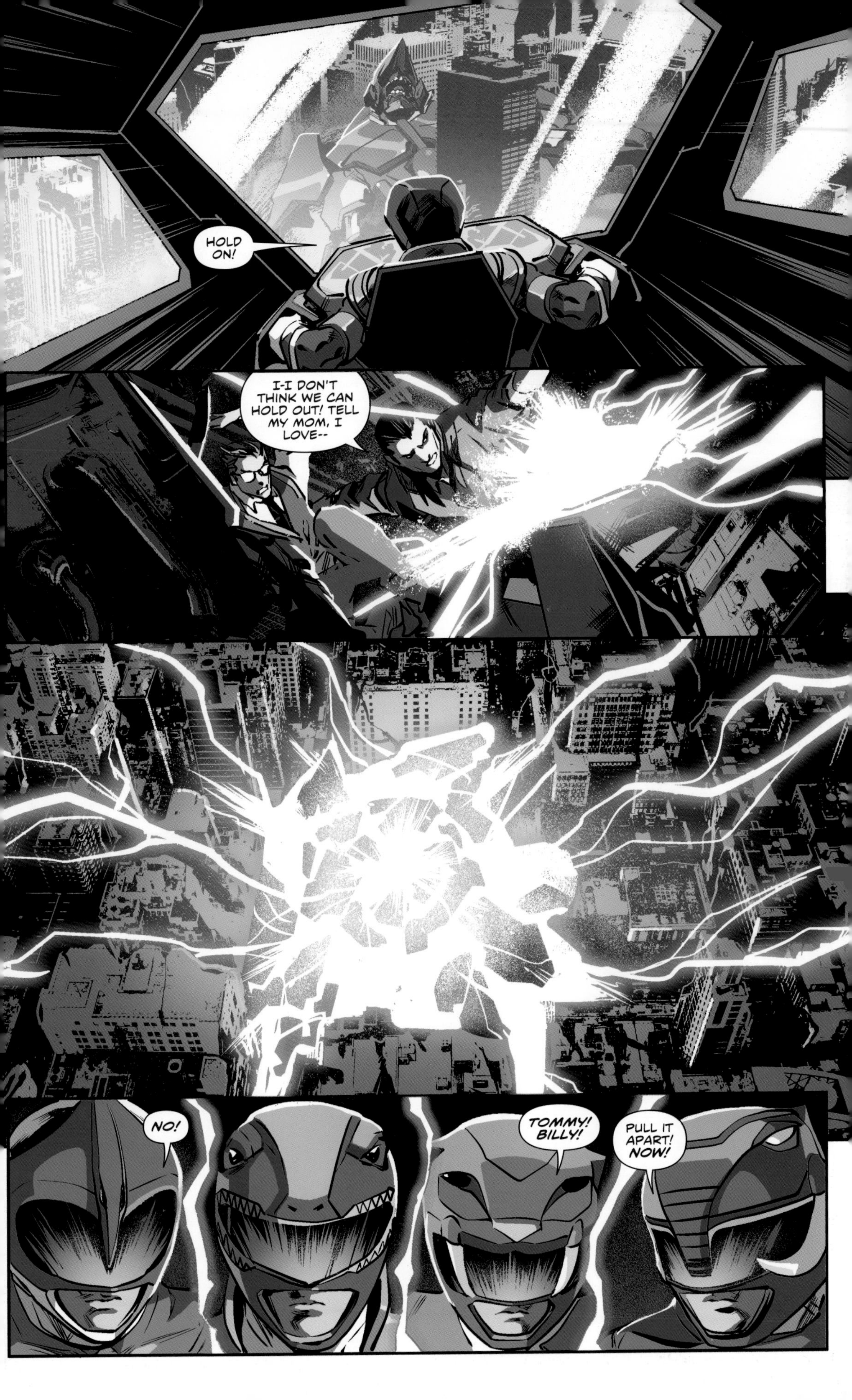
HOLD ON!
I-I DON'T THINK WE CAN HOLD OUT! TELL MY MOM, I LOVE--
NO!
TOMMY! BILLY!
PULL IT APART! NOW!

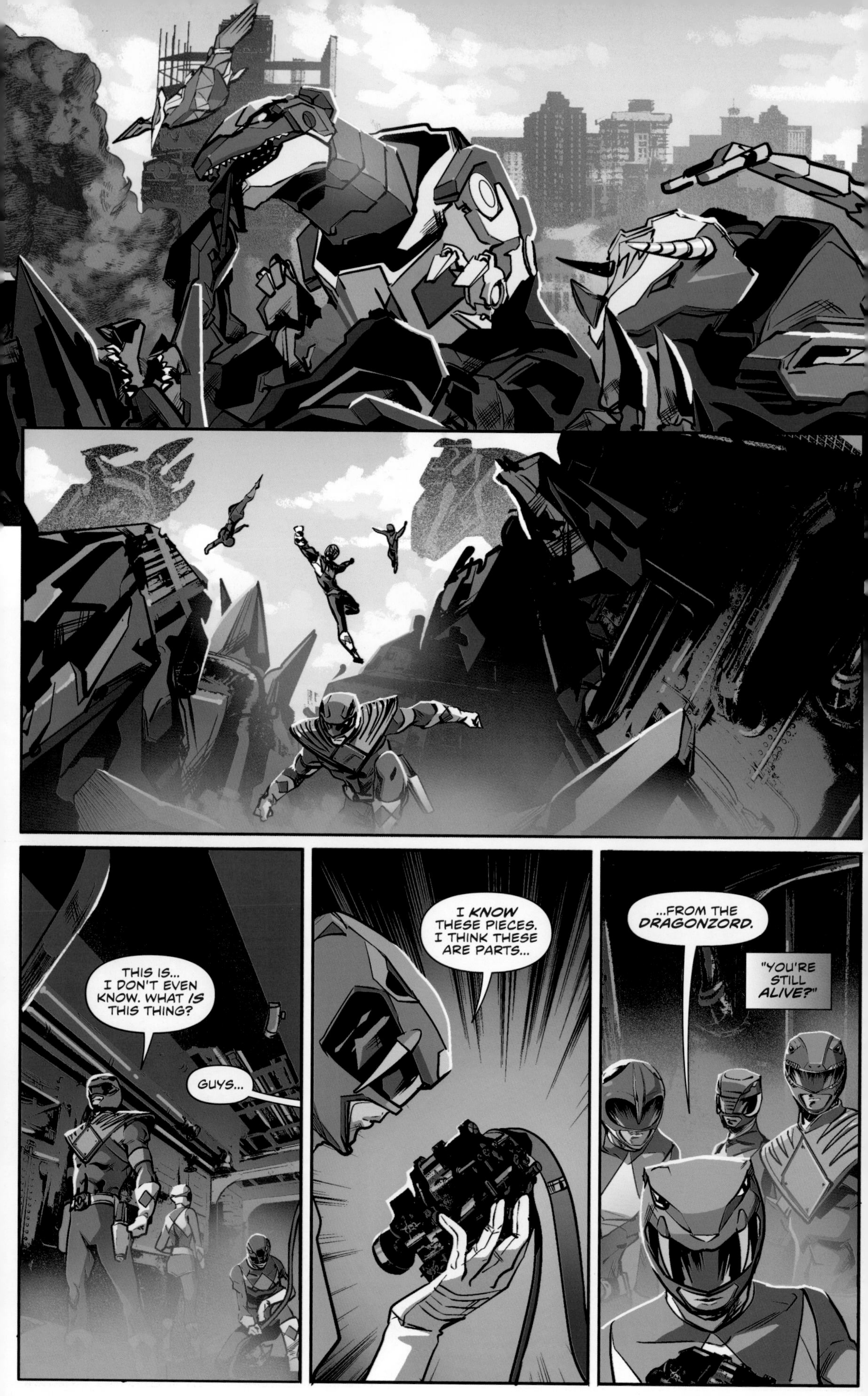
THIS IS... I DON'T EVEN KNOW. WHAT IS THIS THING?
GUYS...
I KNOW THESE PIECES. I THINK THESE ARE PARTS...
...FROM THE DRAGONZORD.
"YOU'RE STILL ALIVE?"

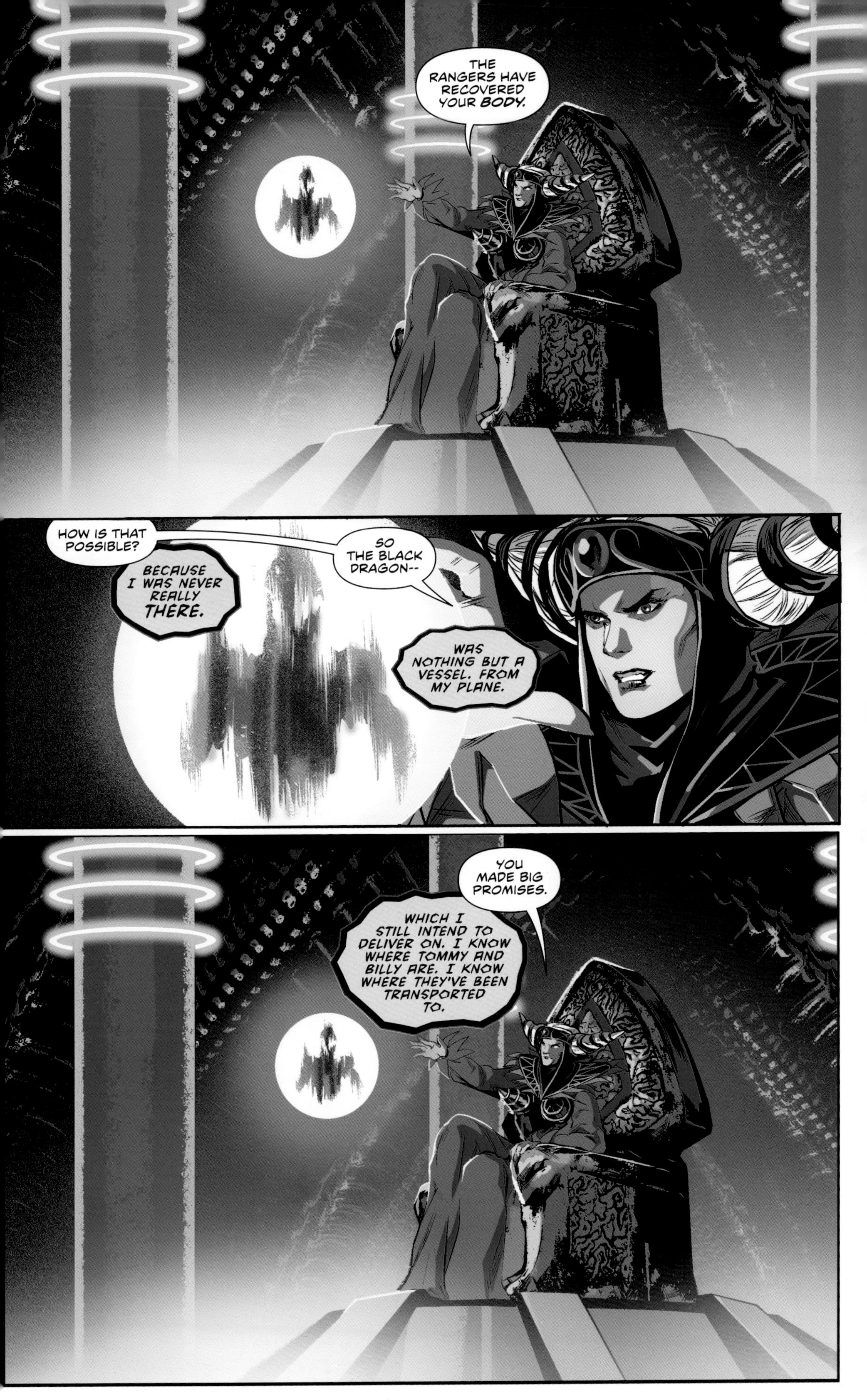
THE RANGERS HAVE RECOVERED YOUR BODY.
HOW IS THAT POSSIBLE?
SO THE BLACK DRAGON--
BECAUSE I WAS NEVER REALLY THERE.
WAS NOTHING BUT A VESSEL. FROM MY PLANE.
YOU MADE BIG PROMISES.
WHICH I STILL INTEND TO DELIVER ON. I KNOW WHERE TOMMY AND BILLY ARE. I KNOW WHERE THEY'VE BEEN TRANSPORTED TO.

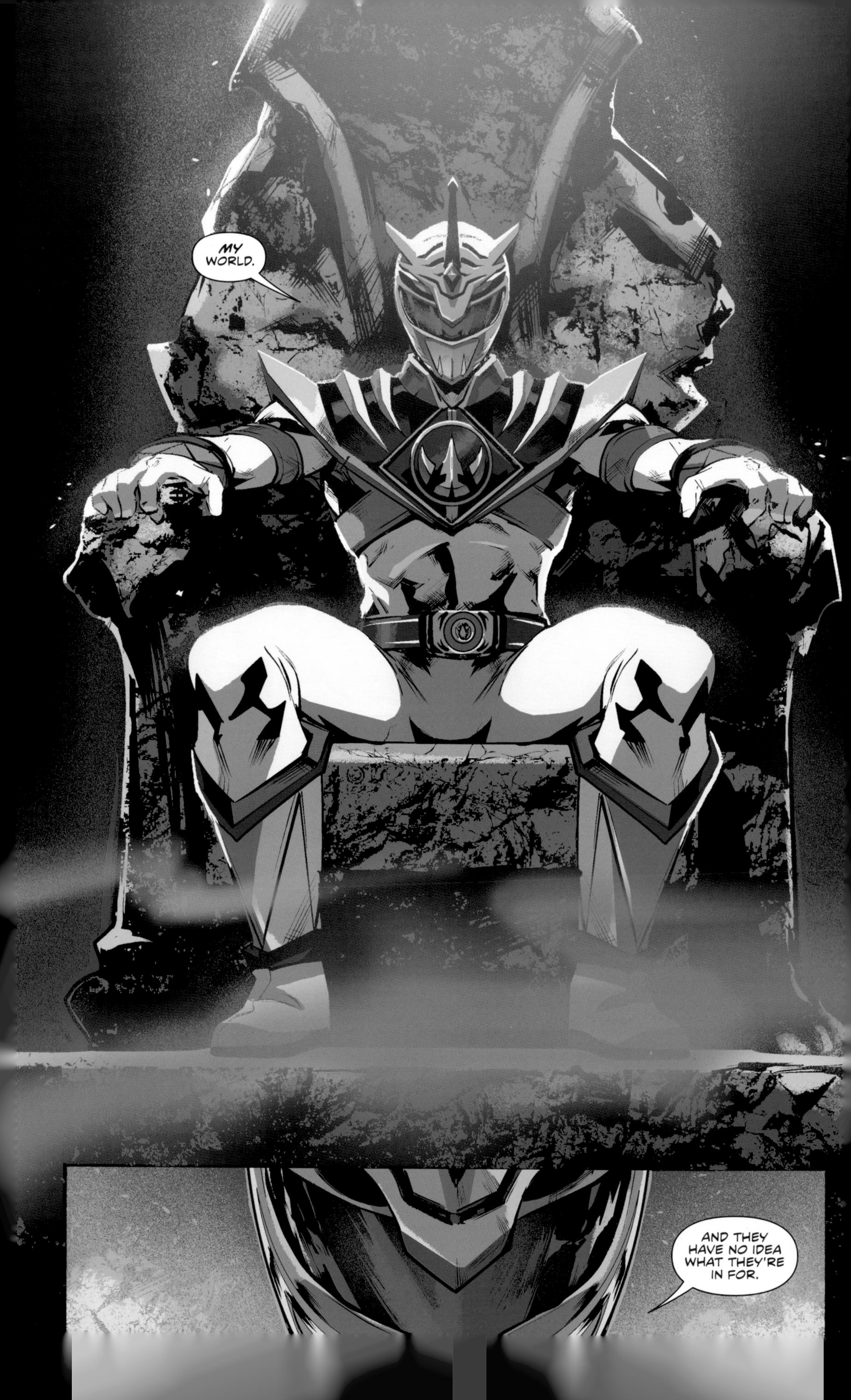
MY WORLD.
AND THEY HAVE NO IDEA WHAT THEY'RE IN FOR.

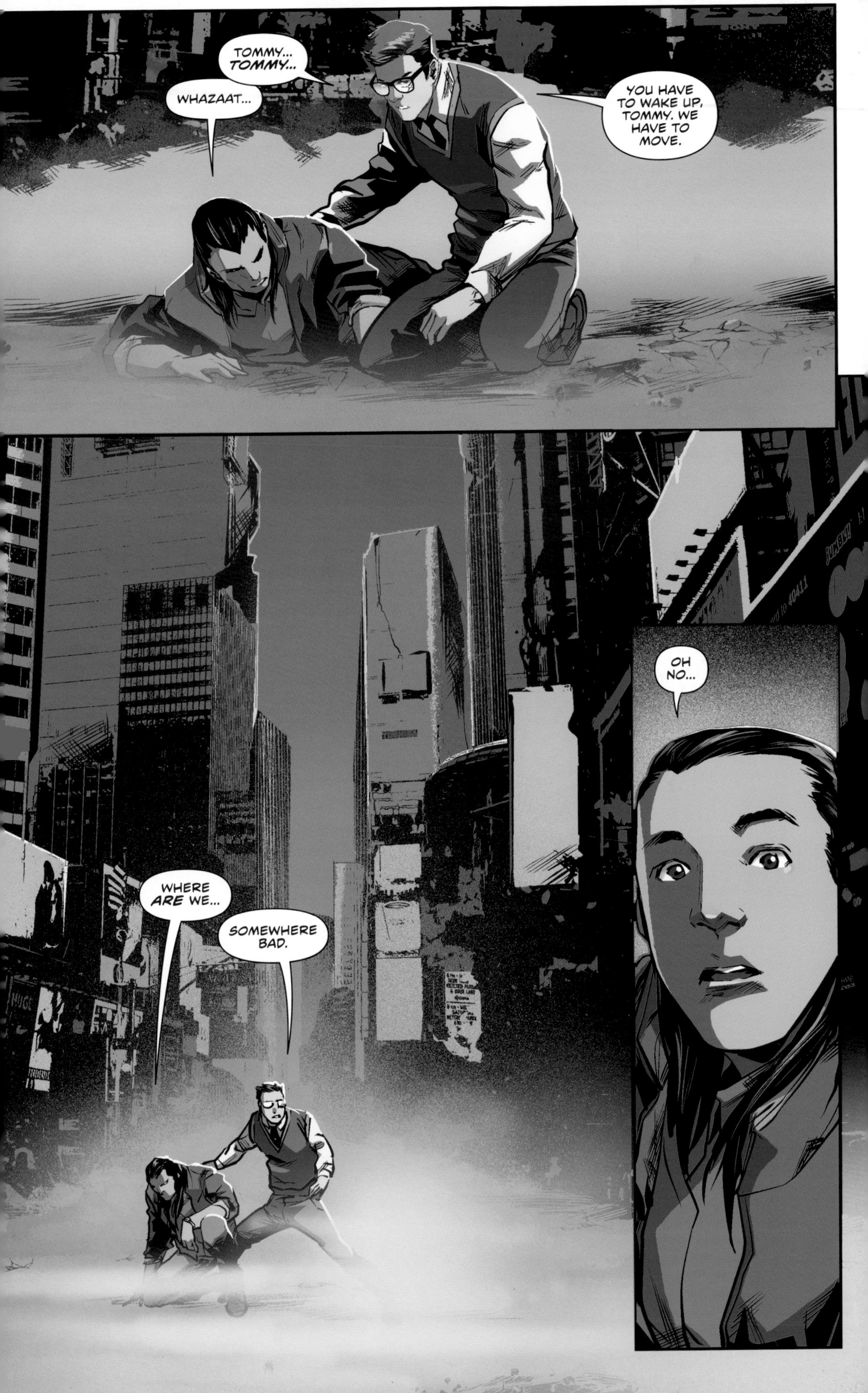
TOMMY... *TOMMY*...
WHAZAAT...
YOU HAVE TO WAKE UP, TOMMY. WE HAVE TO MOVE.
WHERE *ARE* WE...
SOMEWHERE BAD.
OH NO...

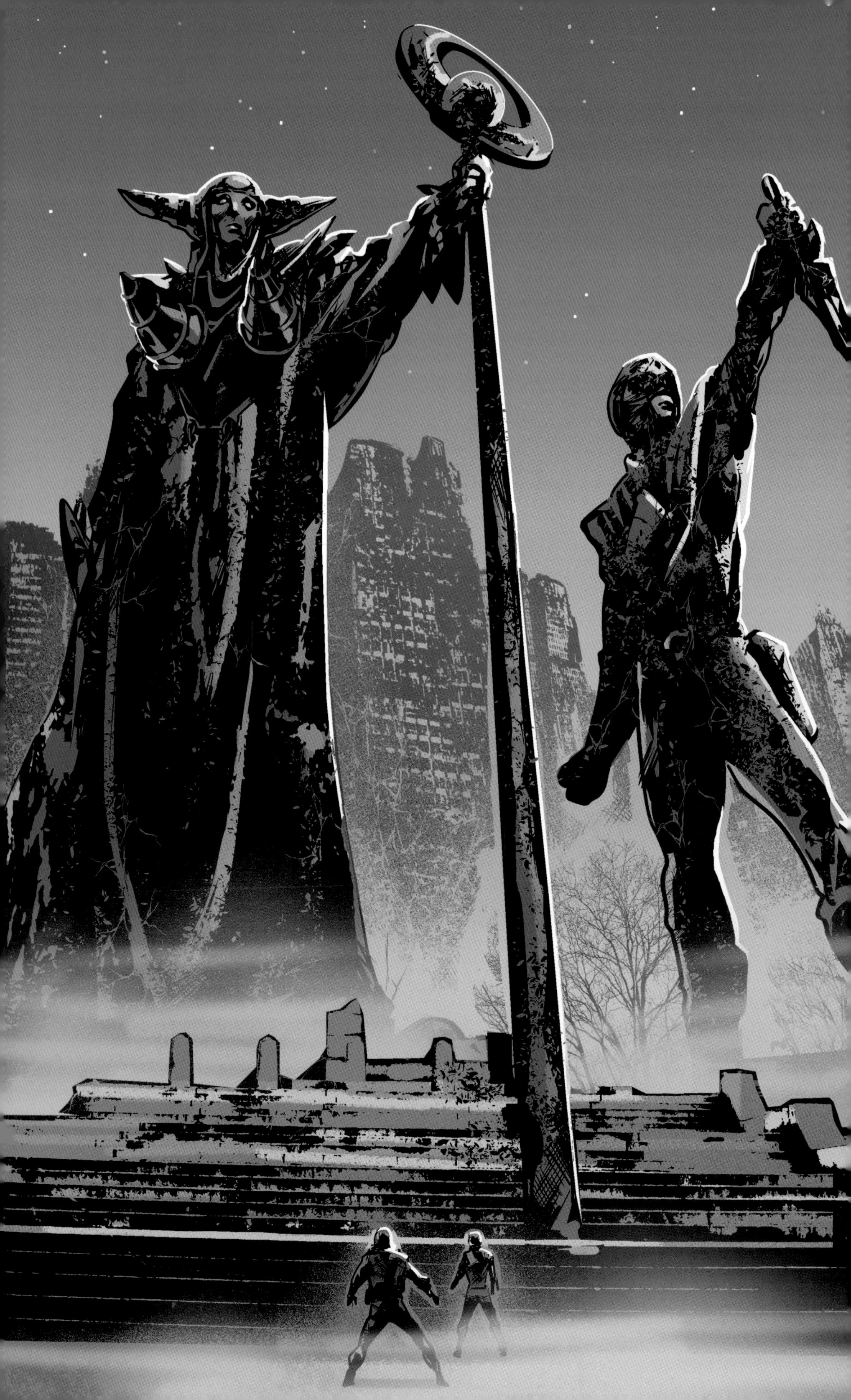

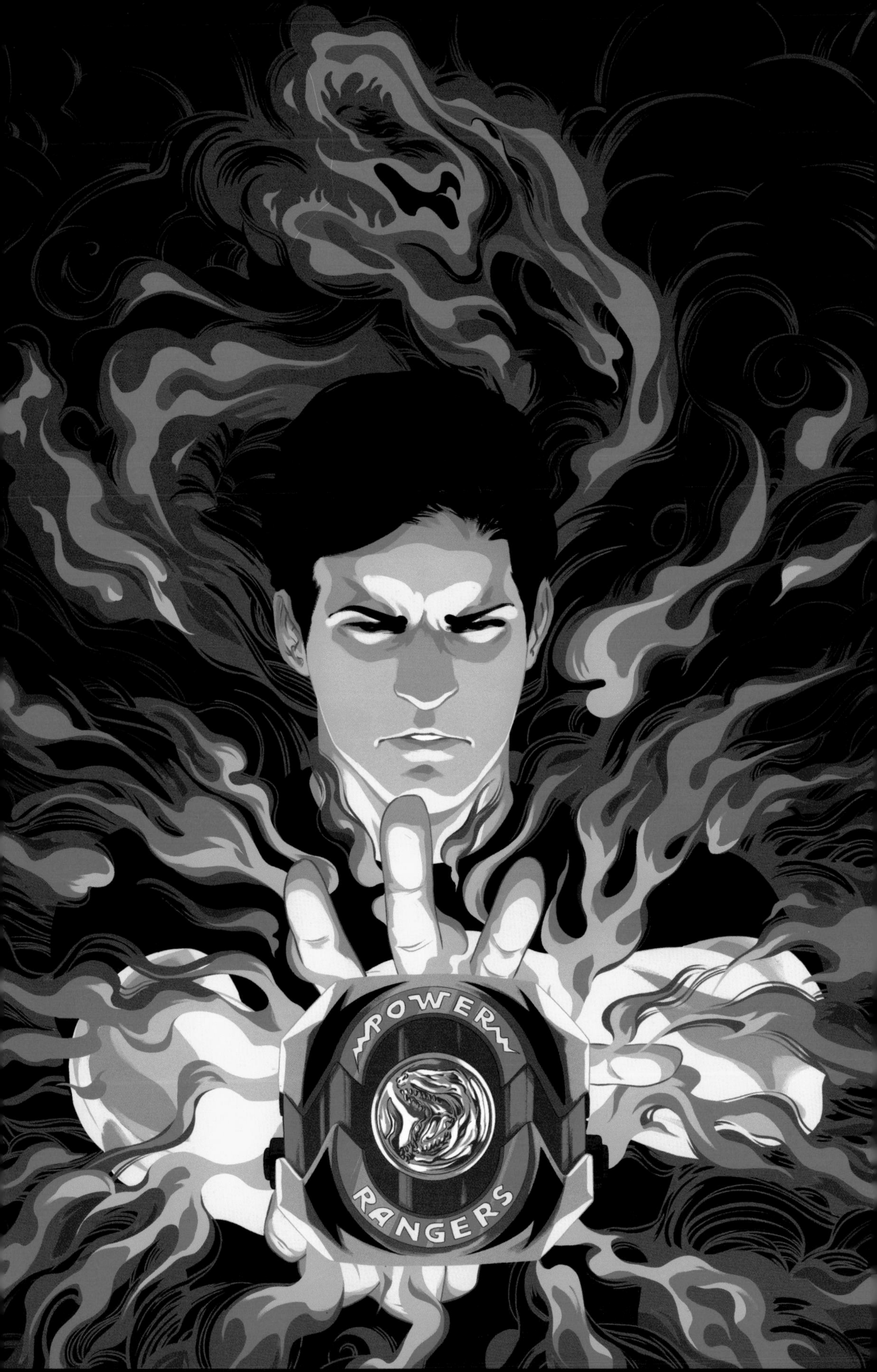
POWER
RANGERS

GOÑI MONTES | ISSUE NINE MORPHIN VARIANT COVER

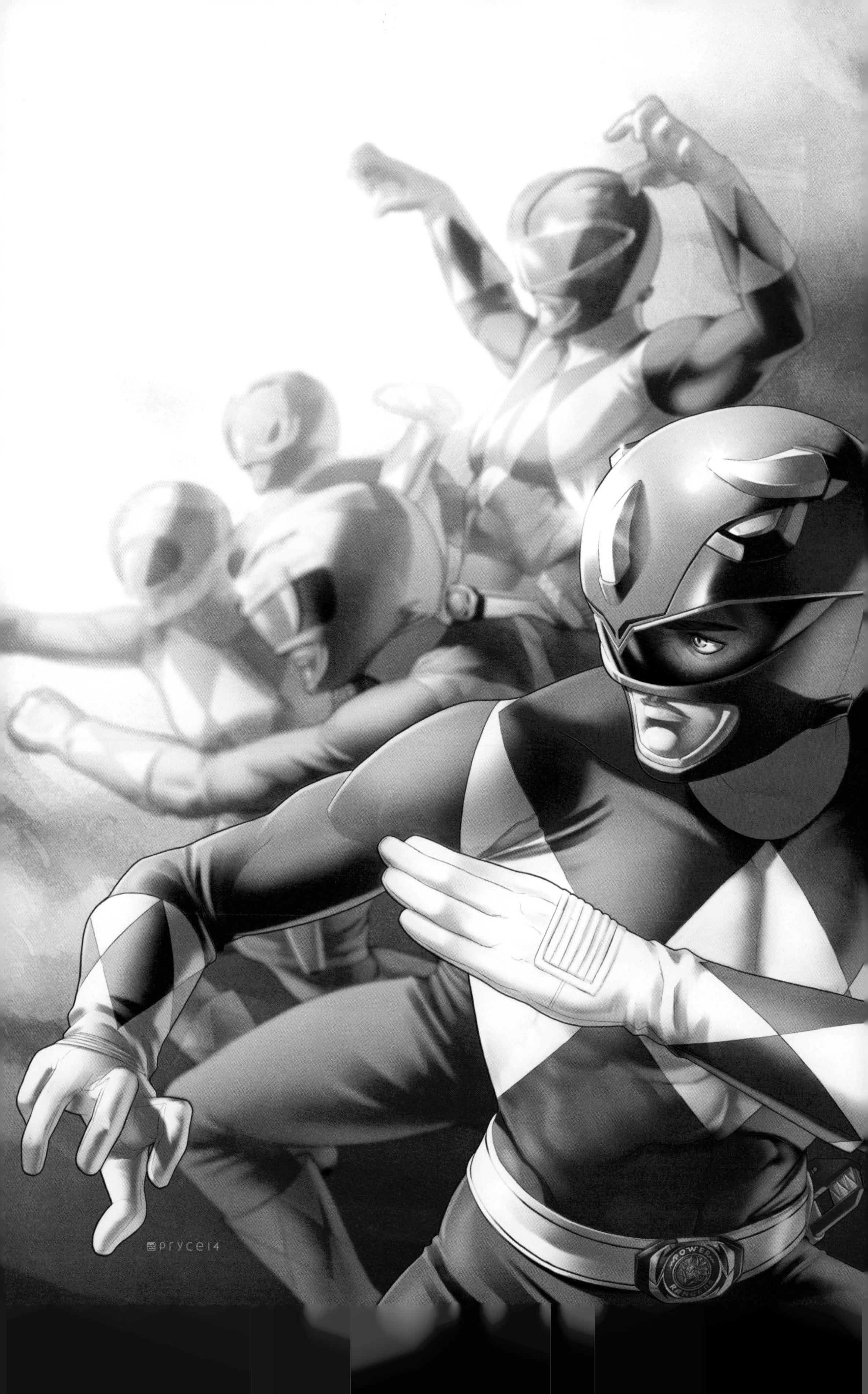
pryce14

WHAT MAKES A HERO?

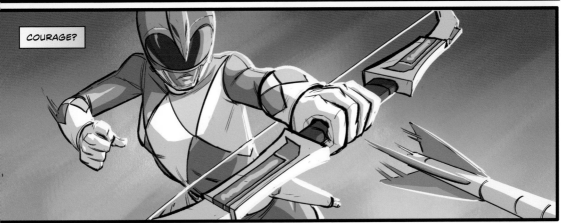

COURAGE?

INTELLIGENCE?

AN ARROW? REALLY? YOU THINK *THAT'S* GETTIN' THROUGH?!

AH!

AN UNWAVERING MORAL COMPASS?

GHNN!

ACK!

OVER TIME, CHARACTERISTICS LIKE THESE HAVE BECOME SYNONYMOUS WITH THE "HERO."

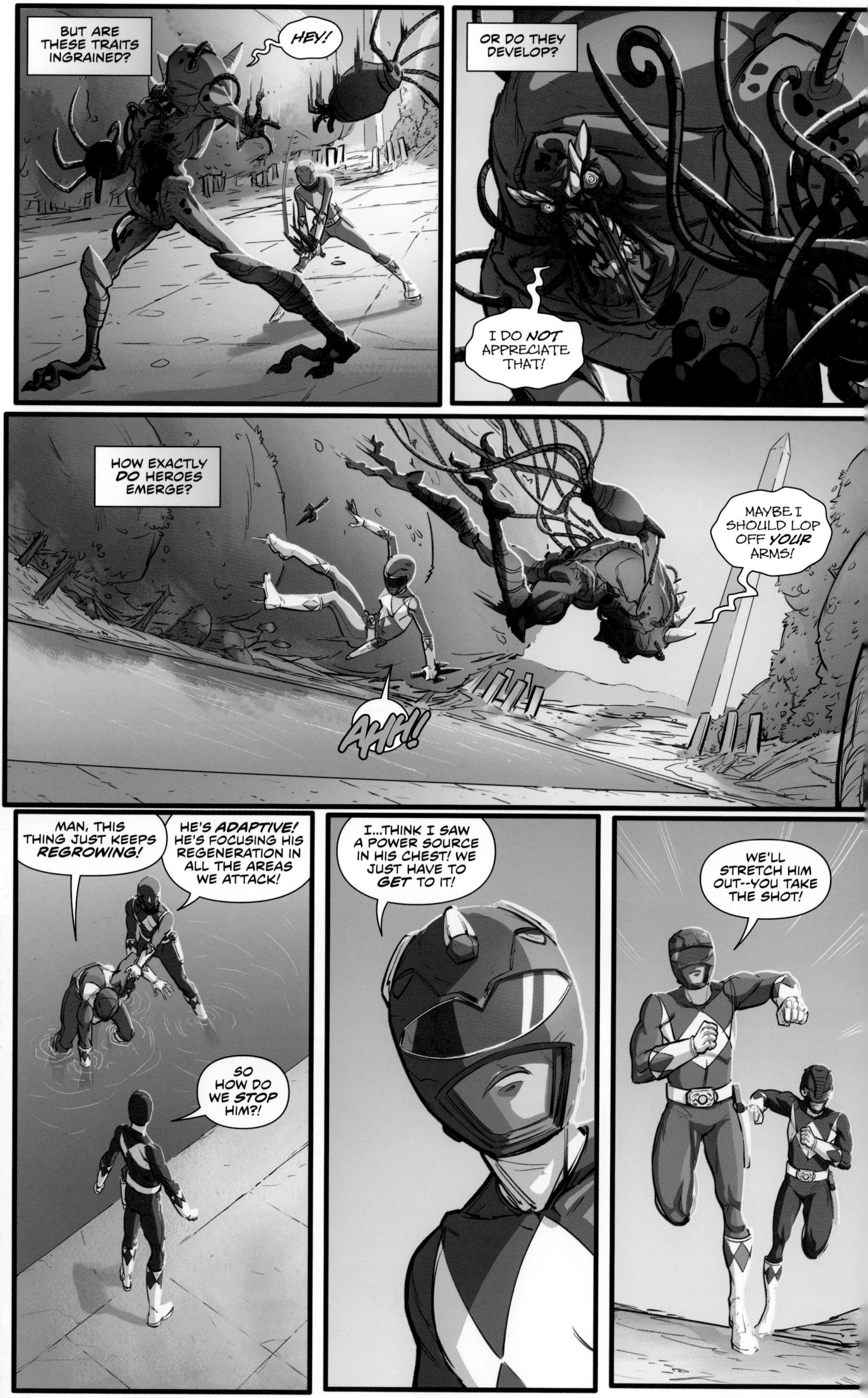

BUT ARE THESE TRAITS INGRAINED?
HEY!
OR DO THEY DEVELOP?
I DO NOT APPRECIATE THAT!
HOW EXACTLY DO HEROES EMERGE?
MAYBE I SHOULD LOP OFF YOUR ARMS!
AHH!
MAN, THIS THING JUST KEEPS REGROWING!
HE'S ADAPTIVE! HE'S FOCUSING HIS REGENERATION IN ALL THE AREAS WE ATTACK!
SO HOW DO WE STOP HIM?!
I...THINK I SAW A POWER SOURCE IN HIS CHEST! WE JUST HAVE TO GET TO IT!
WE'LL STRETCH HIM OUT--YOU TAKE THE SHOT!

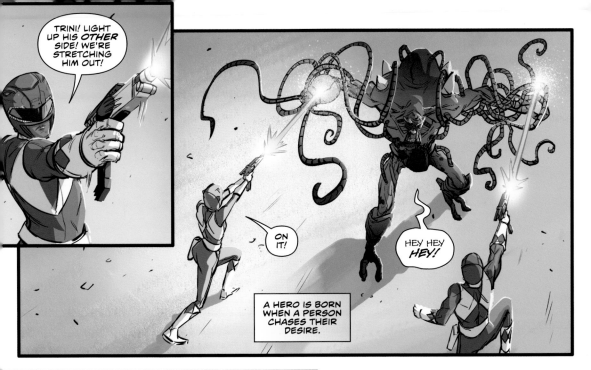

TRINI! LIGHT UP HIS *OTHER* SIDE! WE'RE STRETCHING HIM OUT!

ON IT!

HEY HEY *HEY!*

A HERO IS BORN WHEN A PERSON CHASES THEIR DESIRE.

TAKE THE SHOT, BILLY!

YOU CAN DO THIS, YOU CAN DO THIS--

WHEN THEY FACE UNEXPECTED CONSEQUENCES...

HRWWWWRR

...AND THEN ARE *CHANGED* BY THOSE CONSEQUENCES.

AH!

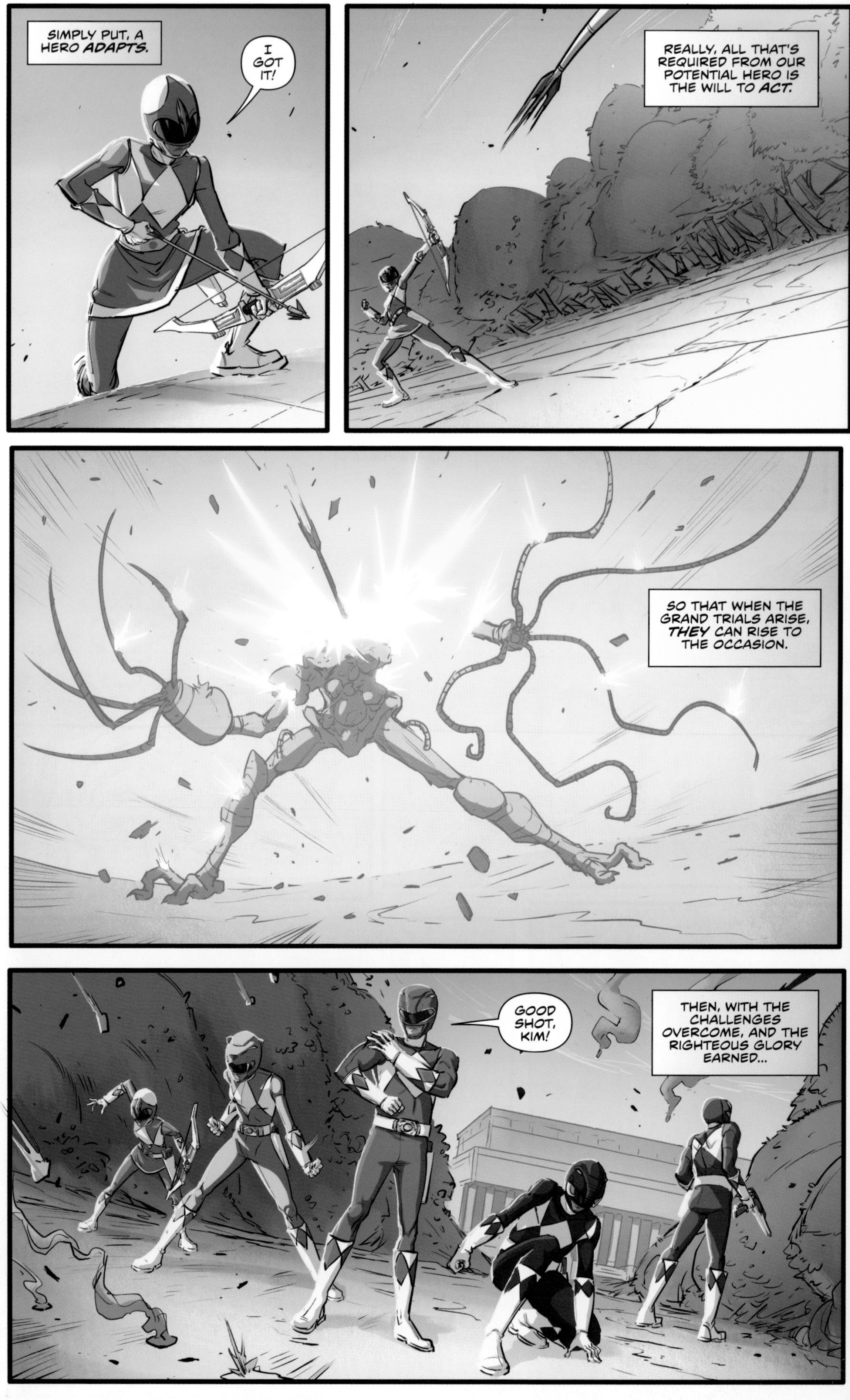
SIMPLY PUT, A HERO ADAPTS.
I GOT IT!
REALLY, ALL THAT'S REQUIRED FROM OUR POTENTIAL HERO IS THE WILL TO ACT.
SO THAT WHEN THE GRAND TRIALS ARISE, THEY CAN RISE TO THE OCCASION.
GOOD SHOT, KIM!
THEN, WITH THE CHALLENGES OVERCOME, AND THE RIGHTEOUS GLORY EARNED...

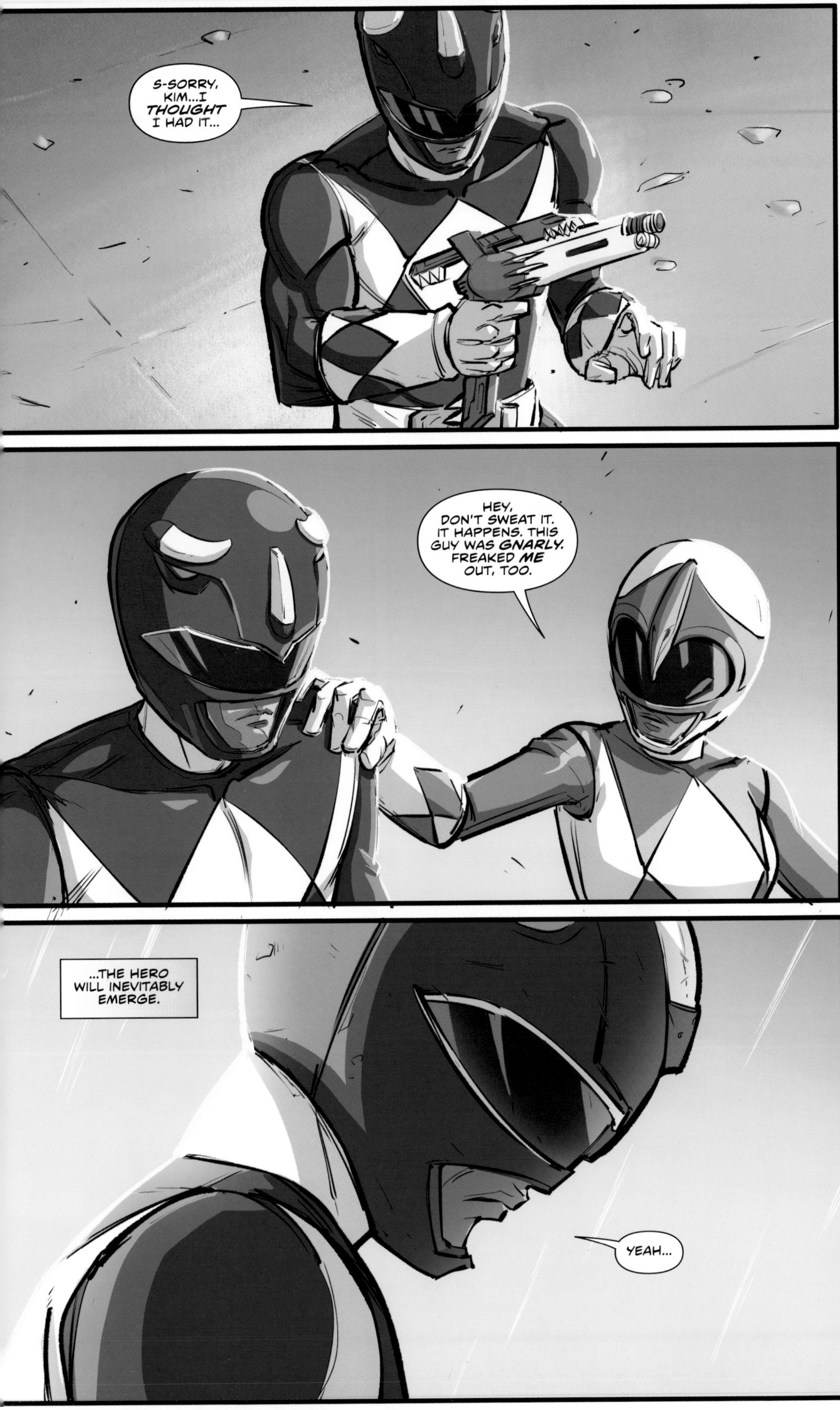
S-SORRY, KIM...I THOUGHT I HAD IT...
HEY, DON'T SWEAT IT. IT HAPPENS. THIS GUY WAS GNARLY. FREAKED ME OUT, TOO.
...THE HERO WILL INEVITABLY EMERGE.
YEAH...

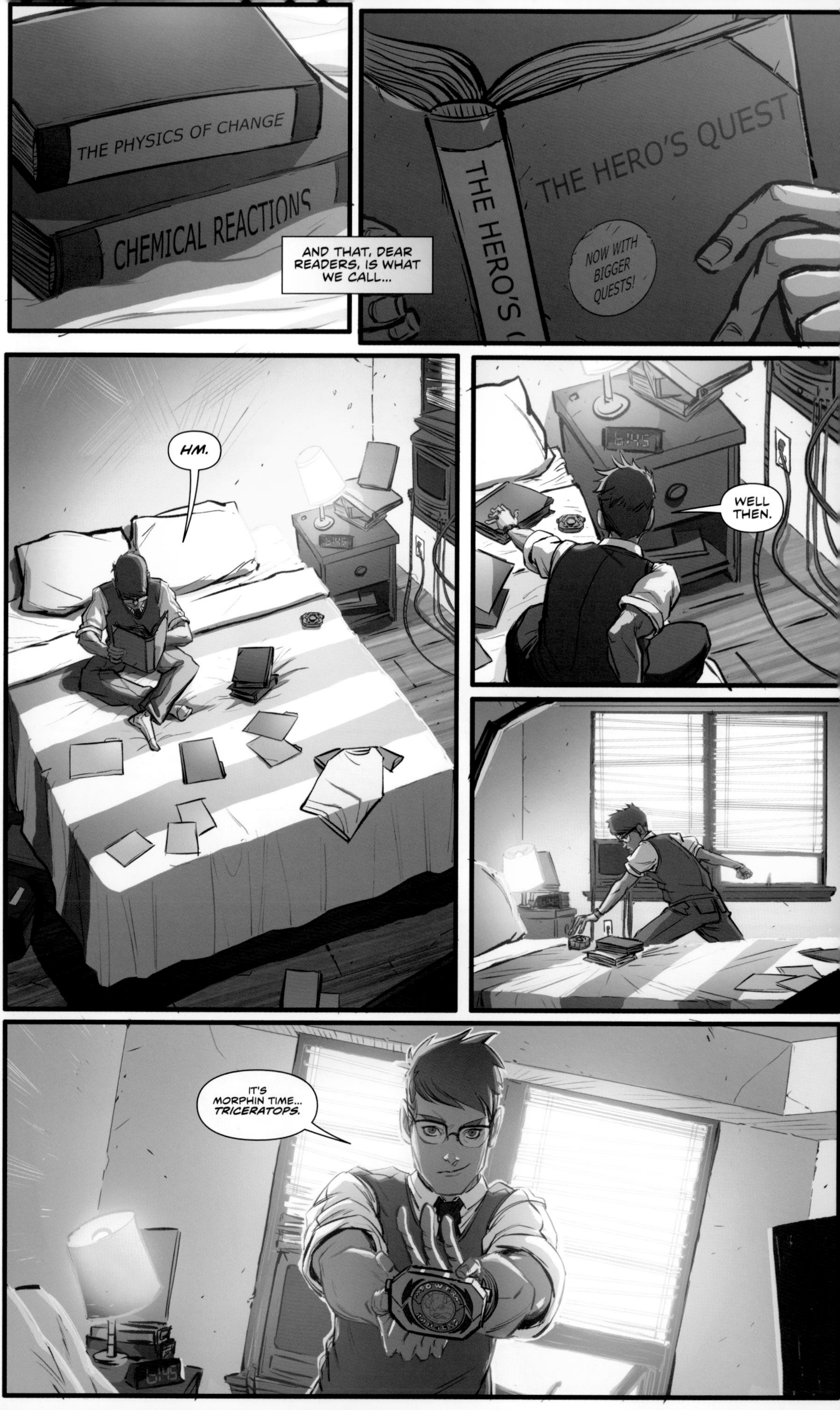
THE PHYSICS OF CHANGE
CHEMICAL REACTIONS
AND THAT, DEAR READERS, IS WHAT WE CALL...
THE HERO'S QUEST
NOW WITH BIGGER QUESTS!
HM.
WELL THEN.
IT'S MORPHIN TIME... TRICERATOPS.

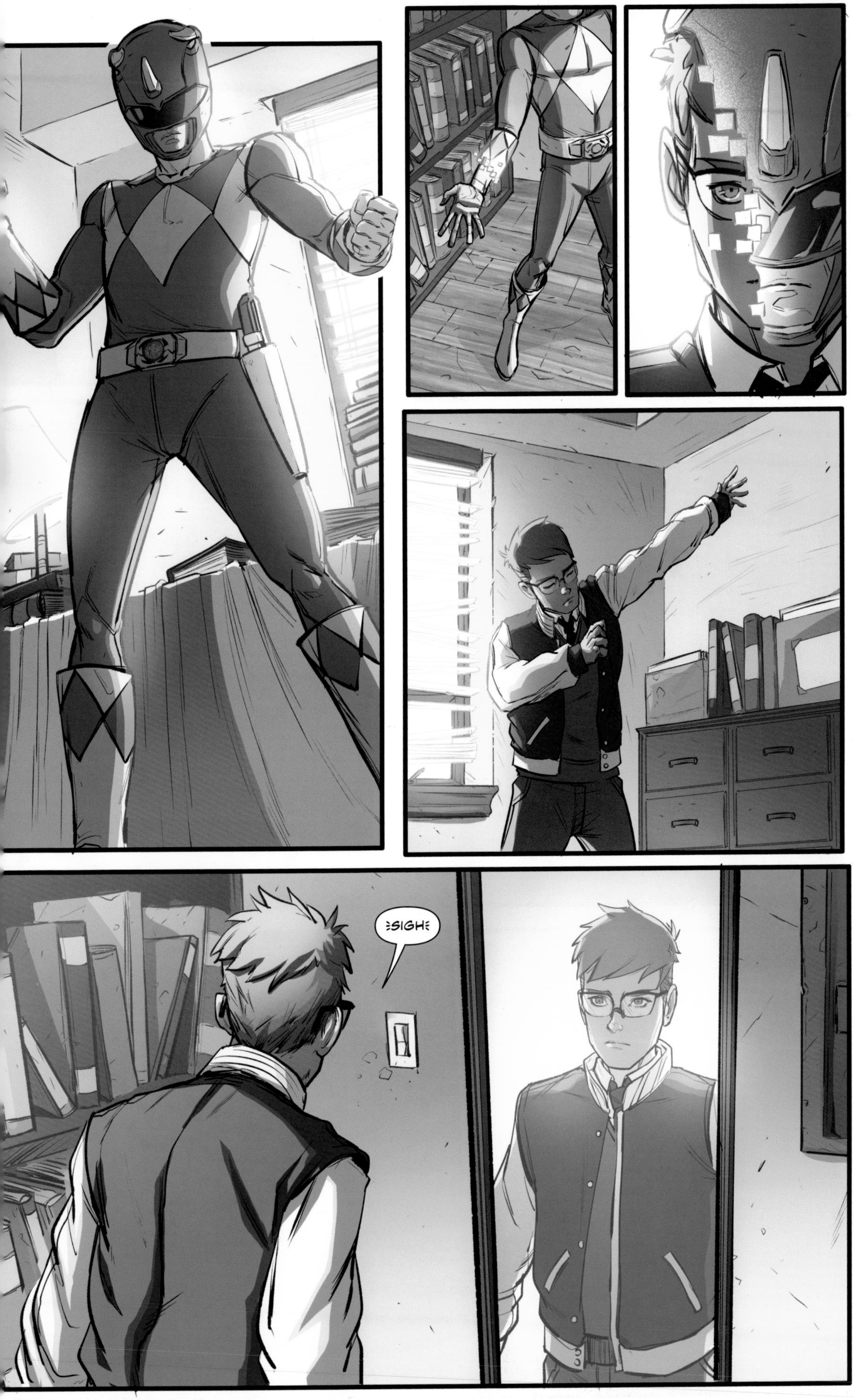
SIGH

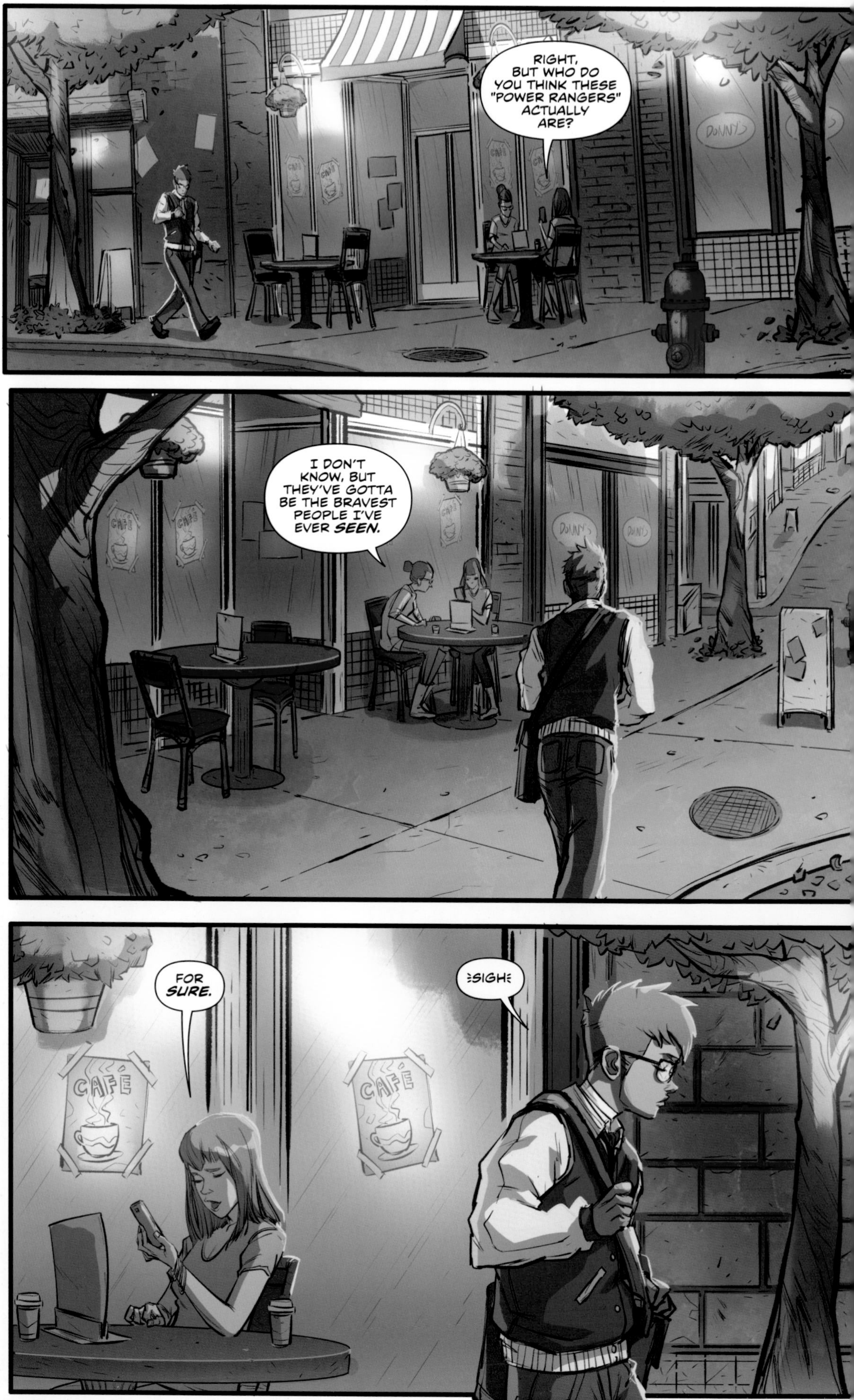
RIGHT, BUT WHO DO YOU THINK THESE "POWER RANGERS" ACTUALLY ARE?
DONNY'S
I DON'T KNOW, BUT THEY'VE GOTTA BE THE BRAVEST PEOPLE I'VE EVER SEEN.
FOR SURE.
SIGH
CAFÉ
CAFÉ

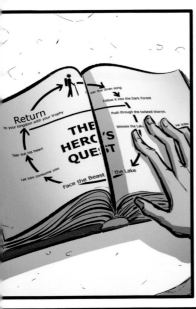

Return to your kingdom with your trophy

THE HERO'S QUEST

Tear out his heart

Hear the siren song

Follow it into the Dark Forest

Push through the twisted thorns

Witness the Lake

Let him consume you

Face the Beast the Lake

WHATCHYA READING?

OH, UH...NOTHING. JUST SOME BOOKS ABOUT... CHANGE.

LIKE, SPARE CHANGE?

NO. I MEAN...YOU KNOW, *HOW* THINGS CHANGE.

OH. RIIIIGHT...

WHEEEEOWWW

WHAT THE--?!

HEY! HEY, RELAX, BILLY. IT'S *NOTHING.* IT'S JUST A SIREN. ALL GOOD.

O-OH...OF COURSE...

ARE YOU SURE YOU'RE OKAY?

Y-YEAH, TRINI...I'M GREAT.

THE HERO'S QUEST IS DEFINED AS FOLLOWS...

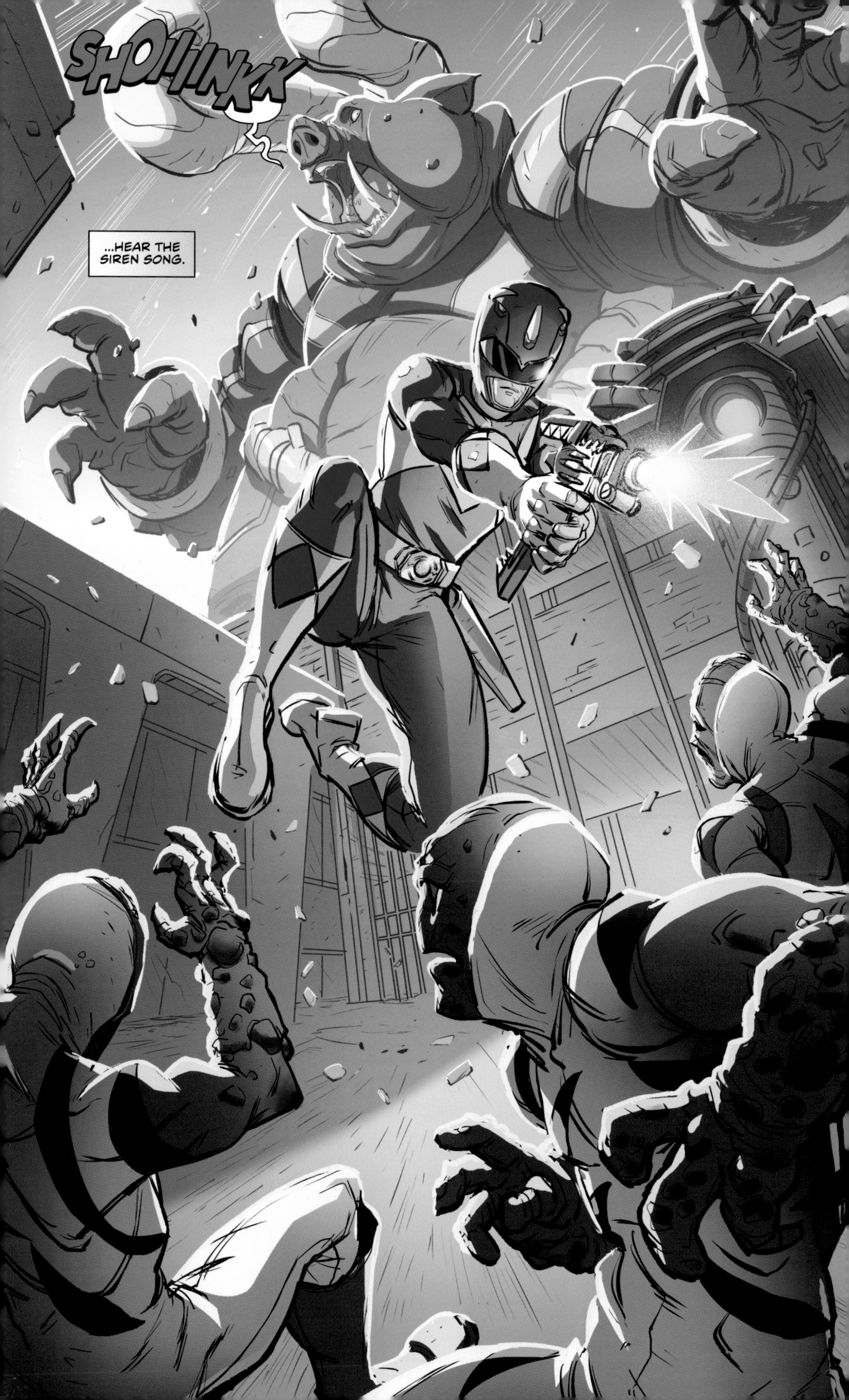
SHOIIIINKK
...HEAR THE SIREN SONG.

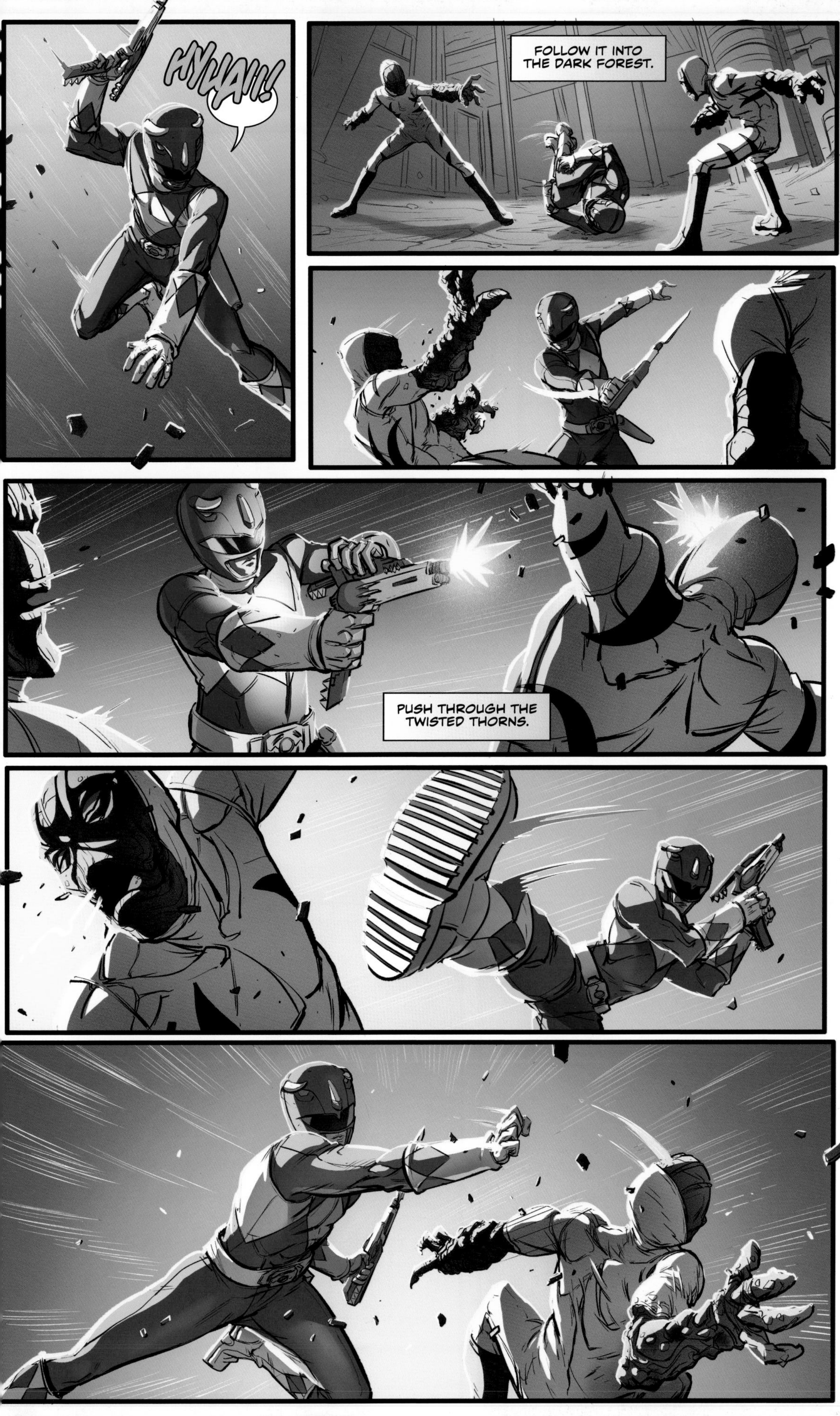
HYUAII!
FOLLOW IT INTO THE DARK FOREST.
PUSH THROUGH THE TWISTED THORNS.

HUYAUUHHU?

HUAUHHH!

HUUUWWWA!

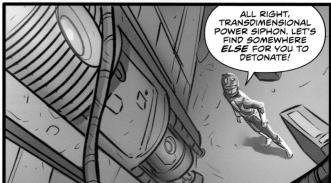

ALL RIGHT, TRANSDIMENSIONAL POWER SIPHON. LET'S FIND SOMEWHERE *ELSE* FOR YOU TO DETONATE!

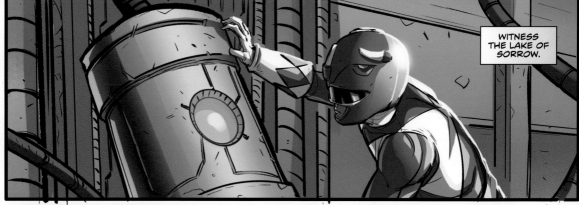

WITNESS THE LAKE OF SORROW.

HUWUHHU!

DIVE INTO IT.

ALL RIGHT, ALL RIGHT...THIRTY SECONDS...

PLENTY OF TIME... YOU'VE GOT THIS...

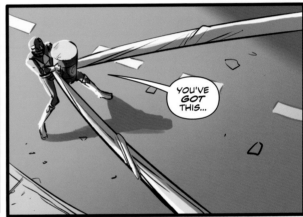

YOU'VE *GOT* THIS...

FACE THE BEAST OF THE LAKE.

SHOOO...

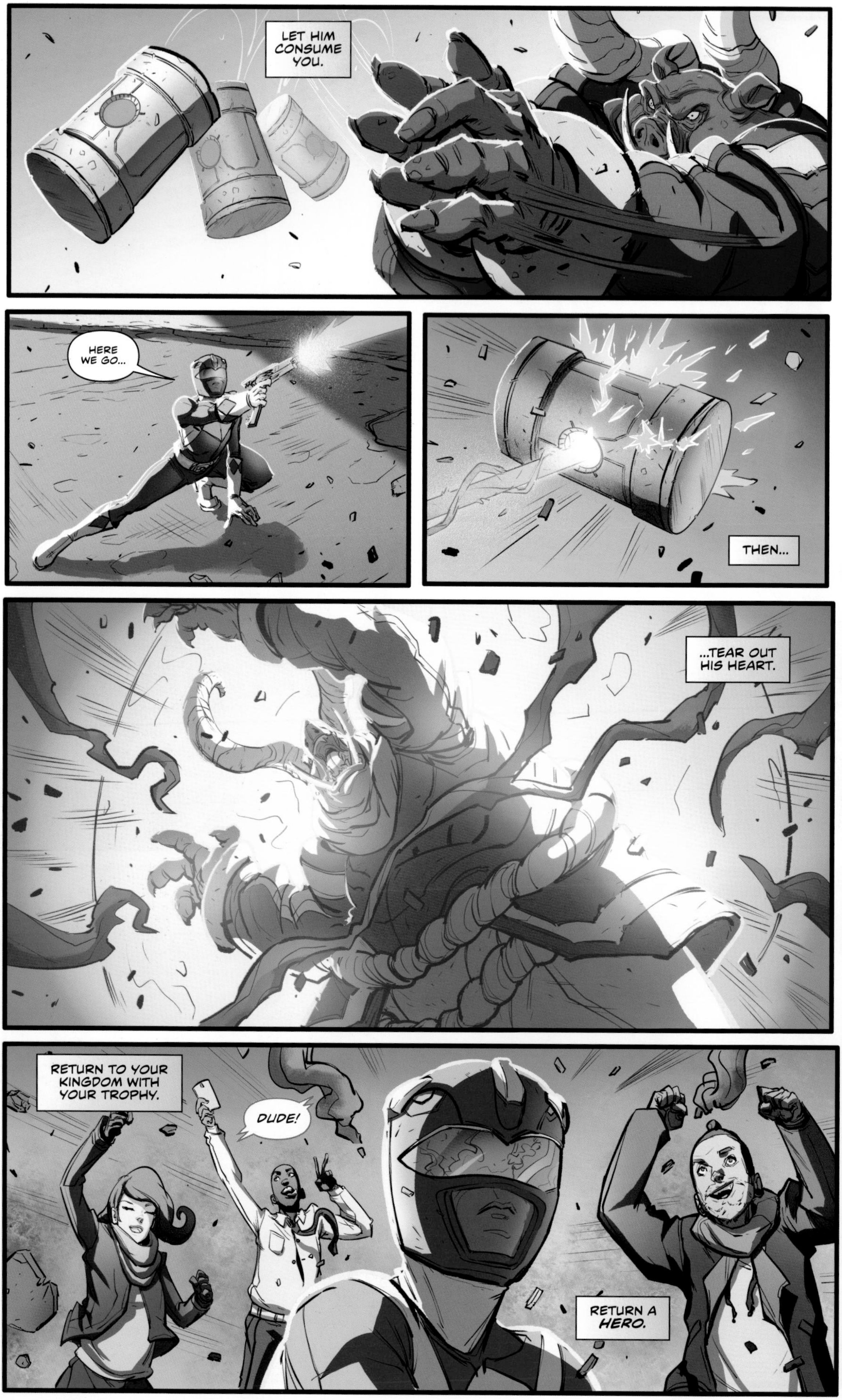
LET HIM CONSUME YOU.
HERE WE GO...
THEN...
...TEAR OUT HIS HEART.
RETURN TO YOUR KINGDOM WITH YOUR TROPHY.
DUDE!
RETURN A *HERO.*

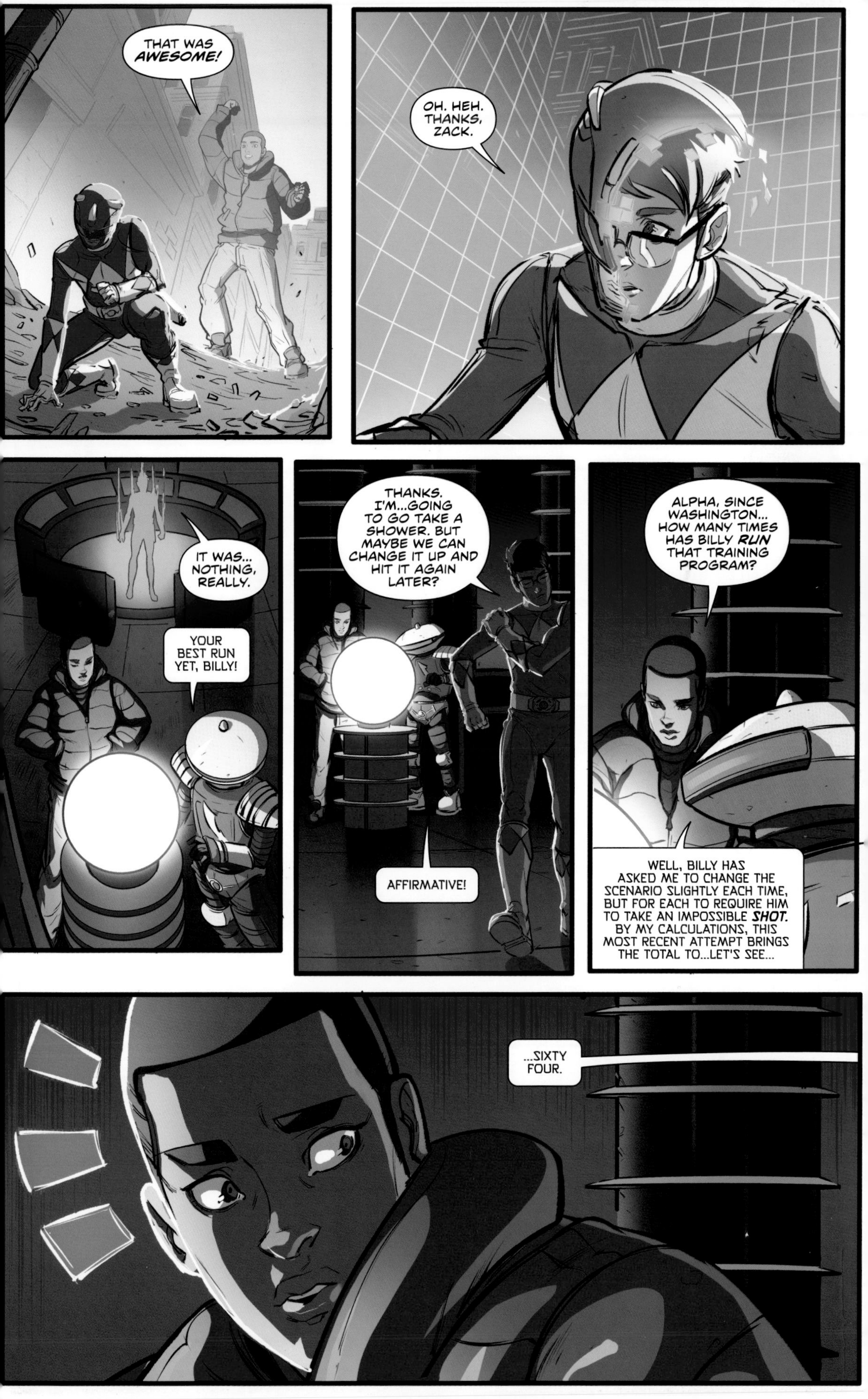
THAT WAS *AWESOME!*
OH. HEH. THANKS, ZACK.
IT WAS... NOTHING, REALLY.
YOUR BEST RUN YET, BILLY!
THANKS. I'M...GOING TO GO TAKE A SHOWER. BUT MAYBE WE CAN CHANGE IT UP AND HIT IT AGAIN LATER?
AFFIRMATIVE!
ALPHA, SINCE WASHINGTON... HOW MANY TIMES HAS BILLY *RUN* THAT TRAINING PROGRAM?
WELL, BILLY HAS ASKED ME TO CHANGE THE SCENARIO SLIGHTLY EACH TIME, BUT FOR EACH TO REQUIRE HIM TO TAKE AN IMPOSSIBLE *SHOT.* BY MY CALCULATIONS, THIS MOST RECENT ATTEMPT BRINGS THE TOTAL TO...LET'S SEE...
...SIXTY FOUR.

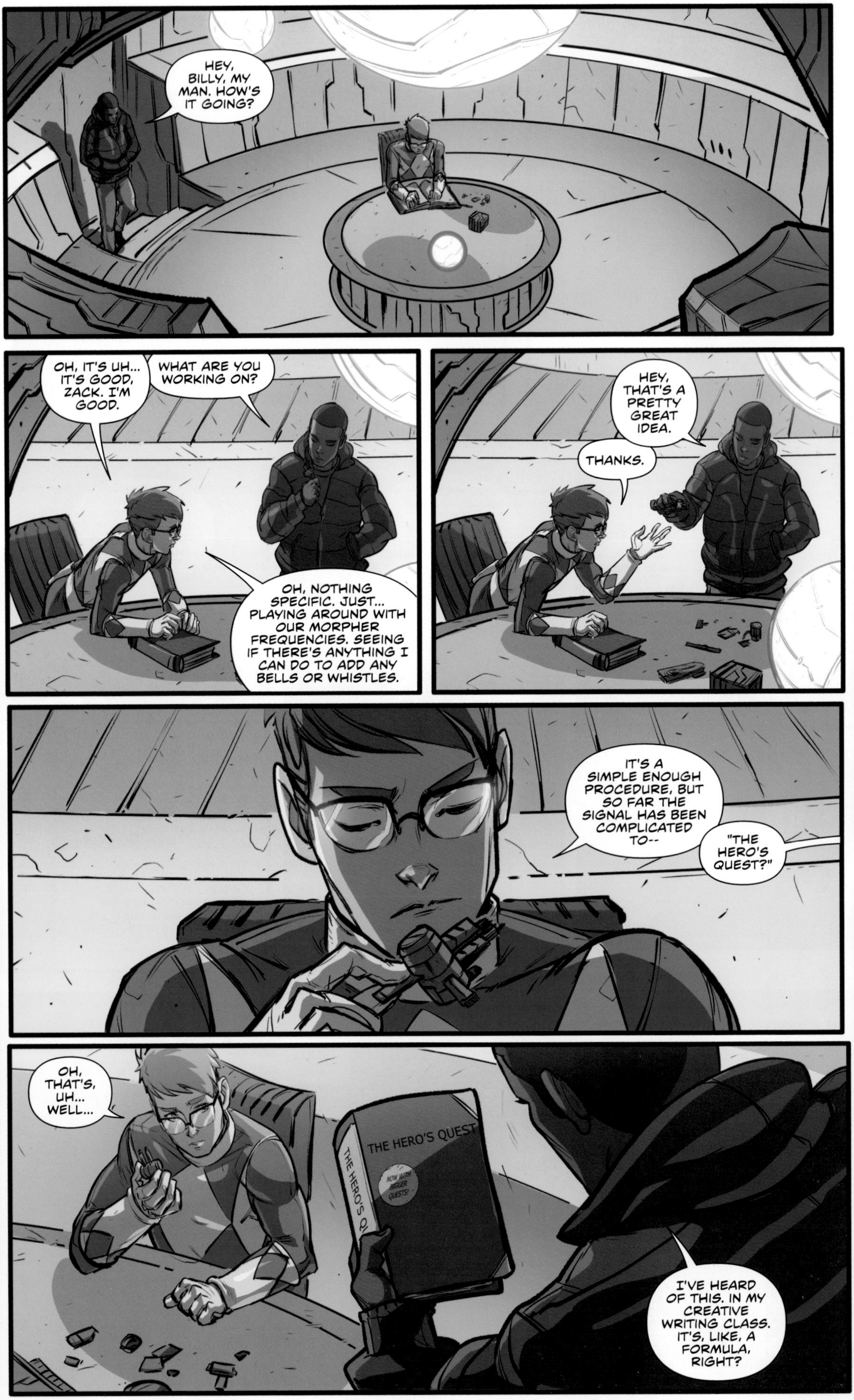
HEY, BILLY, MY MAN. HOW'S IT GOING?
OH, IT'S UH... IT'S GOOD, ZACK. I'M GOOD.
WHAT ARE YOU WORKING ON?
OH, NOTHING SPECIFIC. JUST... PLAYING AROUND WITH OUR MORPHER FREQUENCIES. SEEING IF THERE'S ANYTHING I CAN DO TO ADD ANY BELLS OR WHISTLES.
HEY, THAT'S A PRETTY GREAT IDEA.
THANKS.
IT'S A SIMPLE ENOUGH PROCEDURE, BUT SO FAR THE SIGNAL HAS BEEN COMPLICATED TO--
"THE HERO'S QUEST?"
OH, THAT'S, UH... WELL...
THE HERO'S QUEST
THE HERO'S QU
NOW WITH BIGGER QUESTS!
I'VE HEARD OF THIS. IN MY CREATIVE WRITING CLASS. IT'S, LIKE, A FORMULA, RIGHT?

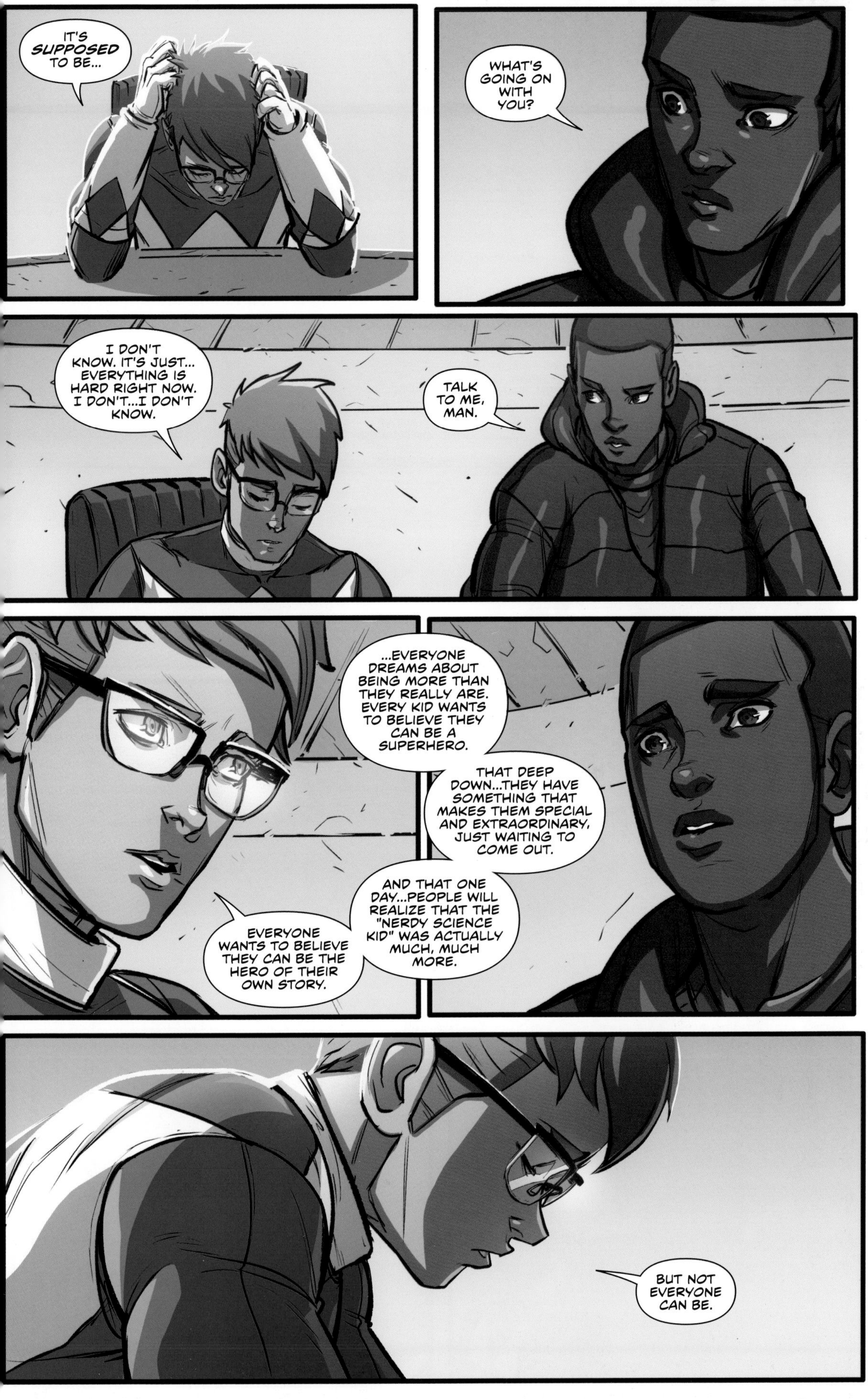
IT'S SUPPOSED TO BE...
WHAT'S GOING ON WITH YOU?
I DON'T KNOW. IT'S JUST... EVERYTHING IS HARD RIGHT NOW. I DON'T...I DON'T KNOW.
TALK TO ME, MAN.
EVERYONE WANTS TO BELIEVE THEY CAN BE THE HERO OF THEIR OWN STORY.
...EVERYONE DREAMS ABOUT BEING MORE THAN THEY REALLY ARE. EVERY KID WANTS TO BELIEVE THEY CAN BE A SUPERHERO.
THAT DEEP DOWN...THEY HAVE SOMETHING THAT MAKES THEM SPECIAL AND EXTRAORDINARY, JUST WAITING TO COME OUT.
AND THAT ONE DAY...PEOPLE WILL REALIZE THAT THE "NERDY SCIENCE KID" WAS ACTUALLY MUCH, MUCH MORE.
BUT NOT EVERYONE CAN BE.

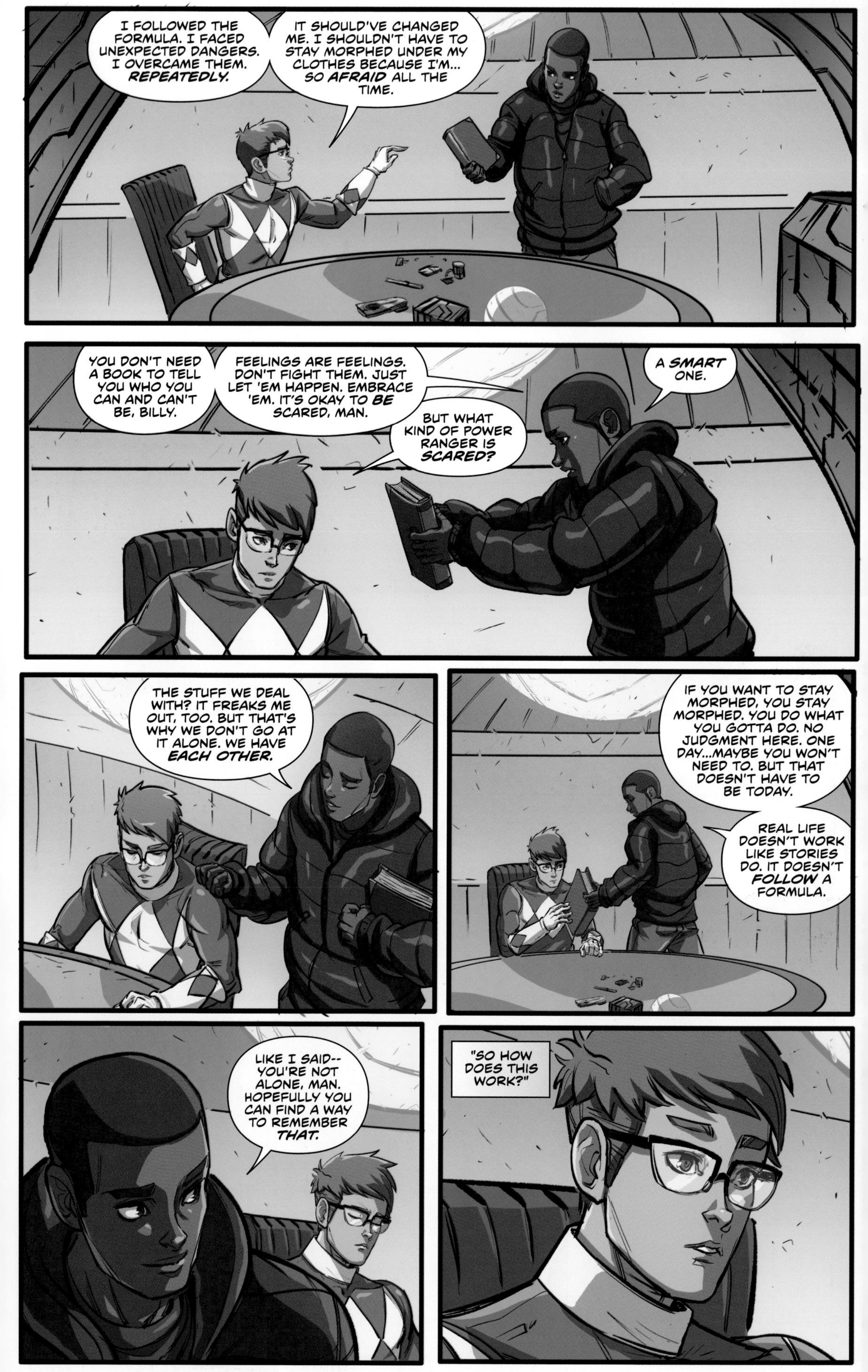
I FOLLOWED THE FORMULA. I FACED UNEXPECTED DANGERS. I OVERCAME THEM. *REPEATEDLY.*
IT SHOULD'VE CHANGED ME. I SHOULDN'T HAVE TO STAY MORPHED UNDER MY CLOTHES BECAUSE I'M... SO *AFRAID* ALL THE TIME.
YOU DON'T NEED A BOOK TO TELL YOU WHO YOU CAN AND CAN'T BE, BILLY.
FEELINGS ARE FEELINGS. DON'T FIGHT THEM. JUST LET 'EM HAPPEN. EMBRACE 'EM. IT'S OKAY TO *BE* SCARED, MAN.
BUT WHAT KIND OF POWER RANGER IS *SCARED?*
A *SMART* ONE.
THE STUFF WE DEAL WITH? IT FREAKS ME OUT, TOO. BUT THAT'S WHY WE DON'T GO AT IT ALONE. WE HAVE *EACH OTHER.*
IF YOU WANT TO STAY MORPHED, YOU STAY MORPHED. YOU DO WHAT YOU GOTTA DO. NO JUDGMENT HERE. ONE DAY...MAYBE YOU WON'T NEED TO. BUT THAT DOESN'T HAVE TO BE TODAY.
REAL LIFE DOESN'T WORK LIKE STORIES DO. IT DOESN'T *FOLLOW* A FORMULA.
LIKE I SAID-- YOU'RE NOT ALONE, MAN. HOPEFULLY YOU CAN FIND A WAY TO REMEMBER *THAT.*
"SO HOW DOES THIS WORK?"

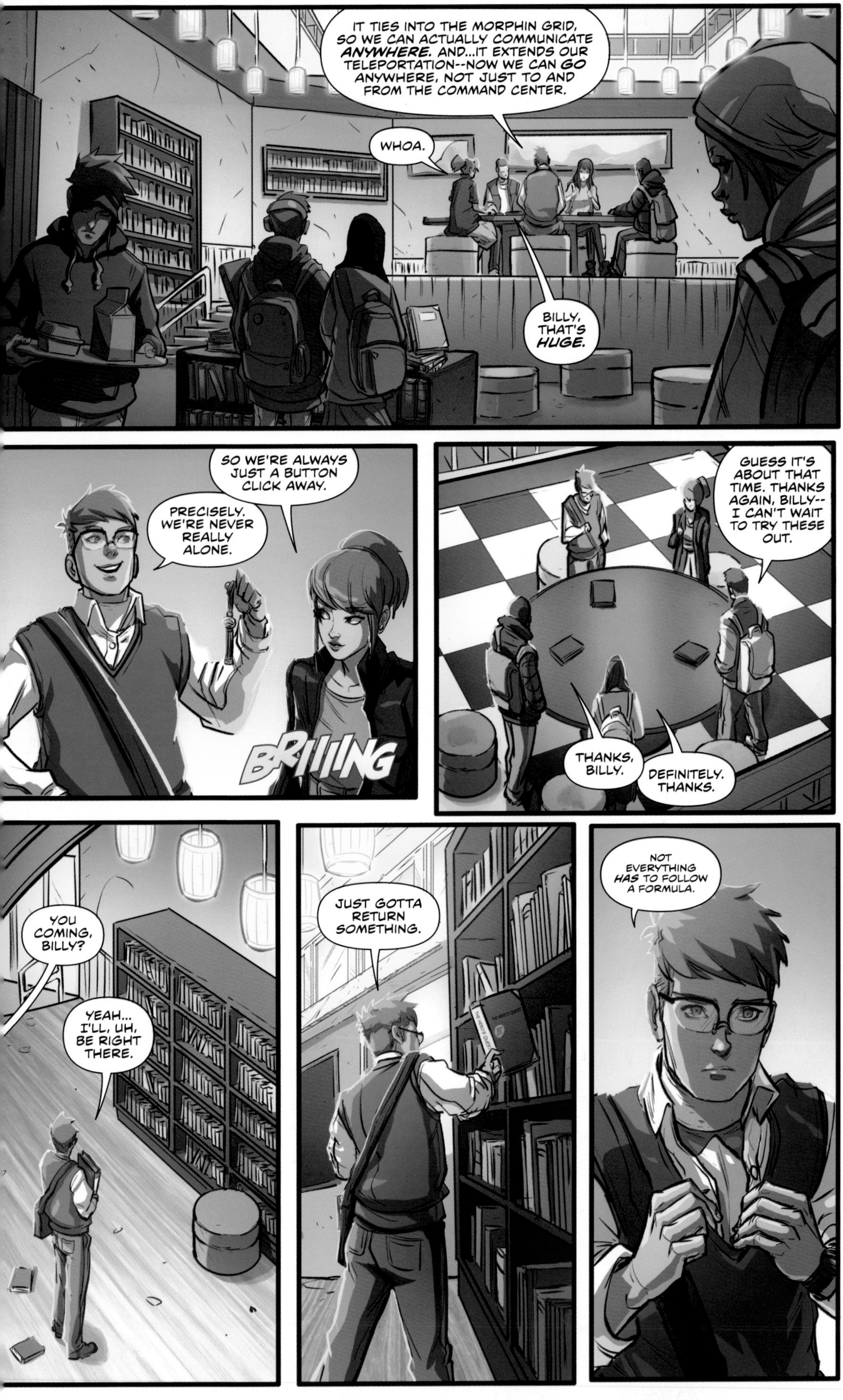
IT TIES INTO THE MORPHIN GRID, SO WE CAN ACTUALLY COMMUNICATE ANYWHERE. AND...IT EXTENDS OUR TELEPORTATION--NOW WE CAN GO ANYWHERE, NOT JUST TO AND FROM THE COMMAND CENTER.
WHOA.
BILLY, THAT'S HUGE.
SO WE'RE ALWAYS JUST A BUTTON CLICK AWAY.
PRECISELY. WE'RE NEVER REALLY ALONE.
BRIIIING
GUESS IT'S ABOUT THAT TIME. THANKS AGAIN, BILLY-- I CAN'T WAIT TO TRY THESE OUT.
THANKS, BILLY.
DEFINITELY. THANKS.
YOU COMING, BILLY?
YEAH... I'LL, UH, BE RIGHT THERE.
JUST GOTTA RETURN SOMETHING.
NOT EVERYTHING HAS TO FOLLOW A FORMULA.

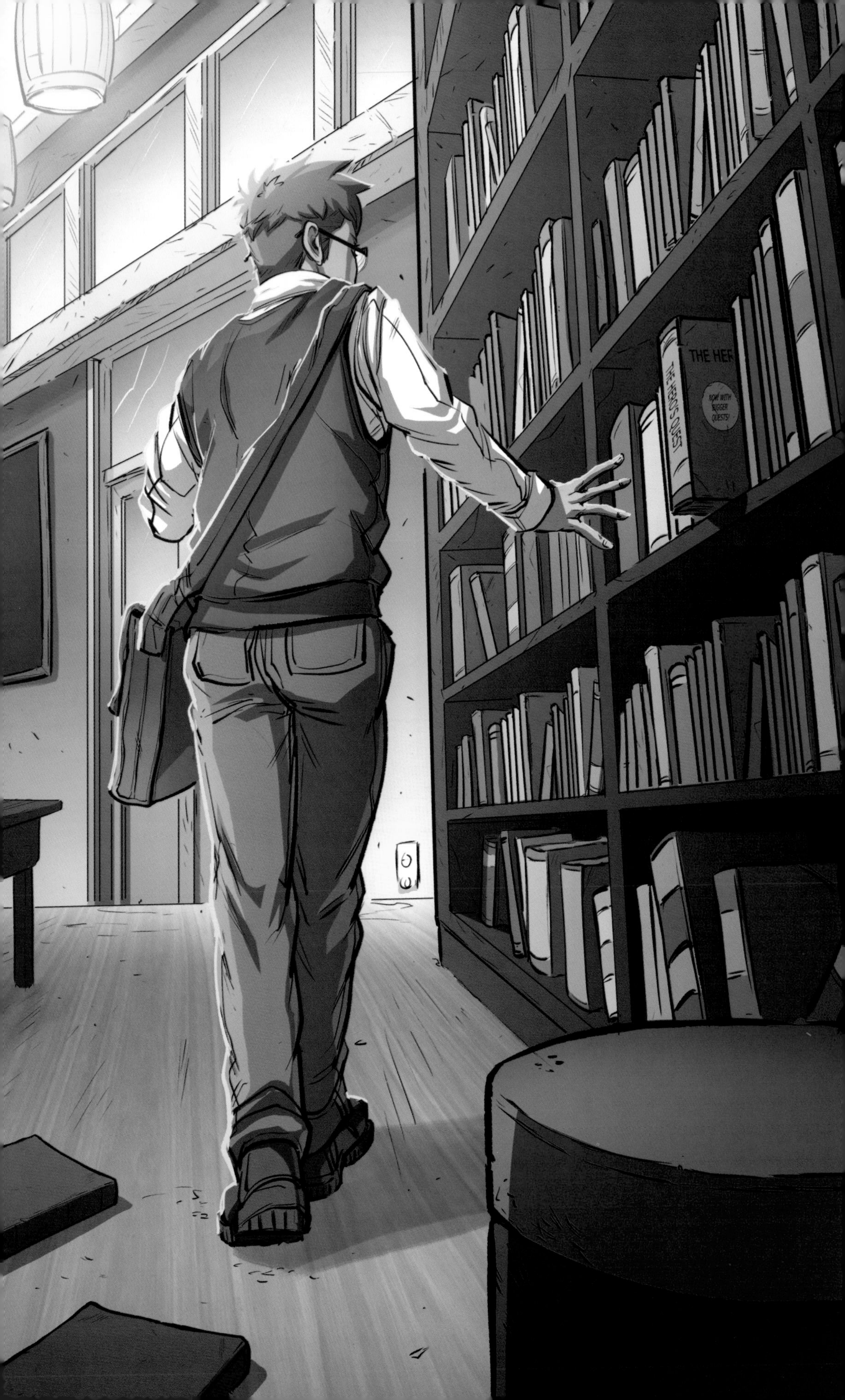
THE HERO'S QUEST
THE HER
NOW WITH BIGGER QUESTS!

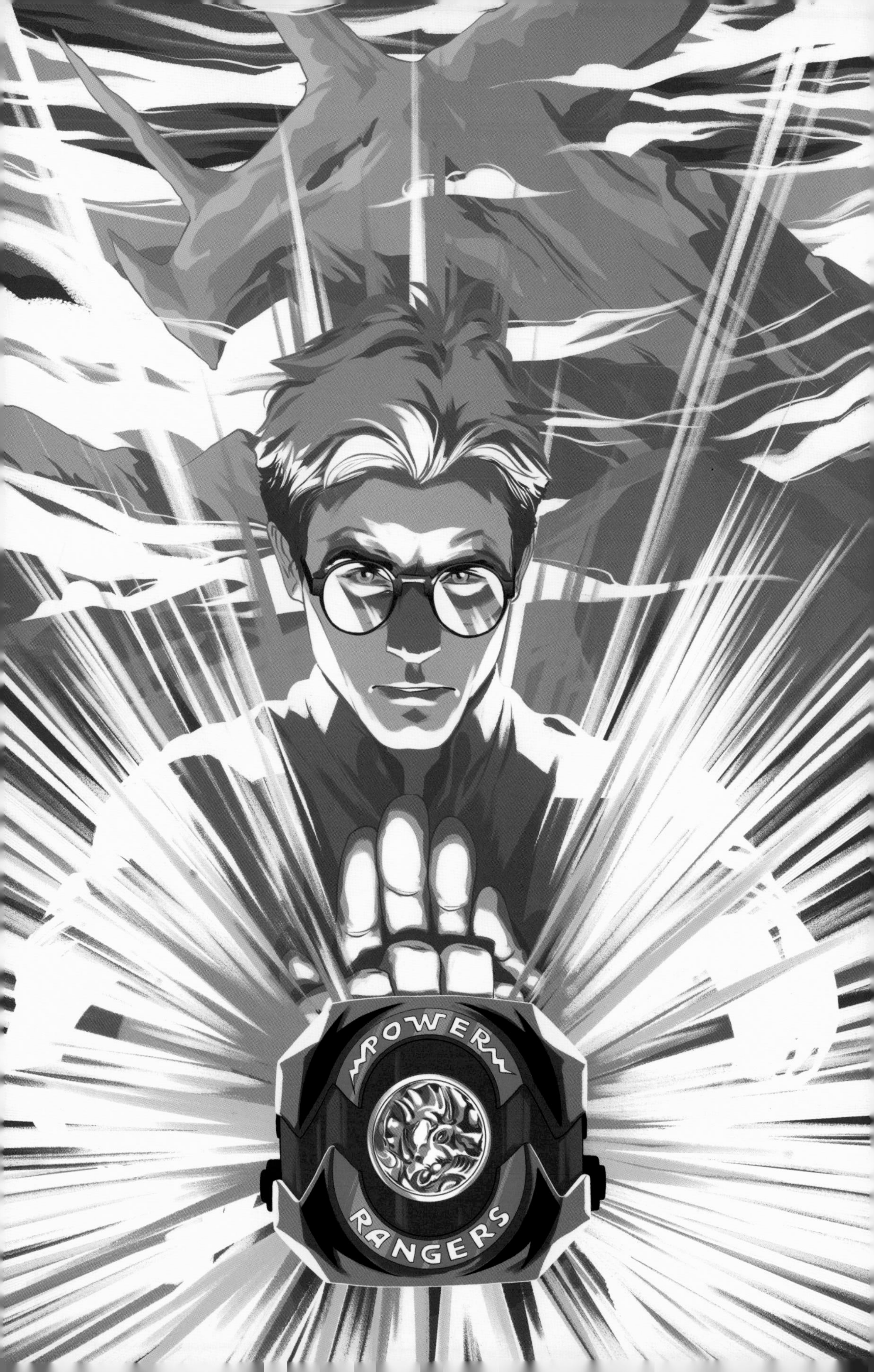
POWER
RANGERS

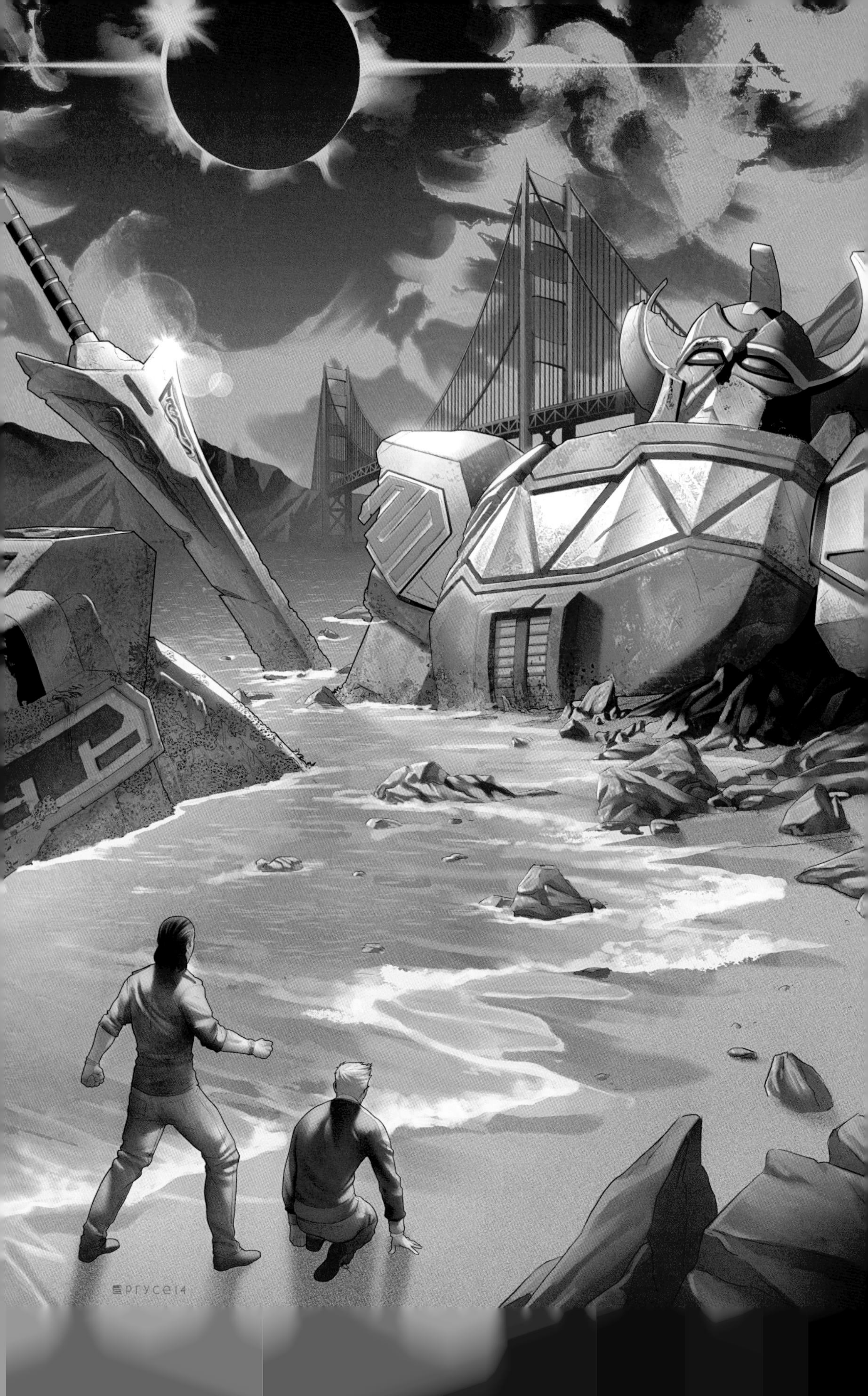
pryce14

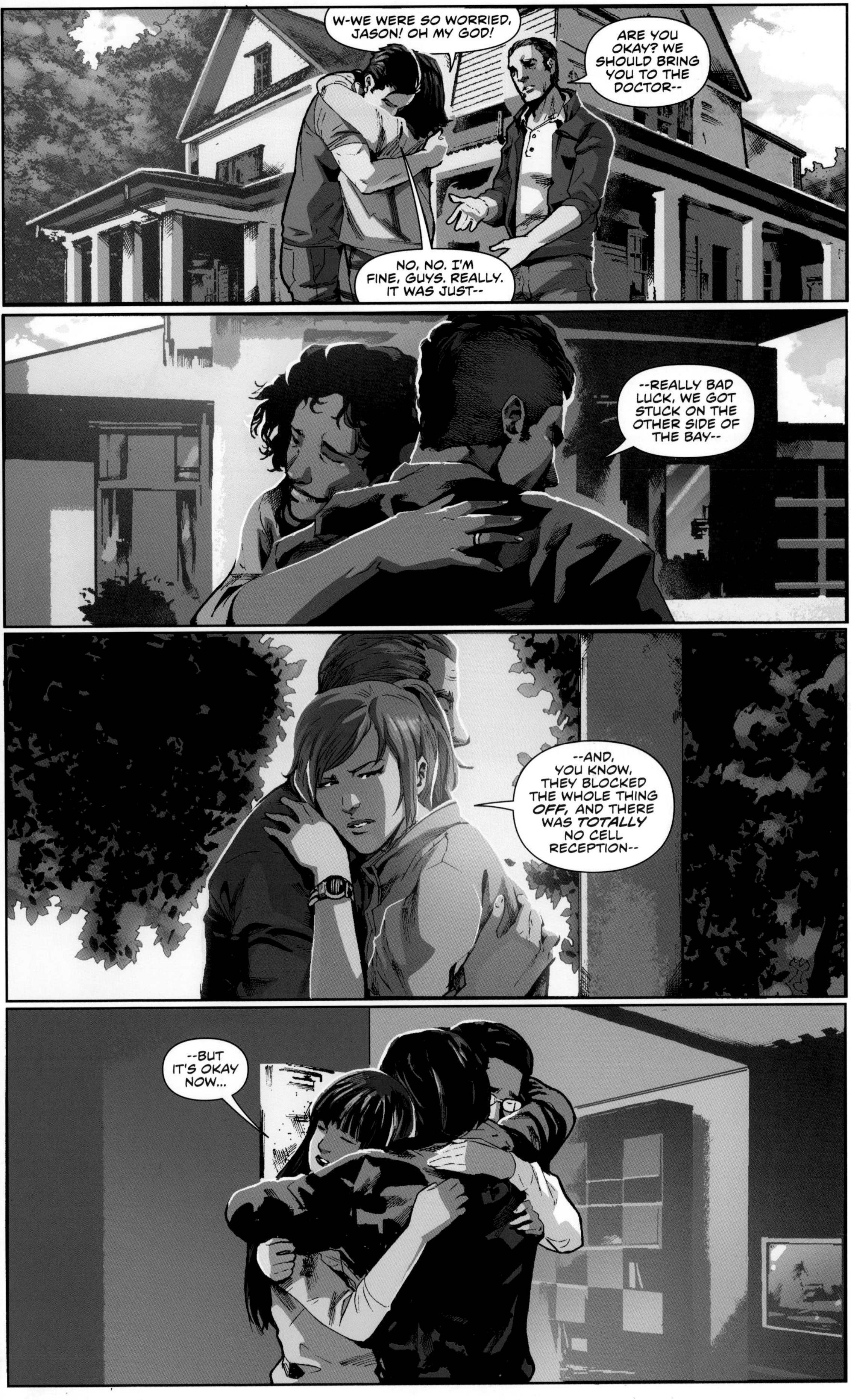
W-WE WERE SO WORRIED, JASON! OH MY GOD!
ARE YOU OKAY? WE SHOULD BRING YOU TO THE DOCTOR--
NO, NO. I'M FINE, GUYS. REALLY. IT WAS JUST--
--REALLY BAD LUCK, WE GOT STUCK ON THE OTHER SIDE OF THE BAY--
--AND, YOU KNOW, THEY BLOCKED THE WHOLE THING OFF, AND THERE WAS TOTALLY NO CELL RECEPTION--
--BUT IT'S OKAY NOW...

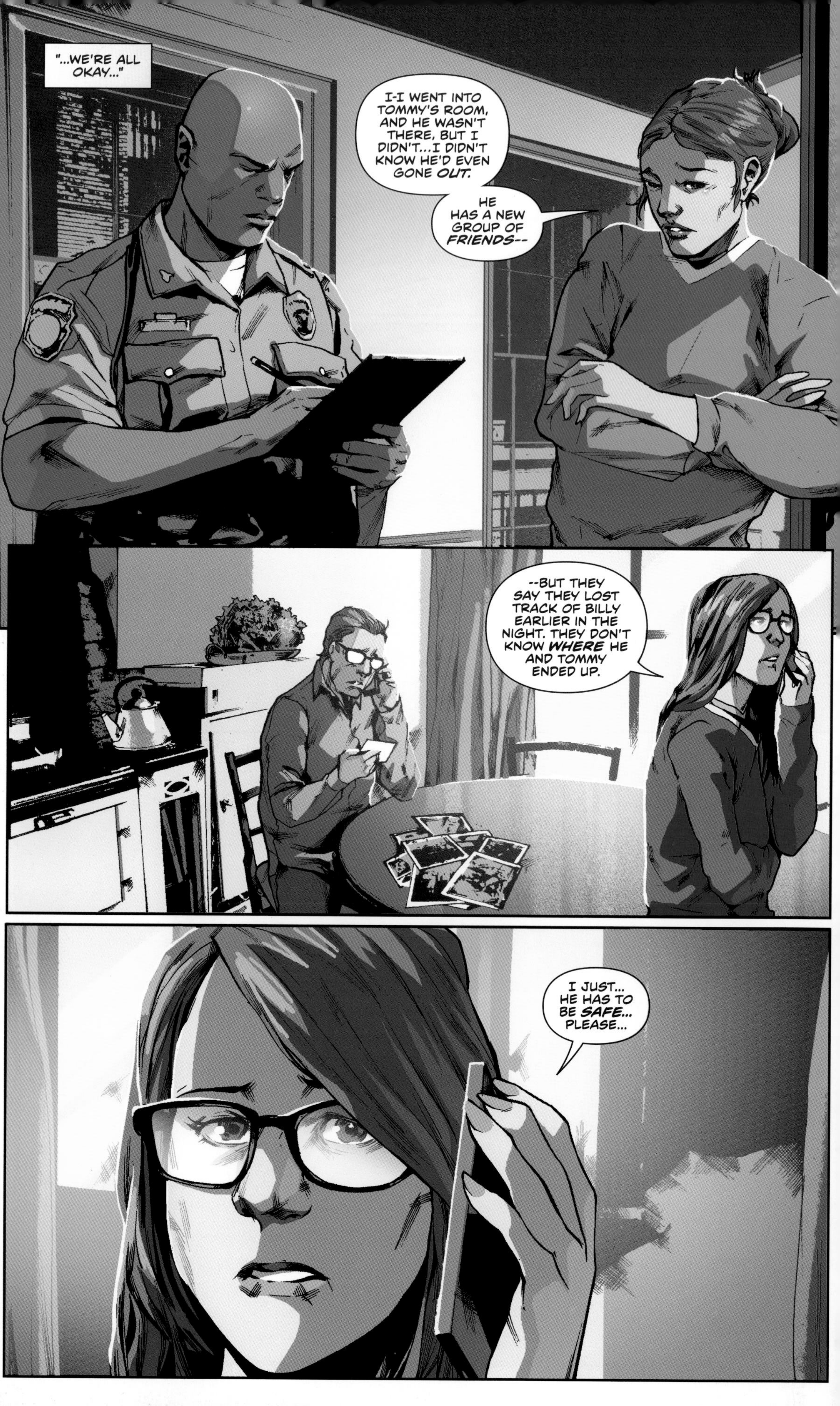
"...WE'RE ALL OKAY..."
I-I WENT INTO TOMMY'S ROOM, AND HE WASN'T THERE, BUT I DIDN'T...I DIDN'T KNOW HE'D EVEN GONE OUT.
HE HAS A NEW GROUP OF FRIENDS--
--BUT THEY SAY THEY LOST TRACK OF BILLY EARLIER IN THE NIGHT. THEY DON'T KNOW WHERE HE AND TOMMY ENDED UP.
I JUST... HE HAS TO BE SAFE... PLEASE...

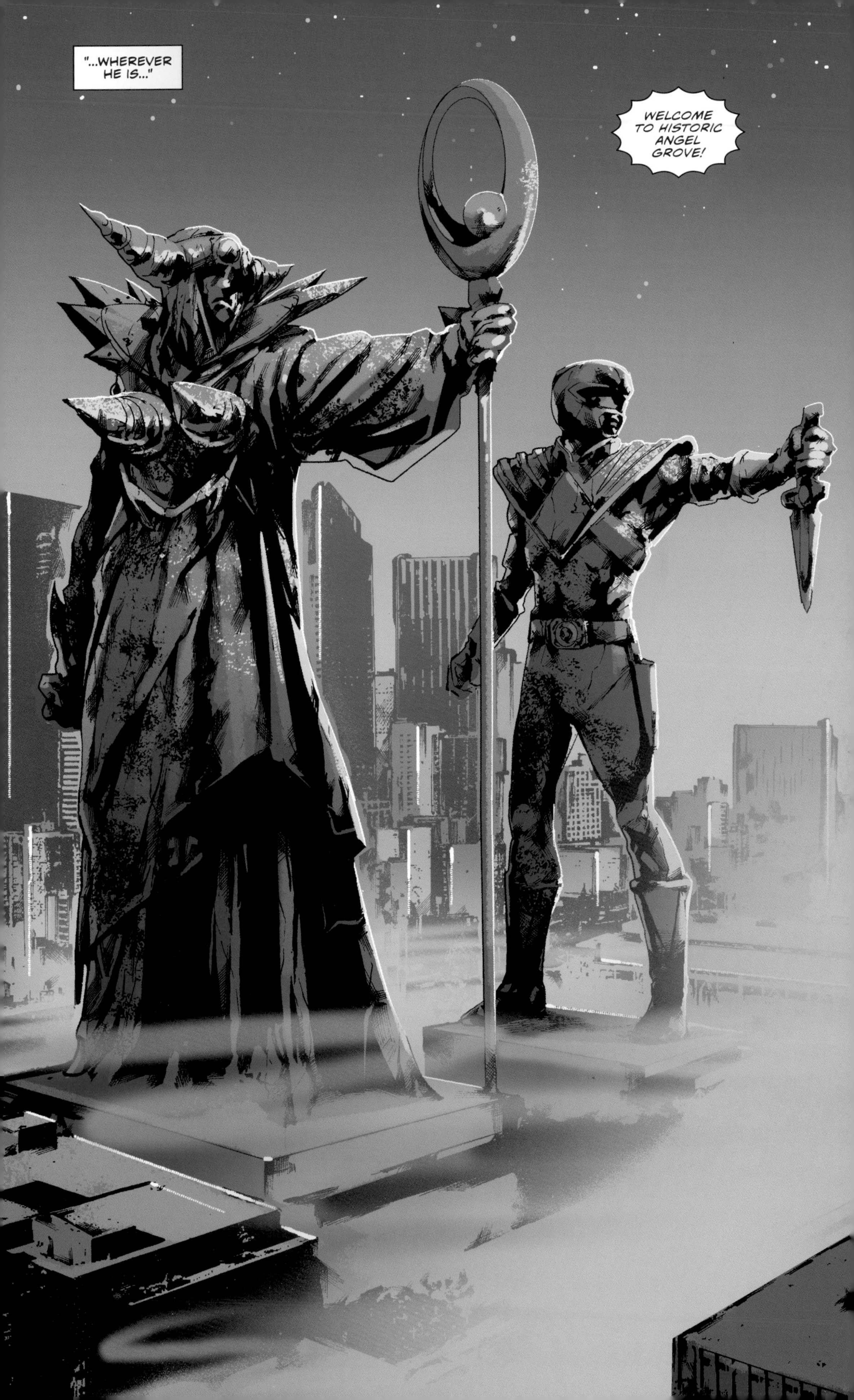
"...WHEREVER HE IS..."
WELCOME TO HISTORIC ANGEL GROVE!

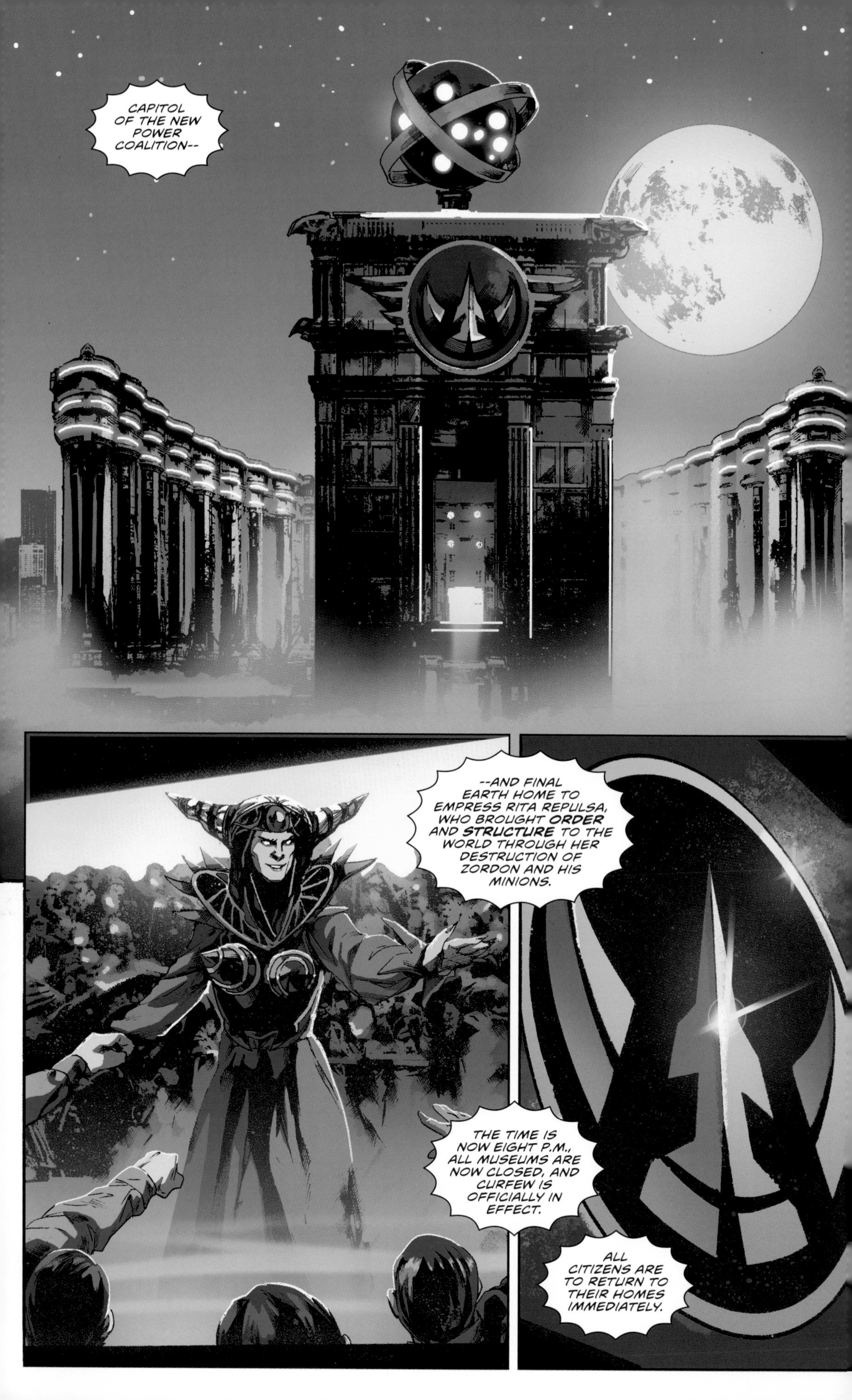
CAPITOL OF THE NEW POWER COALITION--
--AND FINAL EARTH HOME TO EMPRESS RITA REPULSA, WHO BROUGHT ORDER AND STRUCTURE TO THE WORLD THROUGH HER DESTRUCTION OF ZORDON AND HIS MINIONS.
THE TIME IS NOW EIGHT P.M., ALL MUSEUMS ARE NOW CLOSED, AND CURFEW IS OFFICIALLY IN EFFECT.
ALL CITIZENS ARE TO RETURN TO THEIR HOMES IMMEDIATELY.

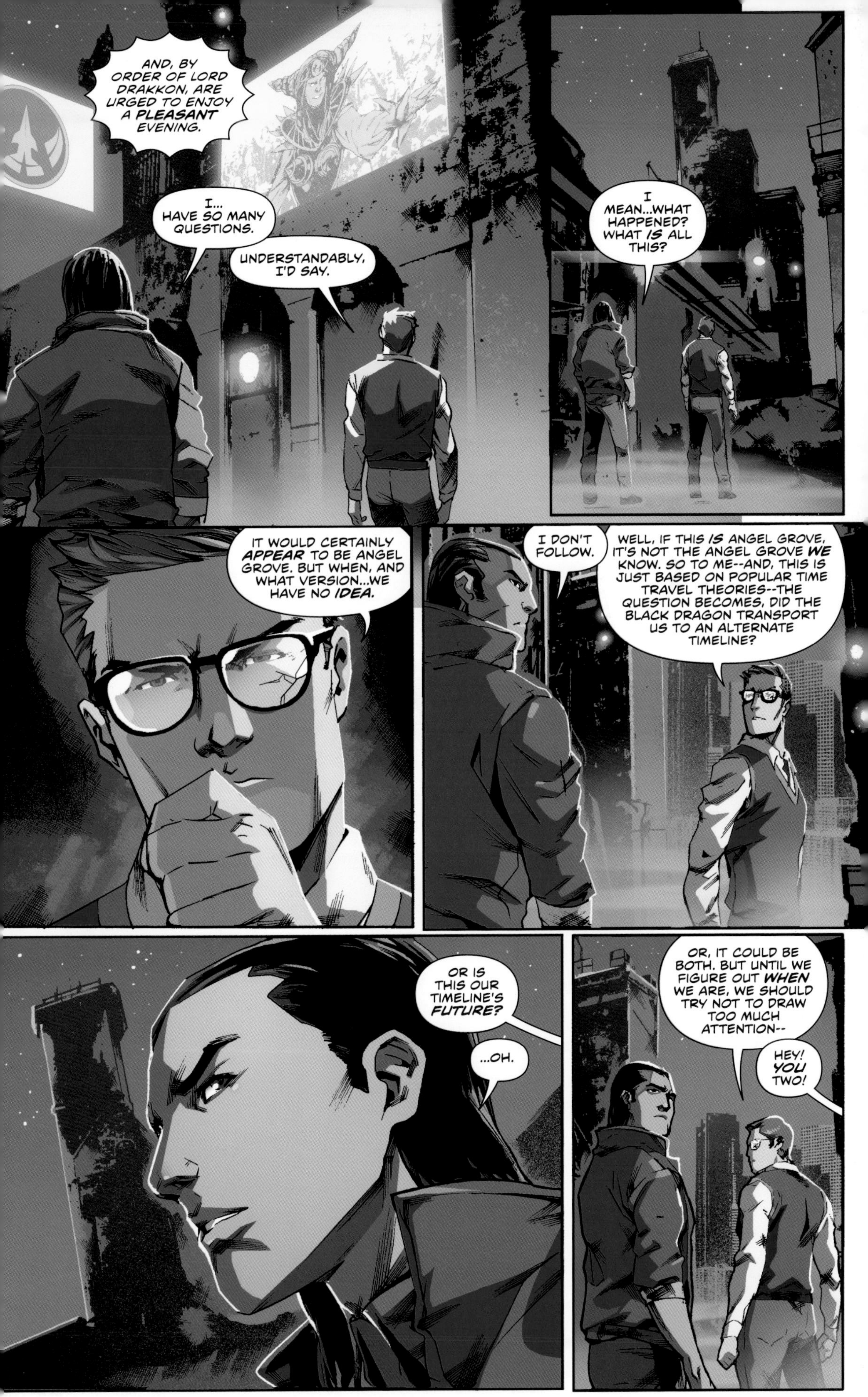
AND, BY ORDER OF LORD DRAKKON, ARE URGED TO ENJOY A **PLEASANT** EVENING.
I... HAVE SO MANY QUESTIONS.
UNDERSTANDABLY, I'D SAY.
I MEAN...WHAT HAPPENED? WHAT *IS* ALL THIS?
IT WOULD CERTAINLY ***APPEAR*** TO BE ANGEL GROVE. BUT WHEN, AND WHAT VERSION...WE HAVE NO *IDEA.*
I DON'T FOLLOW.
WELL, IF THIS *IS* ANGEL GROVE, IT'S NOT THE ANGEL GROVE ***WE*** KNOW. SO TO ME--AND, THIS IS JUST BASED ON POPULAR TIME TRAVEL THEORIES--THE QUESTION BECOMES, DID THE BLACK DRAGON TRANSPORT US TO AN ALTERNATE TIMELINE?
OR IS THIS OUR TIMELINE'S ***FUTURE?***
...OH.
OR, IT COULD BE BOTH. BUT UNTIL WE FIGURE OUT ***WHEN*** WE ARE, WE SHOULD TRY NOT TO DRAW TOO MUCH ATTENTION--
HEY! ***YOU*** TWO!

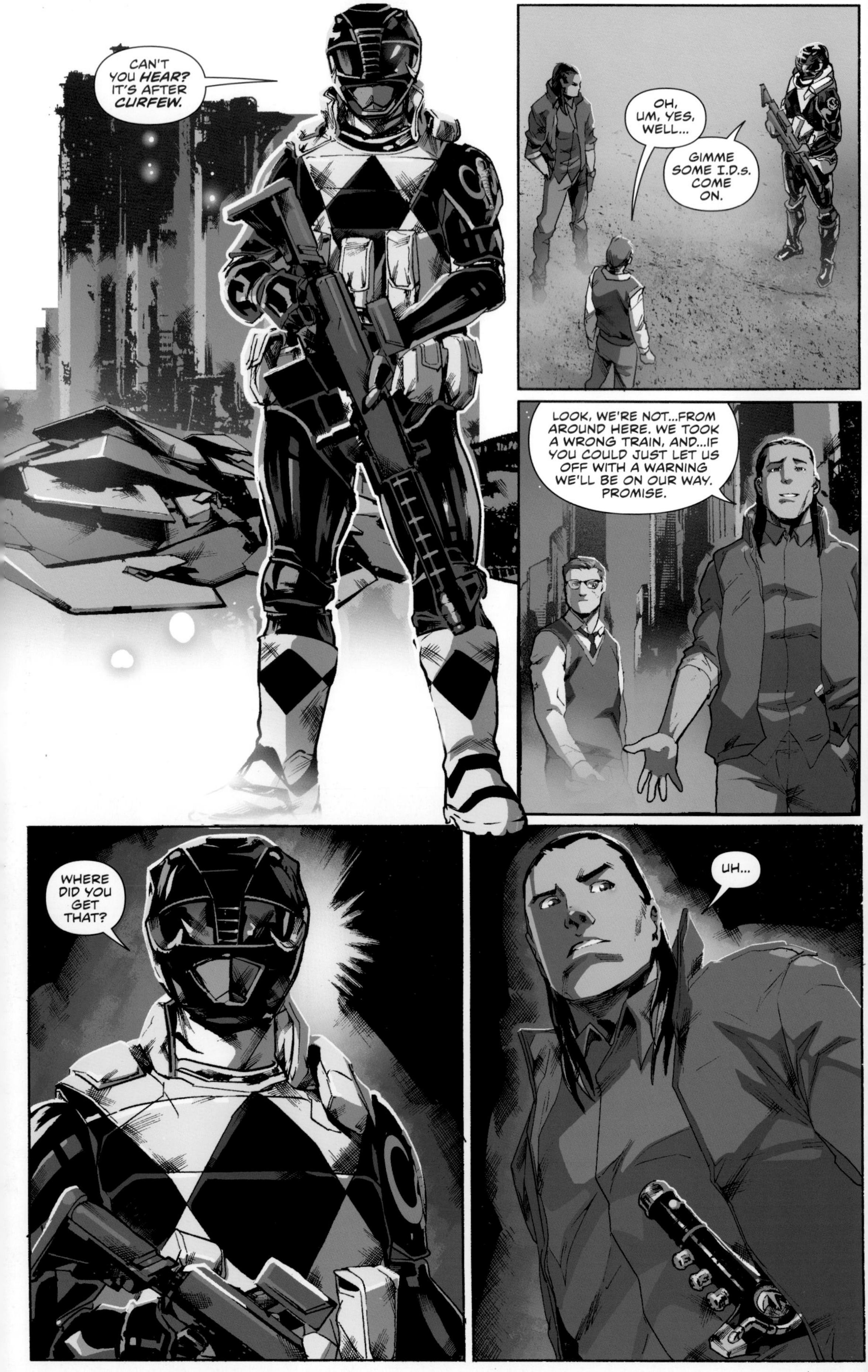
CAN'T YOU HEAR? IT'S AFTER CURFEW.
OH, UM, YES, WELL...
GIMME SOME I.D.s. COME ON.
LOOK, WE'RE NOT...FROM AROUND HERE. WE TOOK A WRONG TRAIN, AND...IF YOU COULD JUST LET US OFF WITH A WARNING WE'LL BE ON OUR WAY. PROMISE.
WHERE DID YOU GET THAT?
UH...

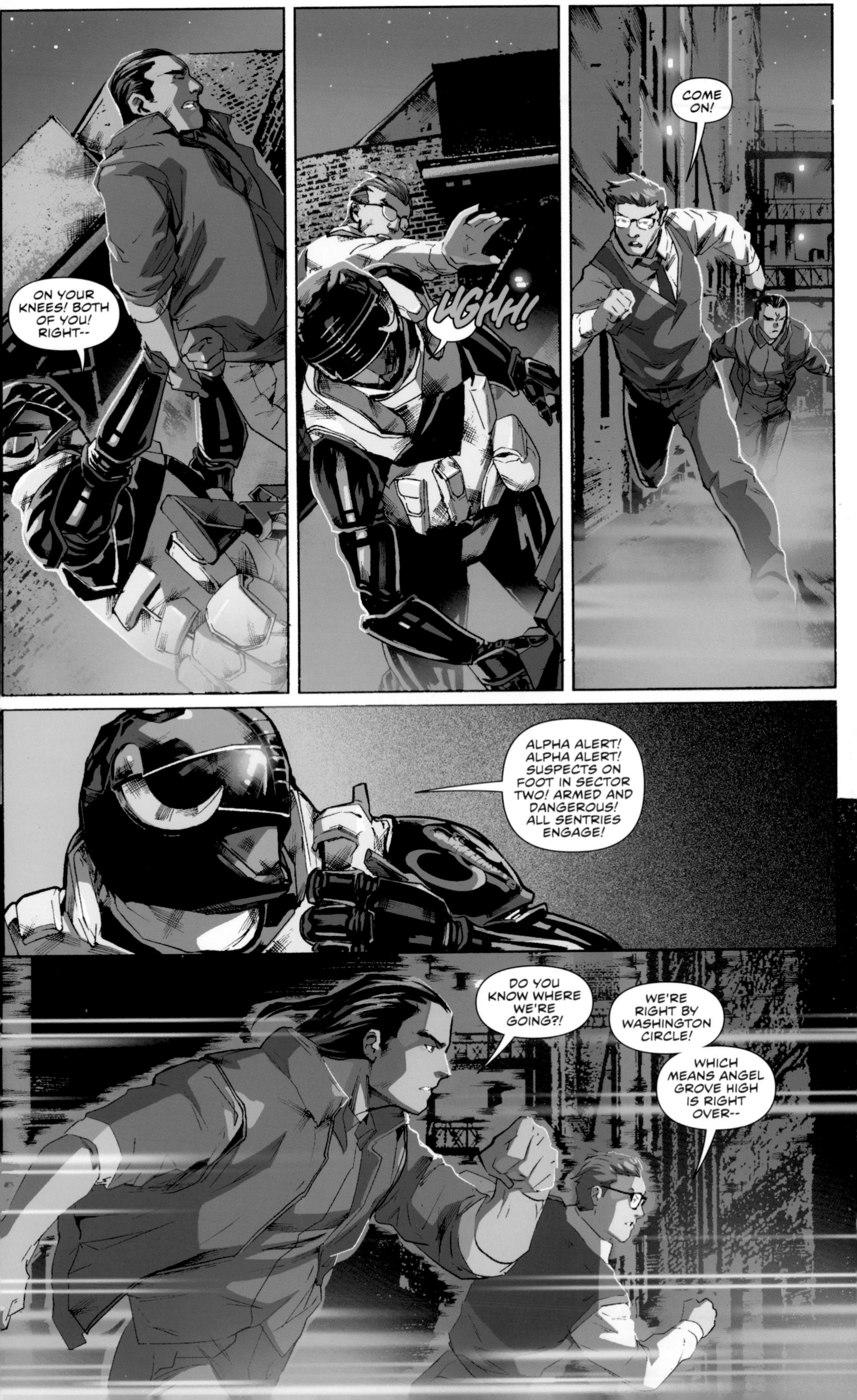
ON YOUR KNEES! BOTH OF YOU! RIGHT--
UGHH!
COME ON!
ALPHA ALERT! ALPHA ALERT! SUSPECTS ON FOOT IN SECTOR TWO! ARMED AND DANGEROUS! ALL SENTRIES ENGAGE!
DO YOU KNOW WHERE WE'RE GOING?!
WE'RE RIGHT BY WASHINGTON CIRCLE!
WHICH MEANS ANGEL GROVE HIGH IS RIGHT OVER--

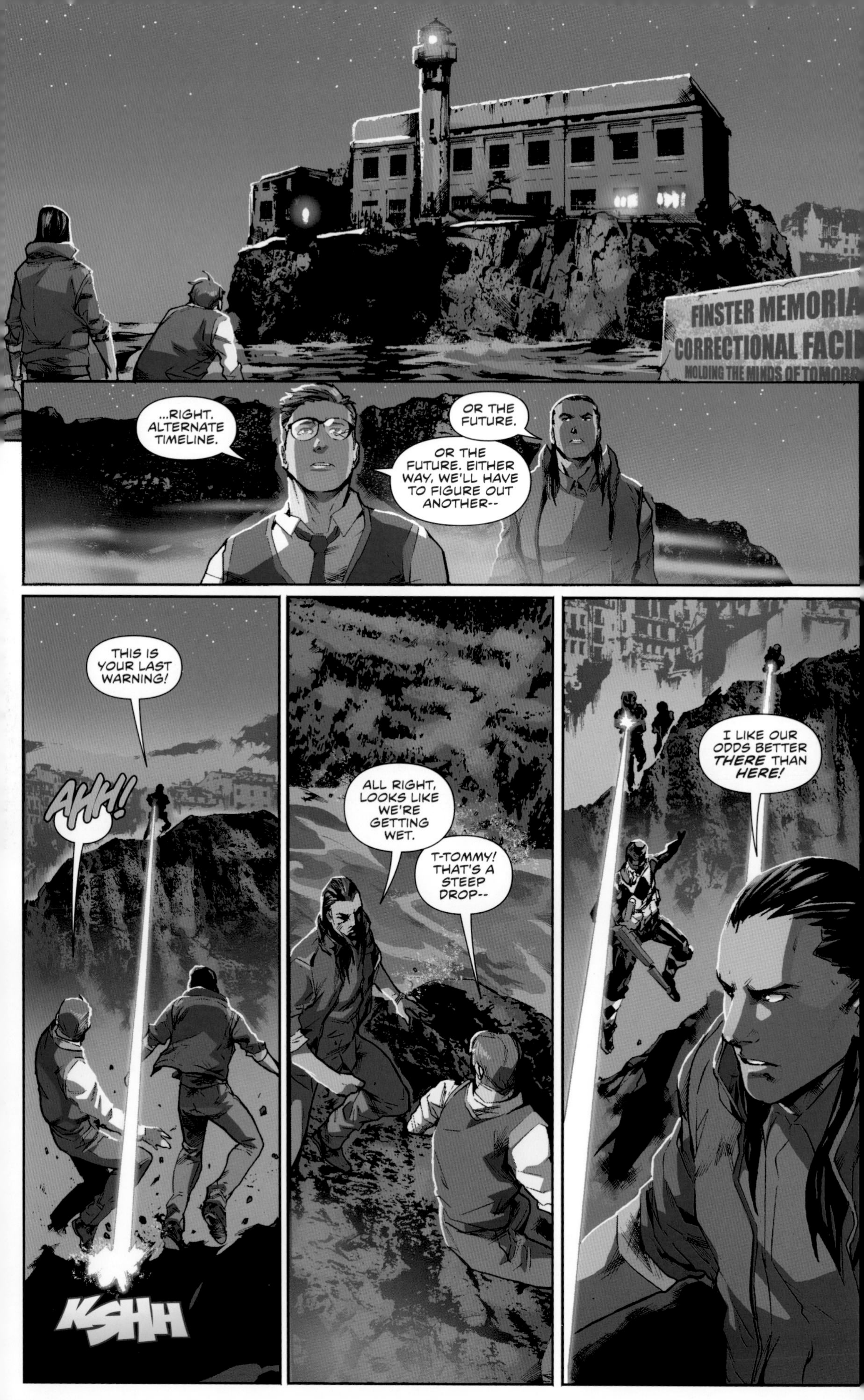

FINSTER MEMORIA
CORRECTIONAL FACI
MOLDING THE MINDS OF TOMORR
...RIGHT. ALTERNATE TIMELINE.
OR THE FUTURE.
OR THE FUTURE. EITHER WAY, WE'LL HAVE TO FIGURE OUT ANOTHER--
THIS IS YOUR LAST WARNING!
AHH!
KSHH
ALL RIGHT, LOOKS LIKE WE'RE GETTING WET.
T-TOMMY! THAT'S A STEEP DROP--
I LIKE OUR ODDS BETTER THERE THAN HERE!

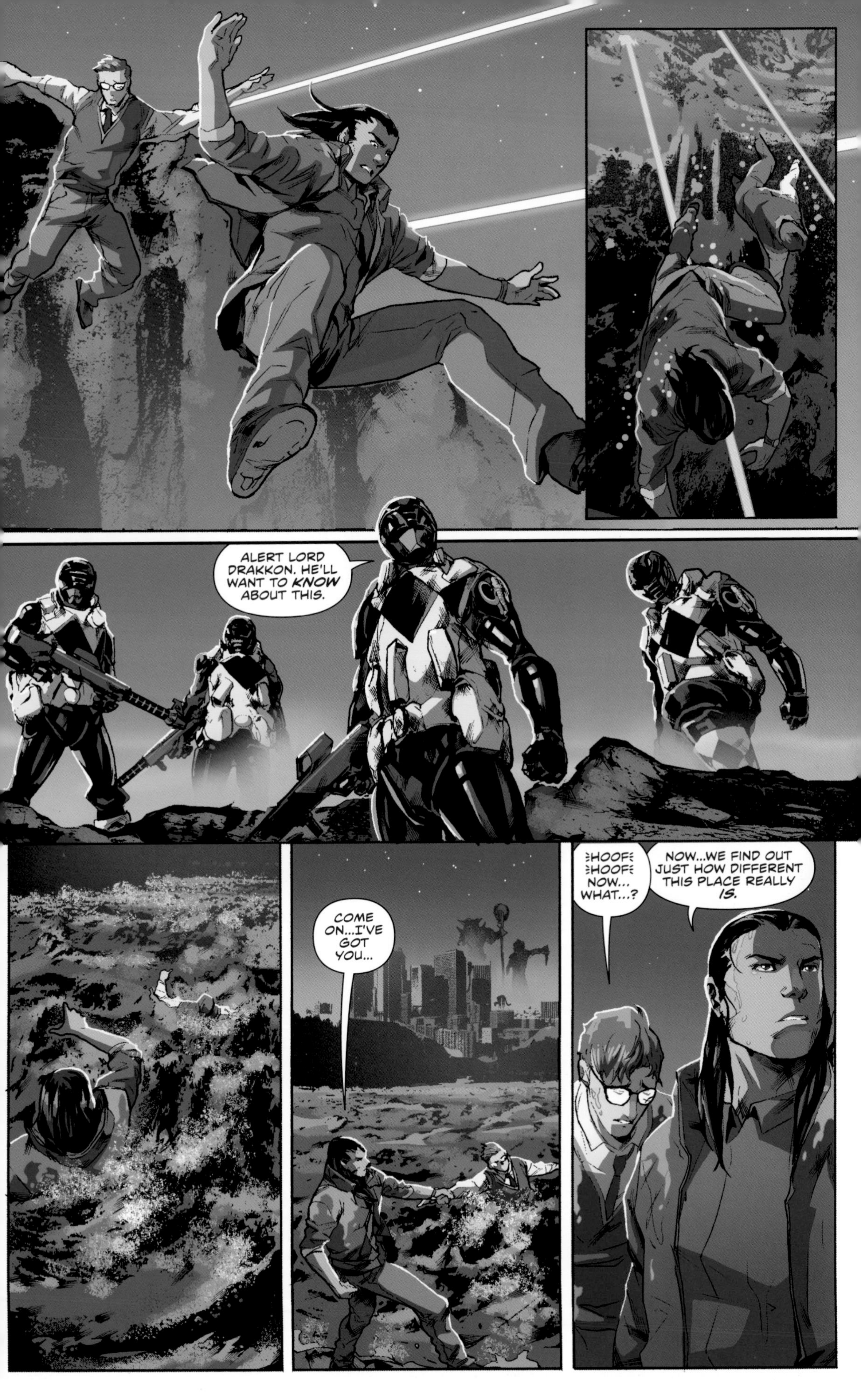
ALERT LORD DRAKKON. HE'LL WANT TO KNOW ABOUT THIS.
COME ON...I'VE GOT YOU...
HOOF HOOF NOW... WHAT...?
NOW...WE FIND OUT JUST HOW DIFFERENT THIS PLACE REALLY IS.

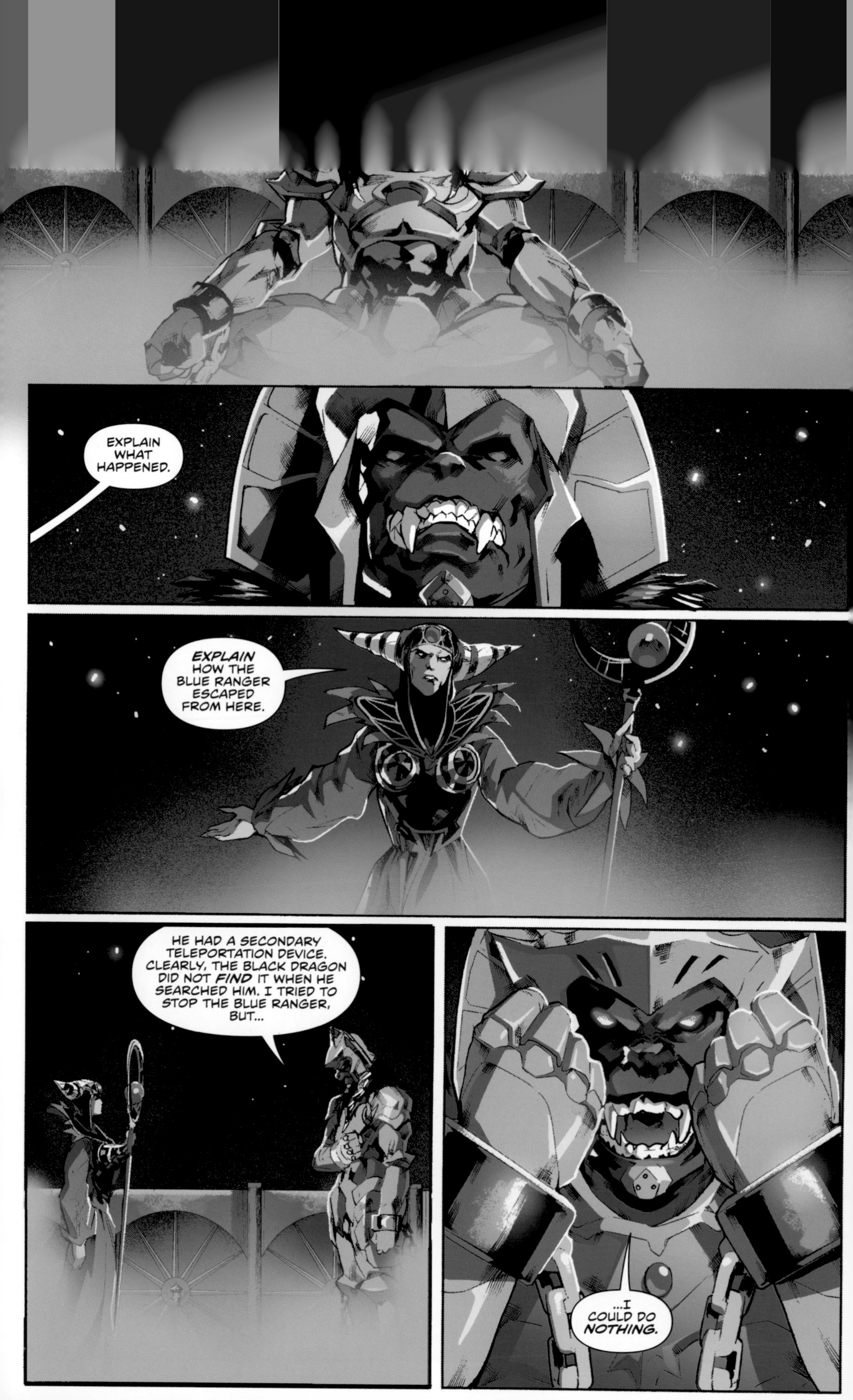
EXPLAIN WHAT HAPPENED.
EXPLAIN HOW THE BLUE RANGER ESCAPED FROM HERE.
HE HAD A SECONDARY TELEPORTATION DEVICE. CLEARLY, THE BLACK DRAGON DID NOT *FIND* IT WHEN HE SEARCHED HIM. I TRIED TO STOP THE BLUE RANGER, BUT...
...I COULD DO *NOTHING.*

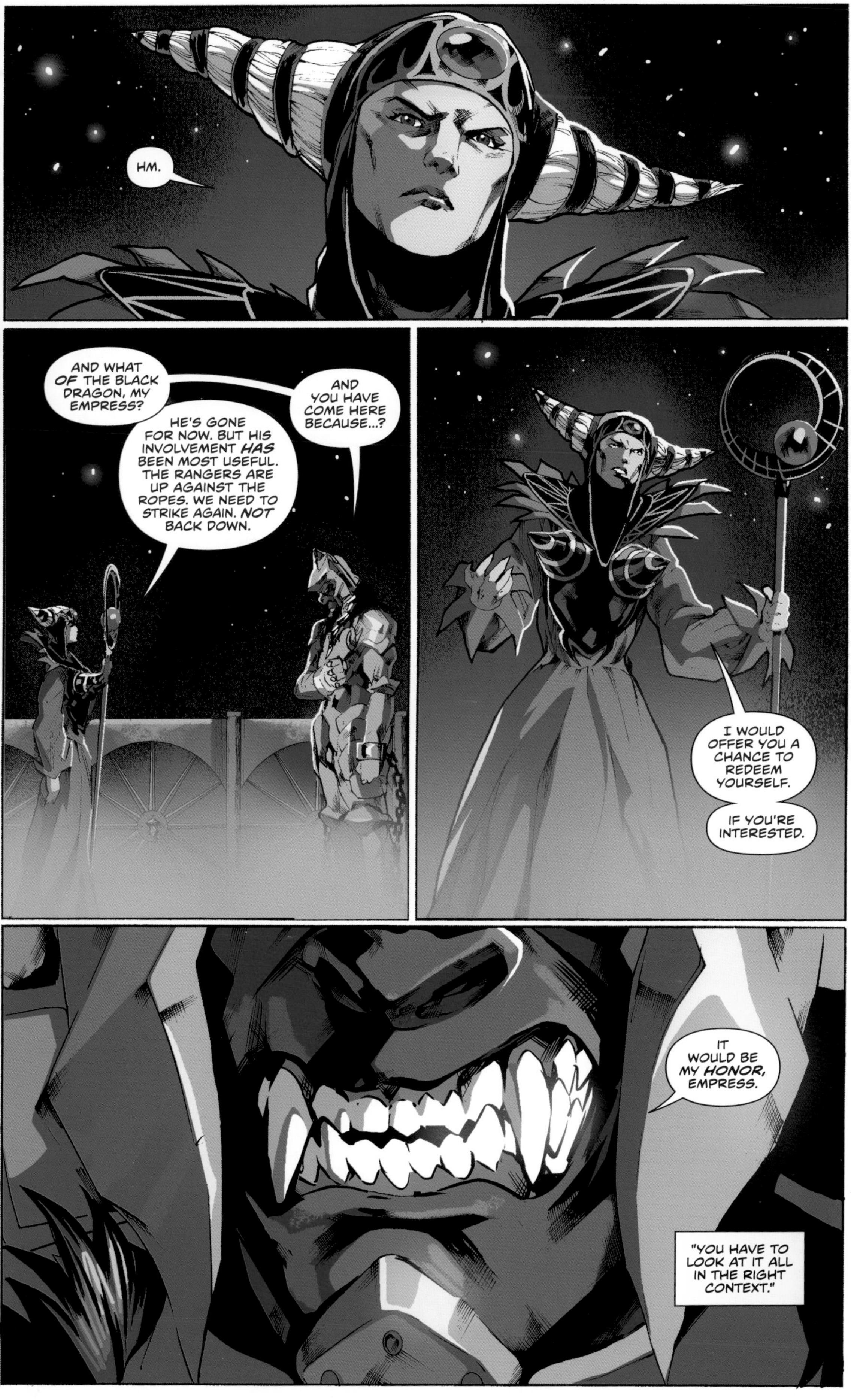
HM.
AND WHAT OF THE BLACK DRAGON, MY EMPRESS?
AND YOU HAVE COME HERE BECAUSE...?
HE'S GONE FOR NOW. BUT HIS INVOLVEMENT HAS BEEN MOST USEFUL. THE RANGERS ARE UP AGAINST THE ROPES. WE NEED TO STRIKE AGAIN. NOT BACK DOWN.
I WOULD OFFER YOU A CHANCE TO REDEEM YOURSELF.
IF YOU'RE INTERESTED.
IT WOULD BE MY HONOR, EMPRESS.
"YOU HAVE TO LOOK AT IT ALL IN THE RIGHT CONTEXT."

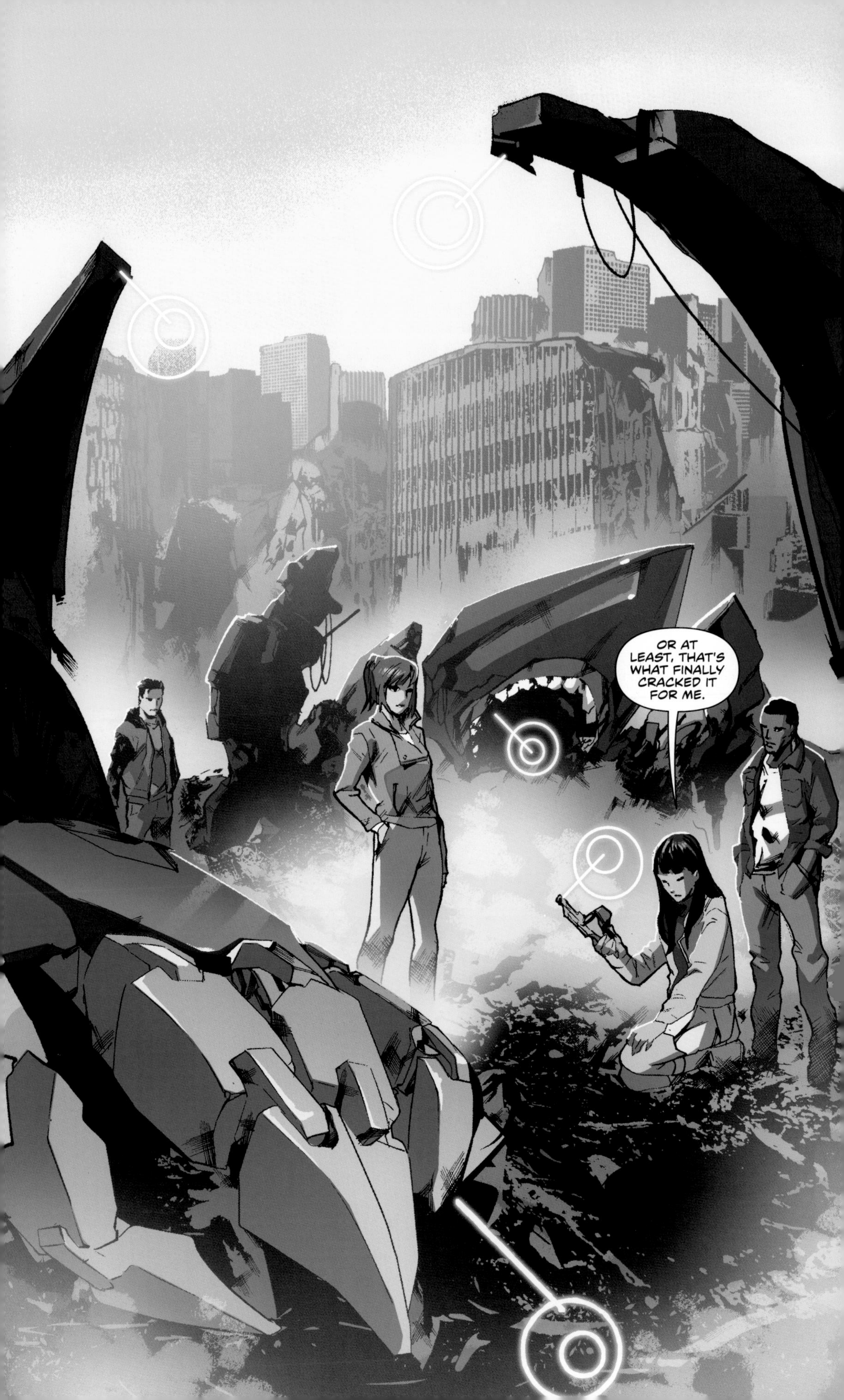
OR AT LEAST, THAT'S WHAT FINALLY CRACKED IT FOR ME.

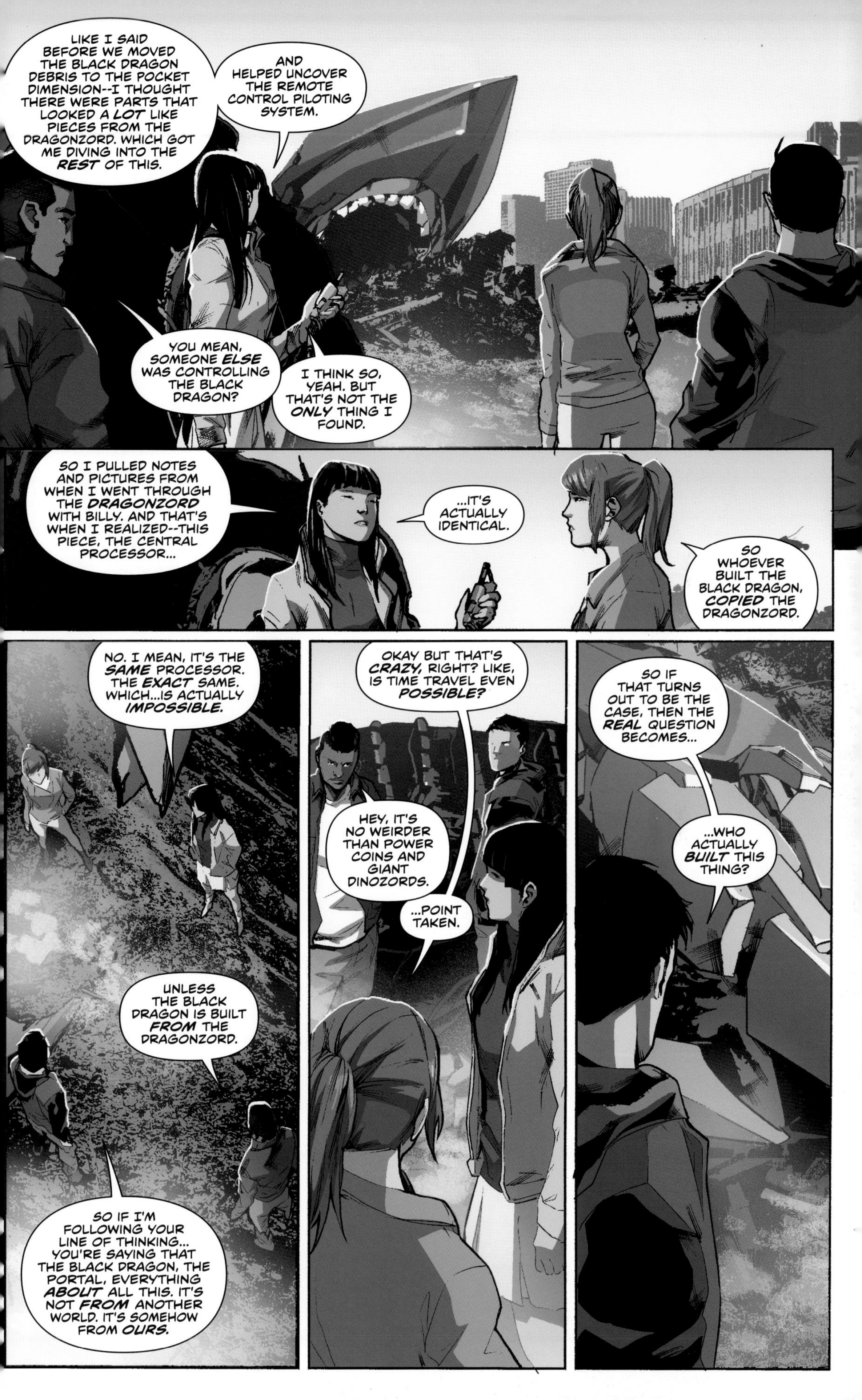
LIKE I SAID BEFORE WE MOVED THE BLACK DRAGON DEBRIS TO THE POCKET DIMENSION--I THOUGHT THERE WERE PARTS THAT LOOKED A *LOT* LIKE PIECES FROM THE DRAGONZORD. WHICH GOT ME DIVING INTO THE *REST* OF THIS.
AND HELPED UNCOVER THE REMOTE CONTROL PILOTING SYSTEM.
YOU MEAN, SOMEONE *ELSE* WAS CONTROLLING THE BLACK DRAGON?
I THINK SO, YEAH. BUT THAT'S NOT THE *ONLY* THING I FOUND.
SO I PULLED NOTES AND PICTURES FROM WHEN I WENT THROUGH THE *DRAGONZORD* WITH BILLY. AND THAT'S WHEN I REALIZED--THIS PIECE, THE CENTRAL PROCESSOR...
...IT'S ACTUALLY IDENTICAL.
SO WHOEVER BUILT THE BLACK DRAGON, *COPIED* THE DRAGONZORD.
NO. I MEAN, IT'S THE *SAME* PROCESSOR. THE *EXACT* SAME. WHICH...IS ACTUALLY *IMPOSSIBLE*.
UNLESS THE BLACK DRAGON IS BUILT *FROM* THE DRAGONZORD.
SO IF I'M FOLLOWING YOUR LINE OF THINKING... YOU'RE SAYING THAT THE BLACK DRAGON, THE PORTAL, EVERYTHING *ABOUT* ALL THIS. IT'S NOT *FROM* ANOTHER WORLD. IT'S SOMEHOW FROM *OURS*.
OKAY BUT THAT'S *CRAZY*, RIGHT? LIKE, IS TIME TRAVEL EVEN *POSSIBLE?*
HEY, IT'S NO WEIRDER THAN POWER COINS AND GIANT DINOZORDS.
...POINT TAKEN.
SO IF THAT TURNS OUT TO BE THE CASE, THEN THE *REAL* QUESTION BECOMES...
...WHO ACTUALLY *BUILT* THIS THING?

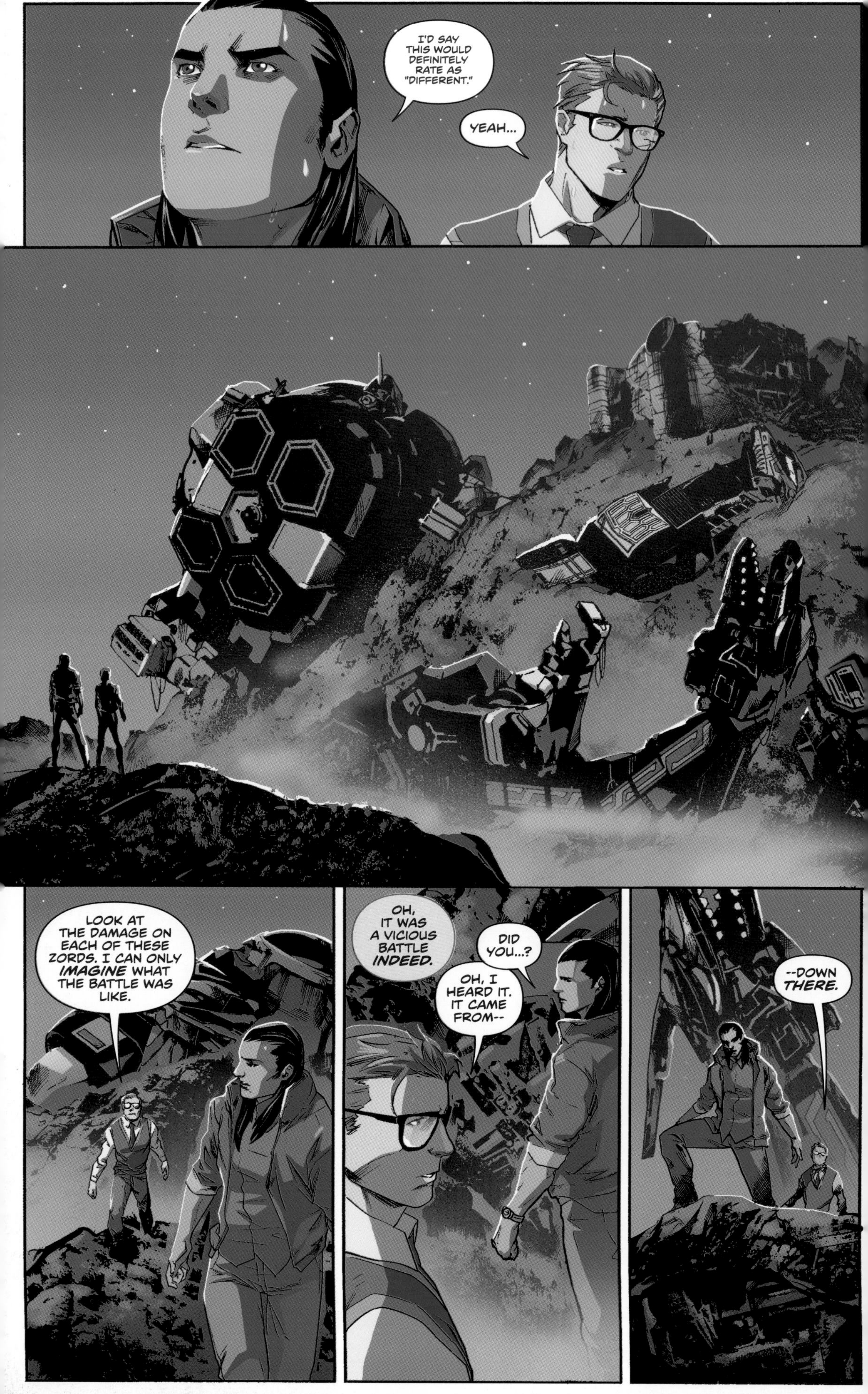
I'D SAY THIS WOULD DEFINITELY RATE AS "DIFFERENT."
YEAH...
LOOK AT THE DAMAGE ON EACH OF THESE ZORDS. I CAN ONLY *IMAGINE* WHAT THE BATTLE WAS LIKE.
OH, IT WAS A VICIOUS BATTLE *INDEED.*
DID YOU...?
OH, I HEARD IT. IT CAME FROM--
--DOWN *THERE.*

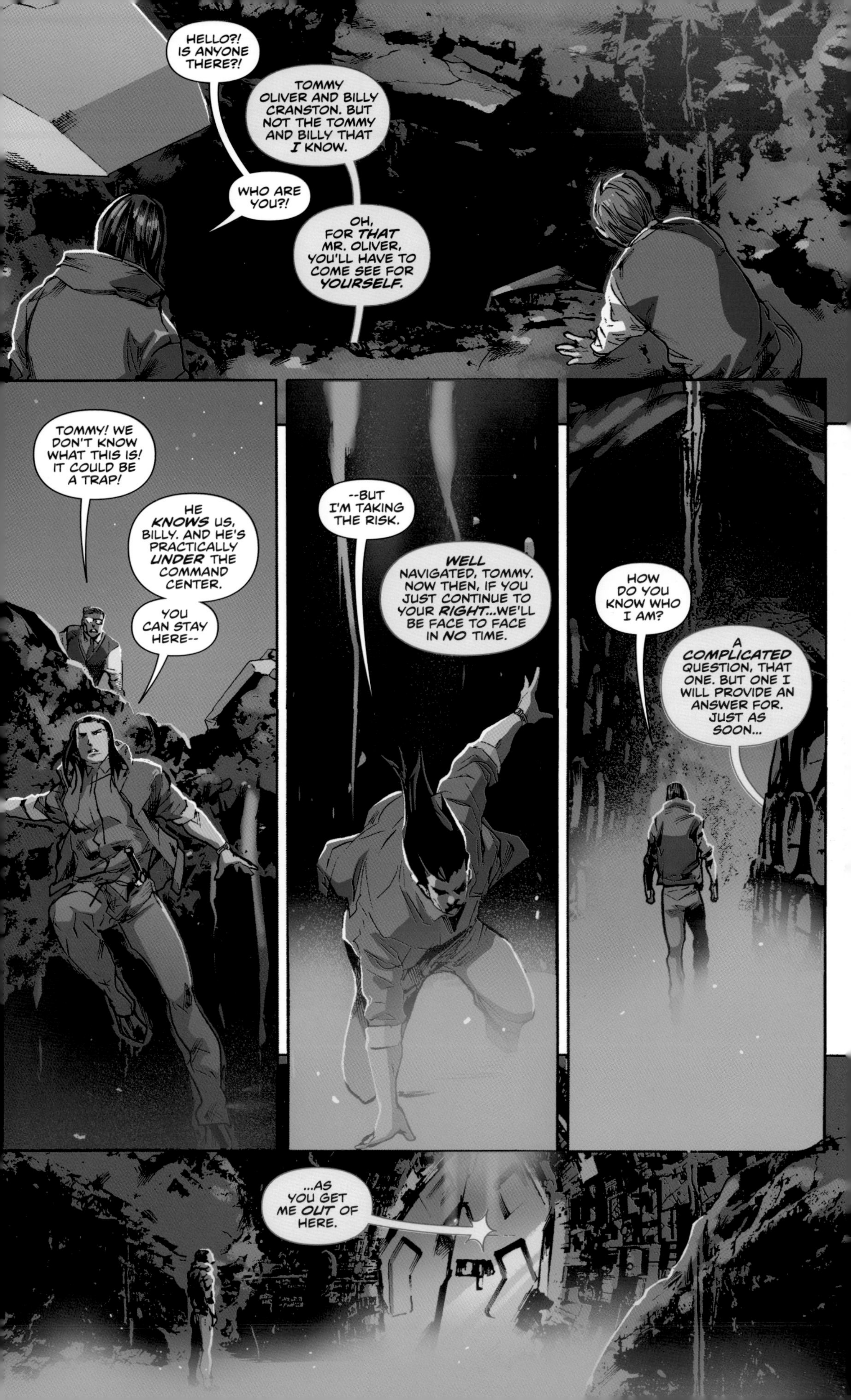
HELLO?! IS ANYONE THERE?!
TOMMY OLIVER AND BILLY CRANSTON. BUT NOT THE TOMMY AND BILLY THAT I KNOW.
WHO ARE YOU?!
OH, FOR THAT MR. OLIVER, YOU'LL HAVE TO COME SEE FOR YOURSELF.
TOMMY! WE DON'T KNOW WHAT THIS IS! IT COULD BE A TRAP!
HE KNOWS US, BILLY. AND HE'S PRACTICALLY UNDER THE COMMAND CENTER.
YOU CAN STAY HERE--
--BUT I'M TAKING THE RISK.
WELL NAVIGATED, TOMMY. NOW THEN, IF YOU JUST CONTINUE TO YOUR RIGHT...WE'LL BE FACE TO FACE IN NO TIME.
HOW DO YOU KNOW WHO I AM?
A COMPLICATED QUESTION, THAT ONE. BUT ONE I WILL PROVIDE AN ANSWER FOR. JUST AS SOON...
...AS YOU GET ME OUT OF HERE.

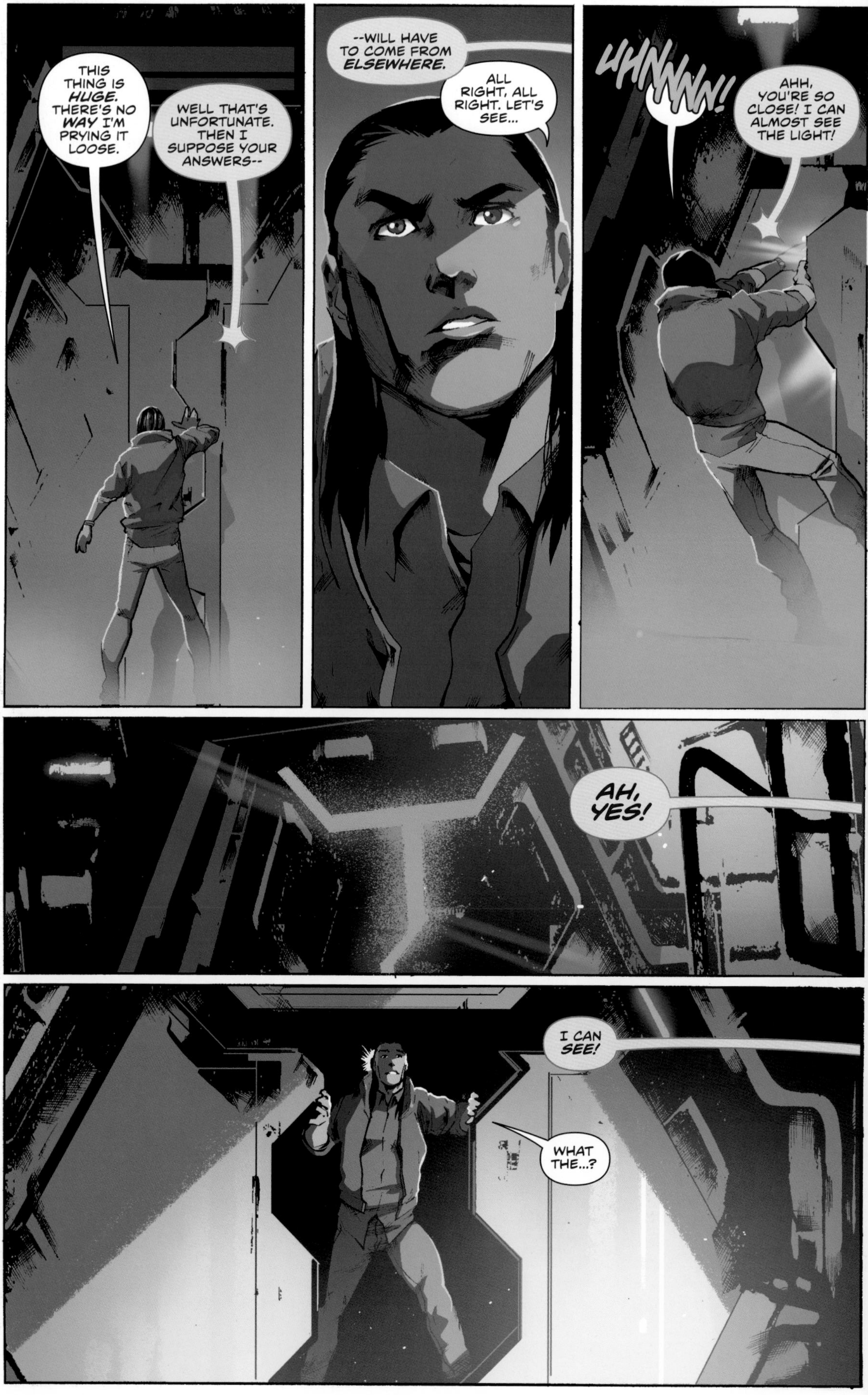
THIS THING IS HUGE. THERE'S NO WAY I'M PRYING IT LOOSE.
WELL THAT'S UNFORTUNATE. THEN I SUPPOSE YOUR ANSWERS--
--WILL HAVE TO COME FROM ELSEWHERE.
ALL RIGHT, ALL RIGHT. LET'S SEE...
UHNNNN!
AHH, YOU'RE SO CLOSE! I CAN ALMOST SEE THE LIGHT!
AH, YES!
I CAN SEE!
WHAT THE...?

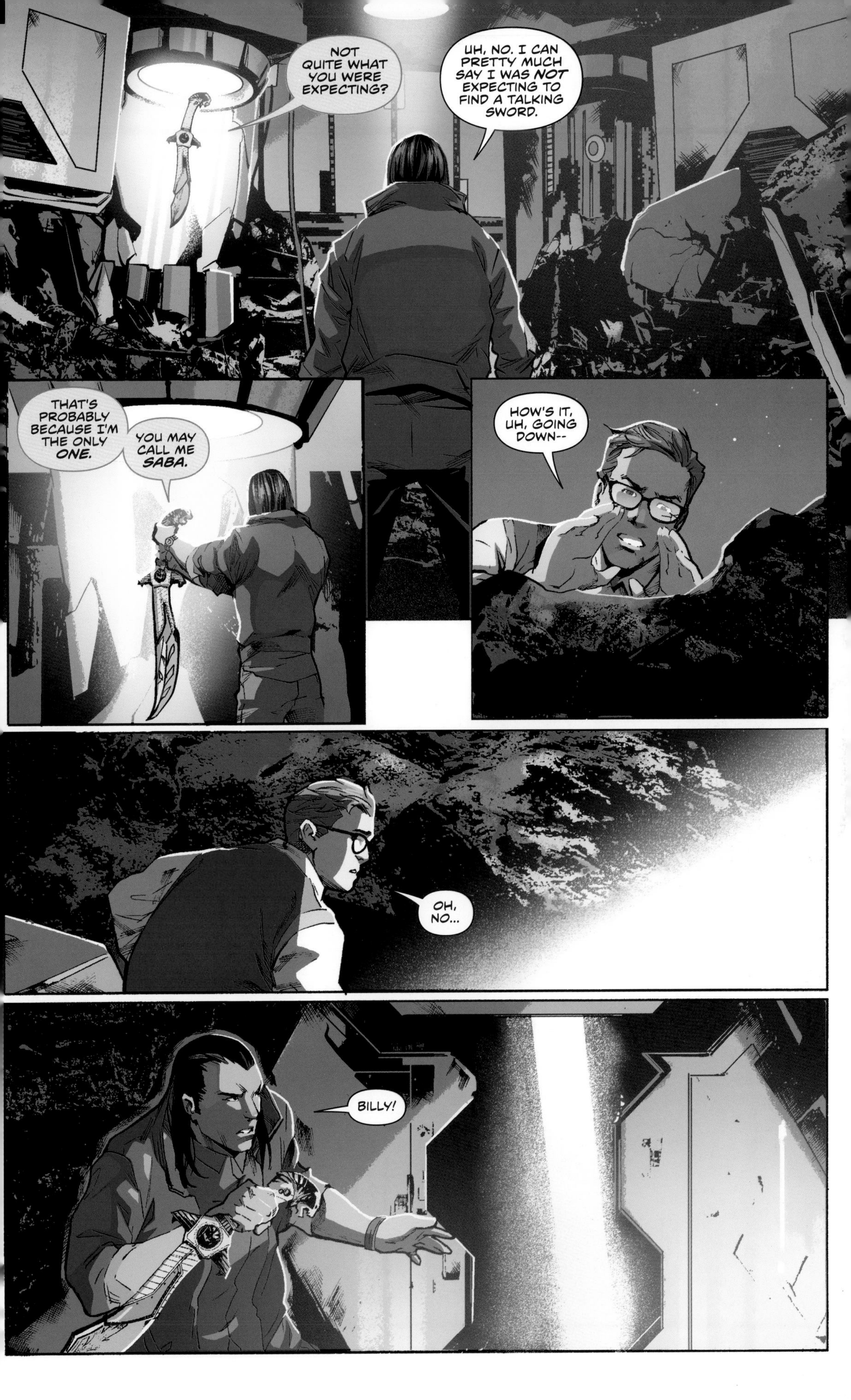
NOT QUITE WHAT YOU WERE EXPECTING?
UH, NO. I CAN PRETTY MUCH SAY I WAS NOT EXPECTING TO FIND A TALKING SWORD.
THAT'S PROBABLY BECAUSE I'M THE ONLY ONE.
YOU MAY CALL ME SABA.
HOW'S IT, UH, GOING DOWN--
OH, NO...
BILLY!

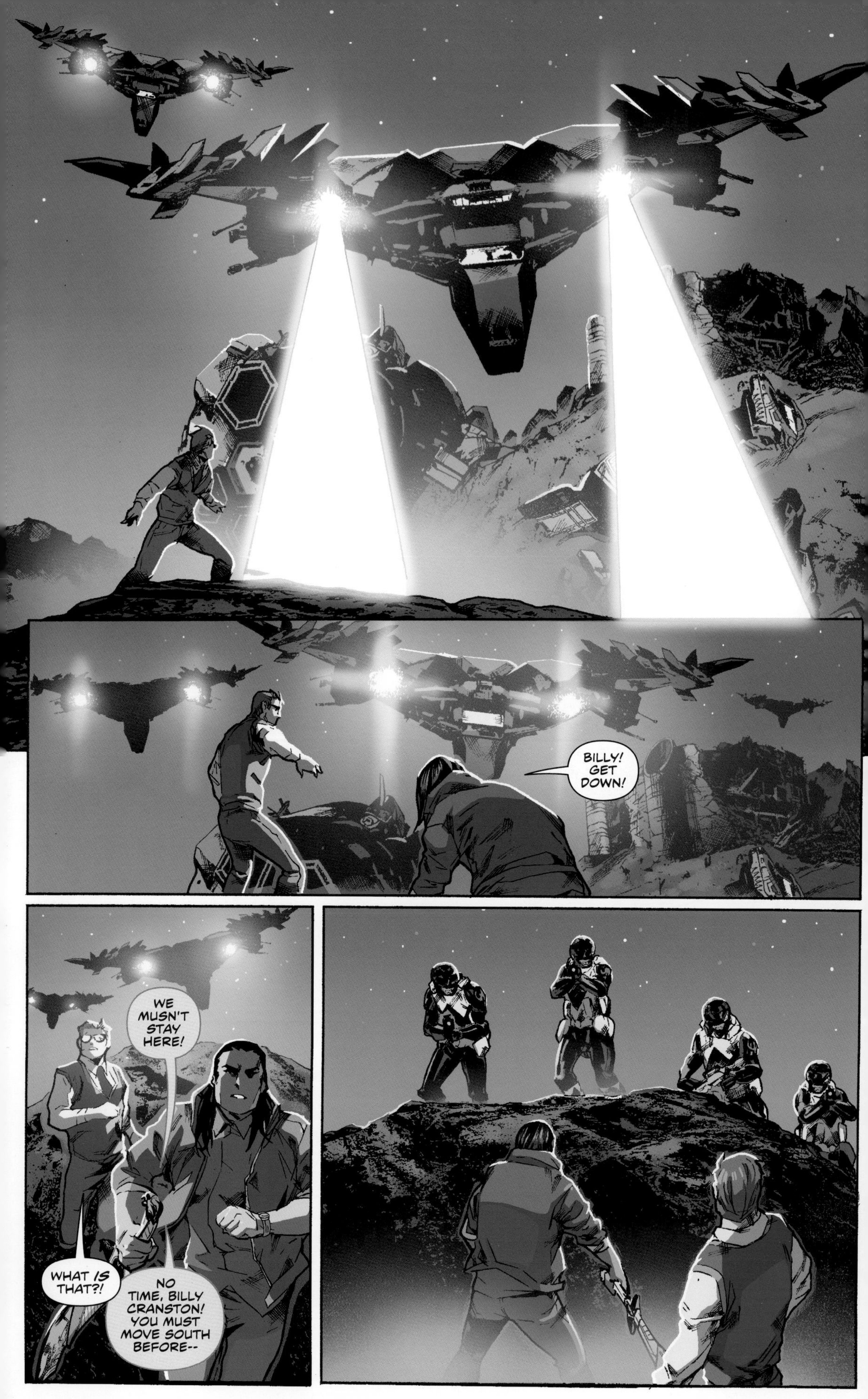
BILLY!
GET
DOWN!
WE
MUSN'T
STAY
HERE!
WHAT IS
THAT?!
NO
TIME, BILLY
CRANSTON!
YOU MUST
MOVE SOUTH
BEFORE--

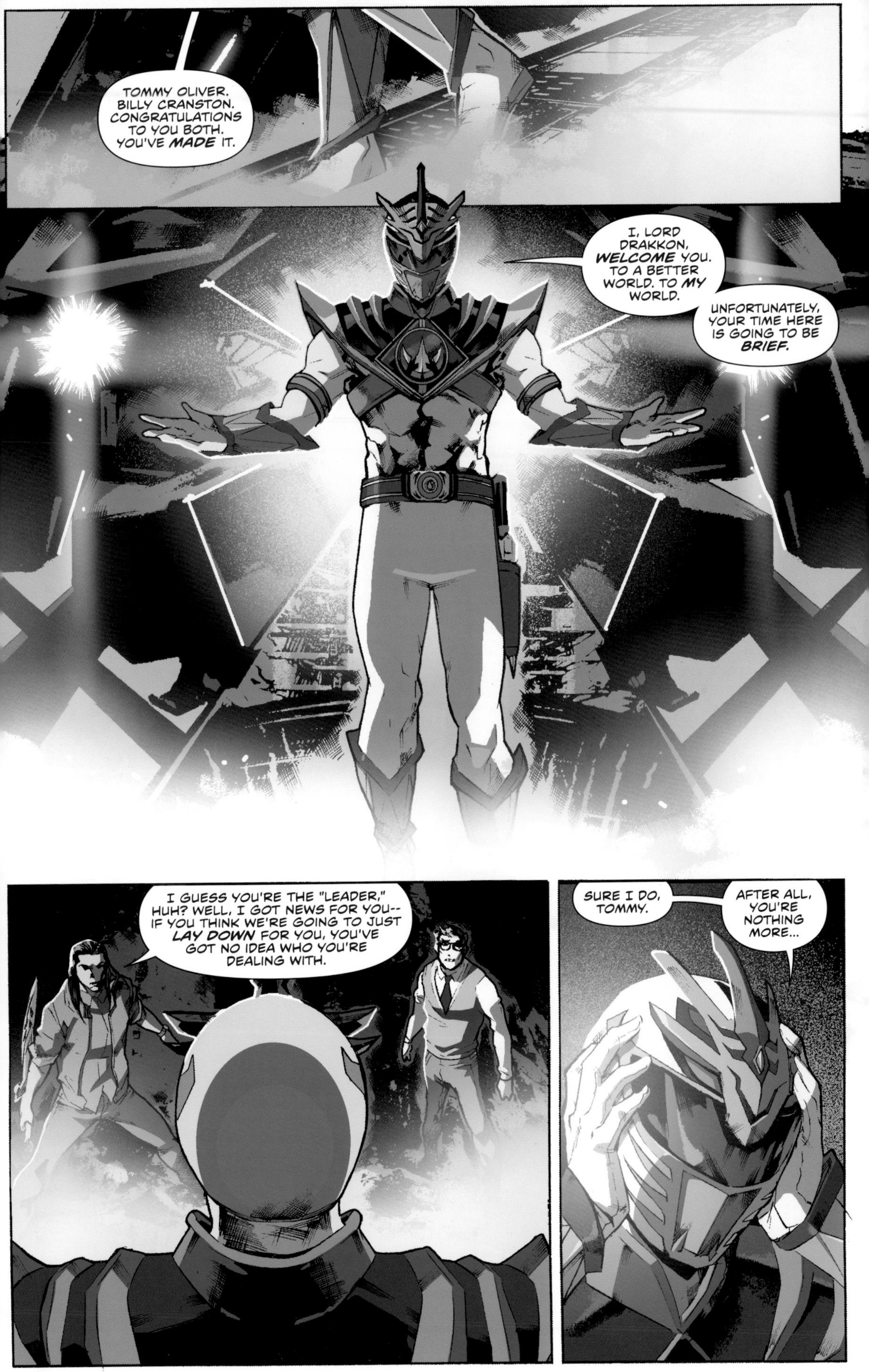
TOMMY OLIVER. BILLY CRANSTON. CONGRATULATIONS TO YOU BOTH. YOU'VE MADE IT.
I, LORD DRAKKON, WELCOME YOU. TO A BETTER WORLD. TO MY WORLD.
UNFORTUNATELY, YOUR TIME HERE IS GOING TO BE BRIEF.
I GUESS YOU'RE THE "LEADER," HUH? WELL, I GOT NEWS FOR YOU-- IF YOU THINK WE'RE GOING TO JUST LAY DOWN FOR YOU, YOU'VE GOT NO IDEA WHO YOU'RE DEALING WITH.
SURE I DO, TOMMY.
AFTER ALL, YOU'RE NOTHING MORE...

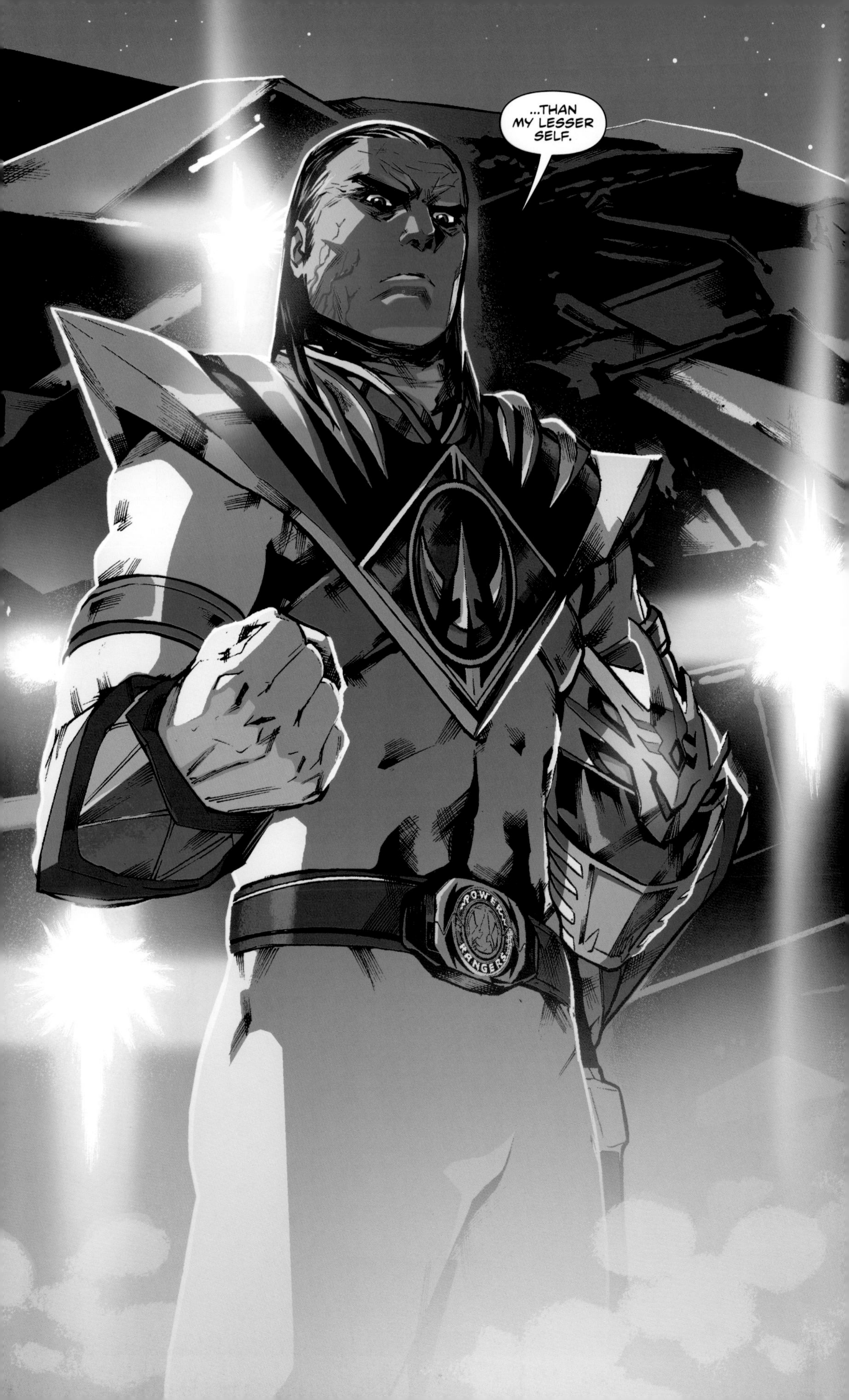
...THAN MY LESSER SELF.
POWER RANGERS

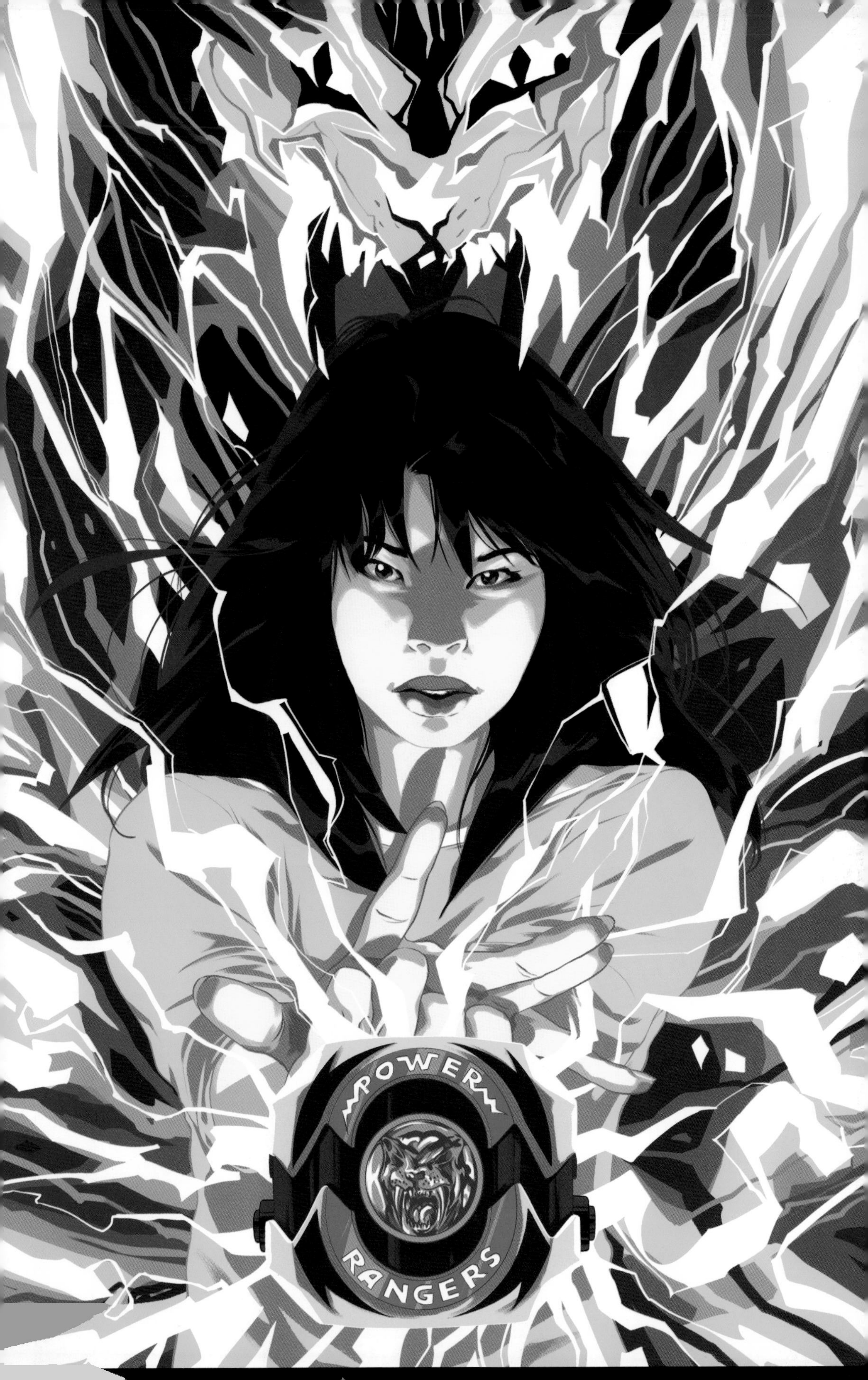
POWER
RANGERS

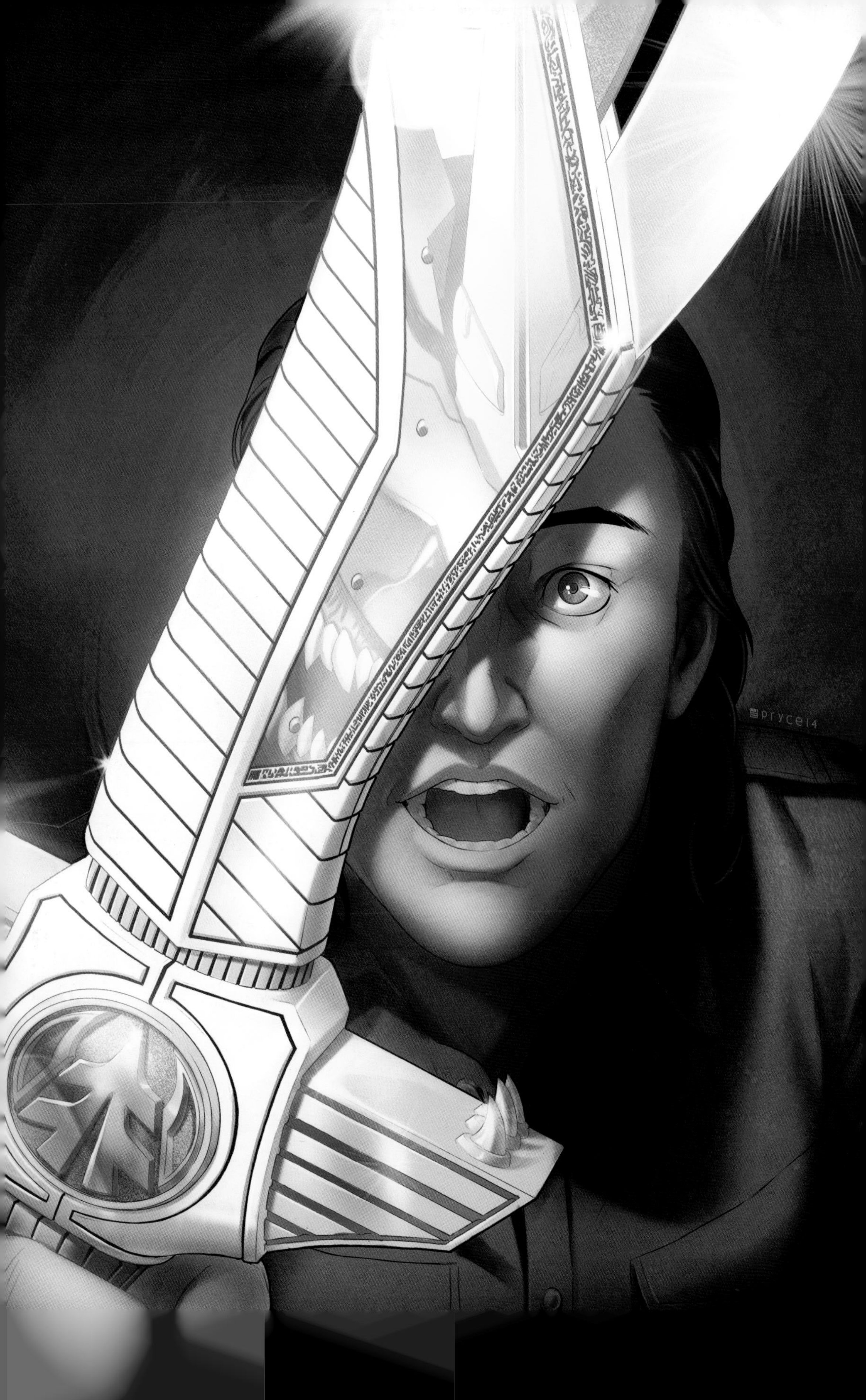
pryce14

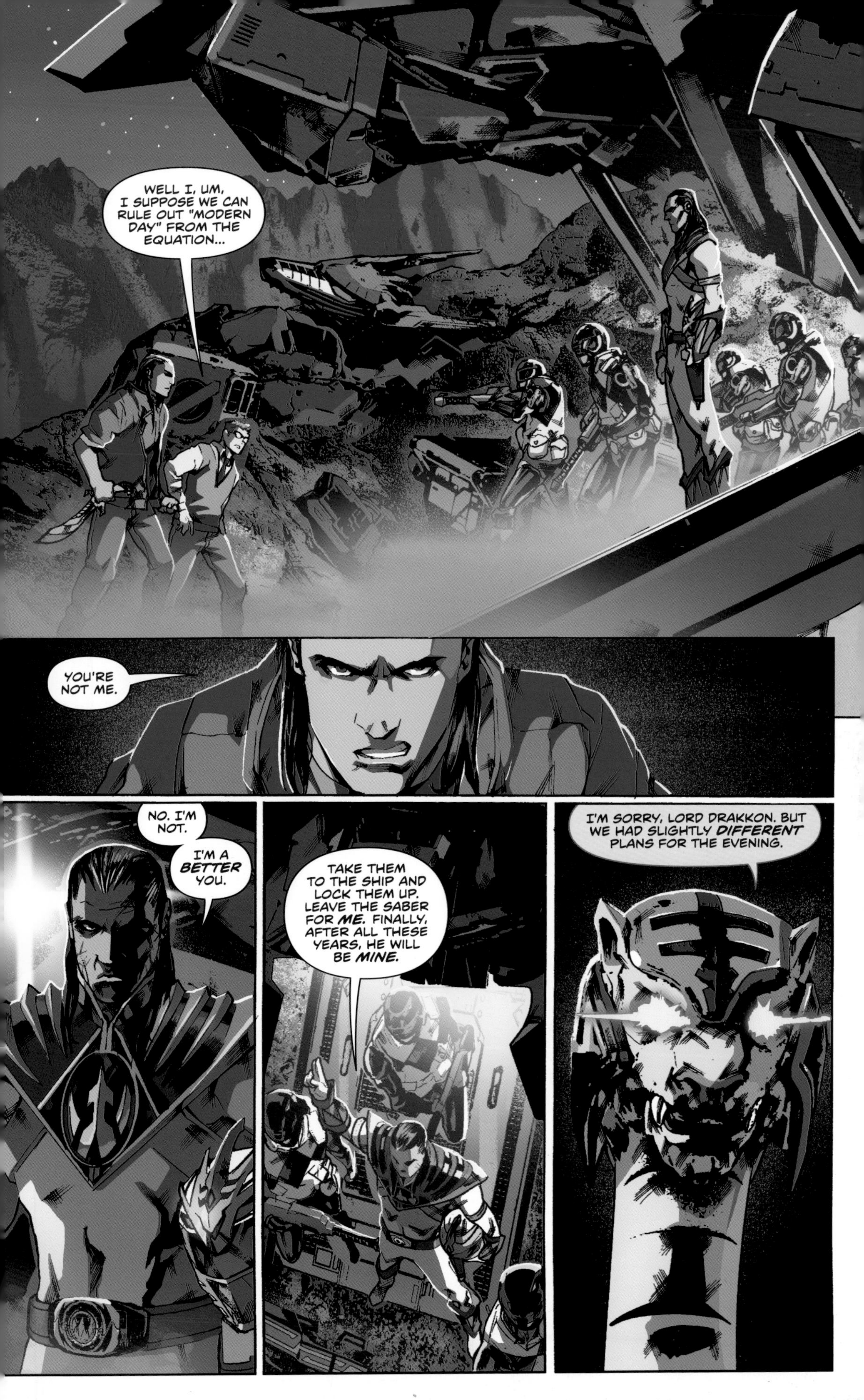
WELL I, UM, I SUPPOSE WE CAN RULE OUT "MODERN DAY" FROM THE EQUATION...
YOU'RE NOT ME.
NO. I'M NOT.
I'M A *BETTER* YOU.
TAKE THEM TO THE SHIP AND LOCK THEM UP. LEAVE THE SABER FOR *ME*. FINALLY, AFTER ALL THESE YEARS, HE WILL BE *MINE*.
I'M SORRY, LORD DRAKKON. BUT WE HAD SLIGHTLY *DIFFERENT* PLANS FOR THE EVENING.

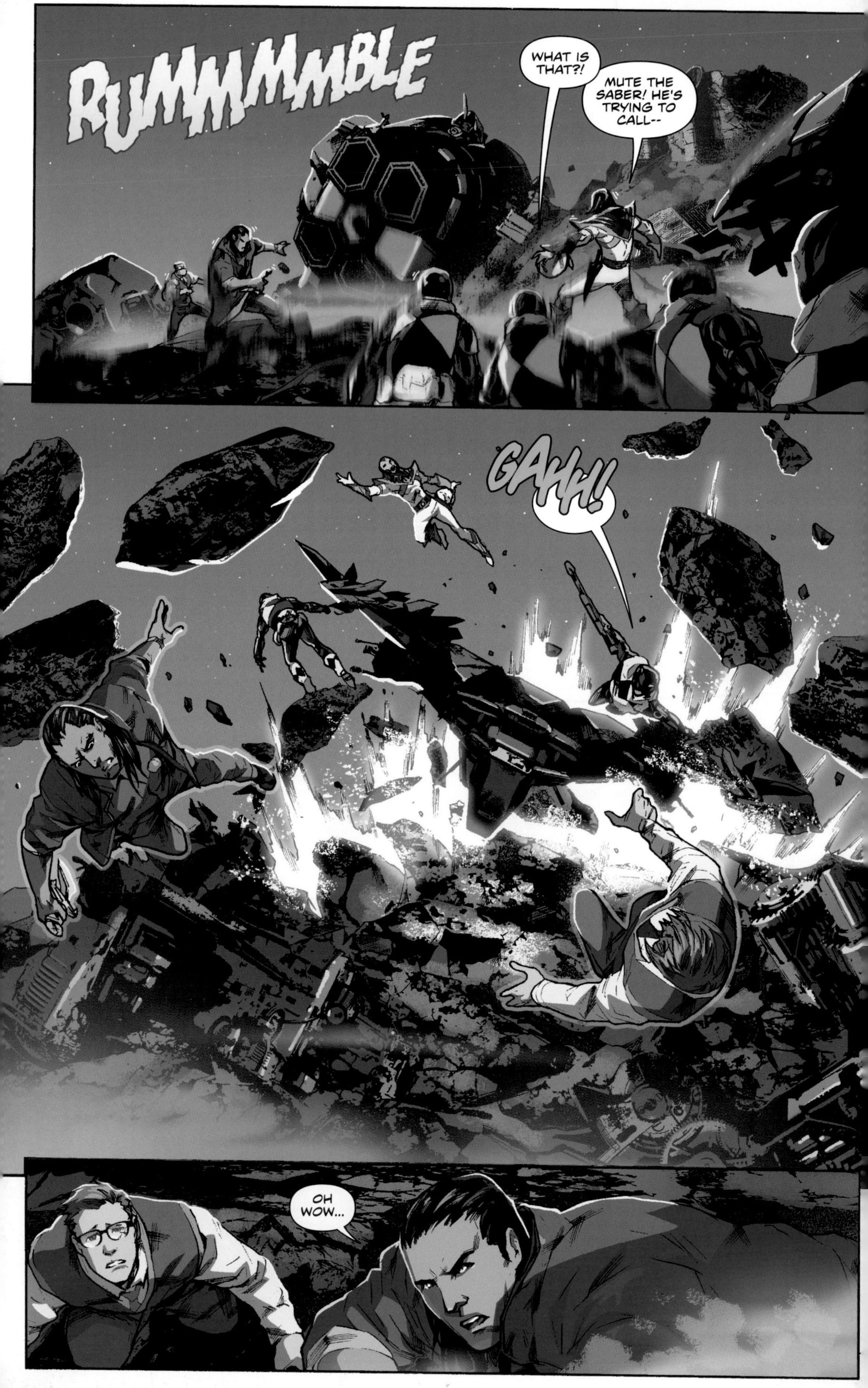
RUMMMMBLE
WHAT IS THAT?!
MUTE THE SABER! HE'S TRYING TO CALL--
GAHH!
OH WOW...

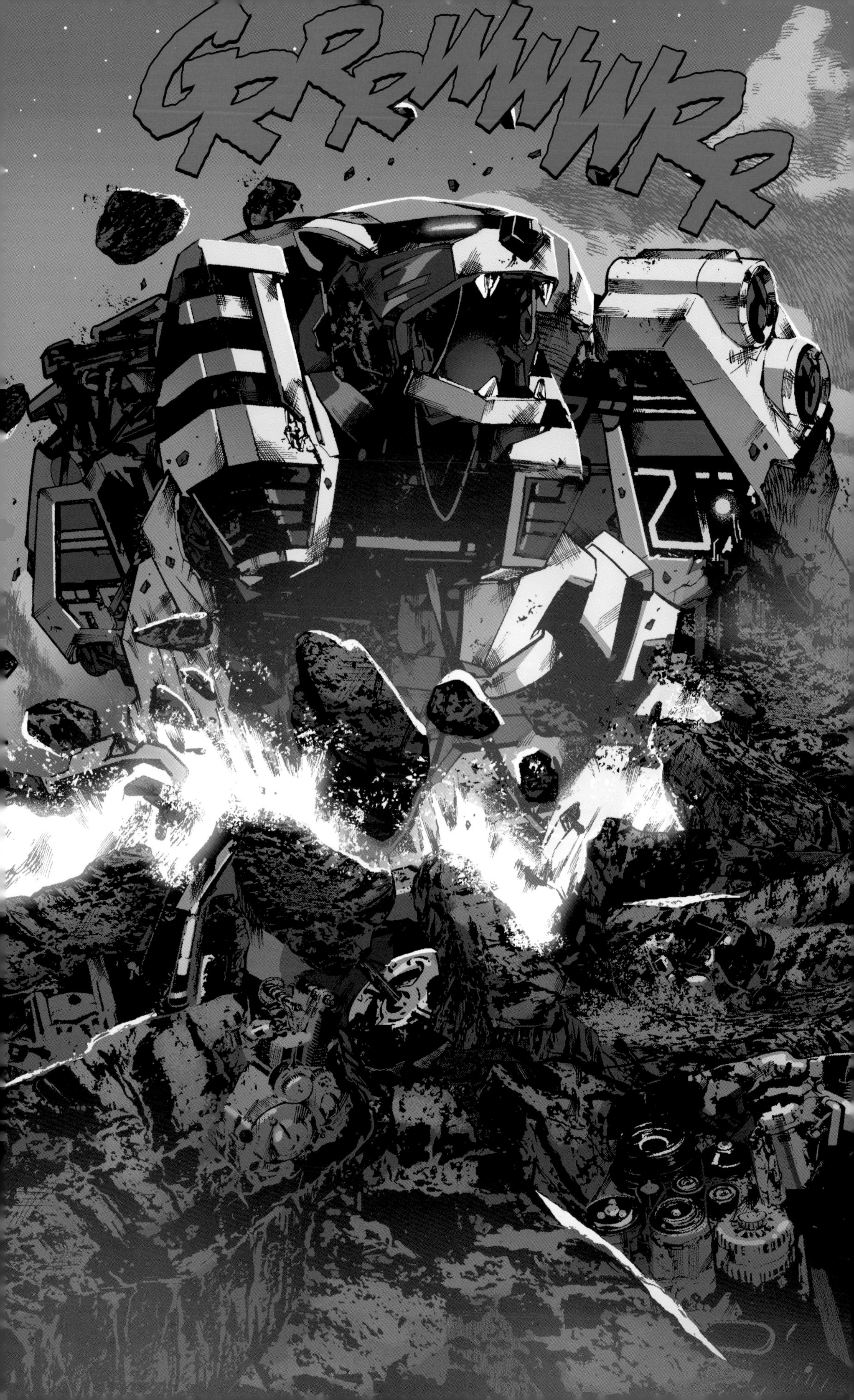
GRRRWWRR

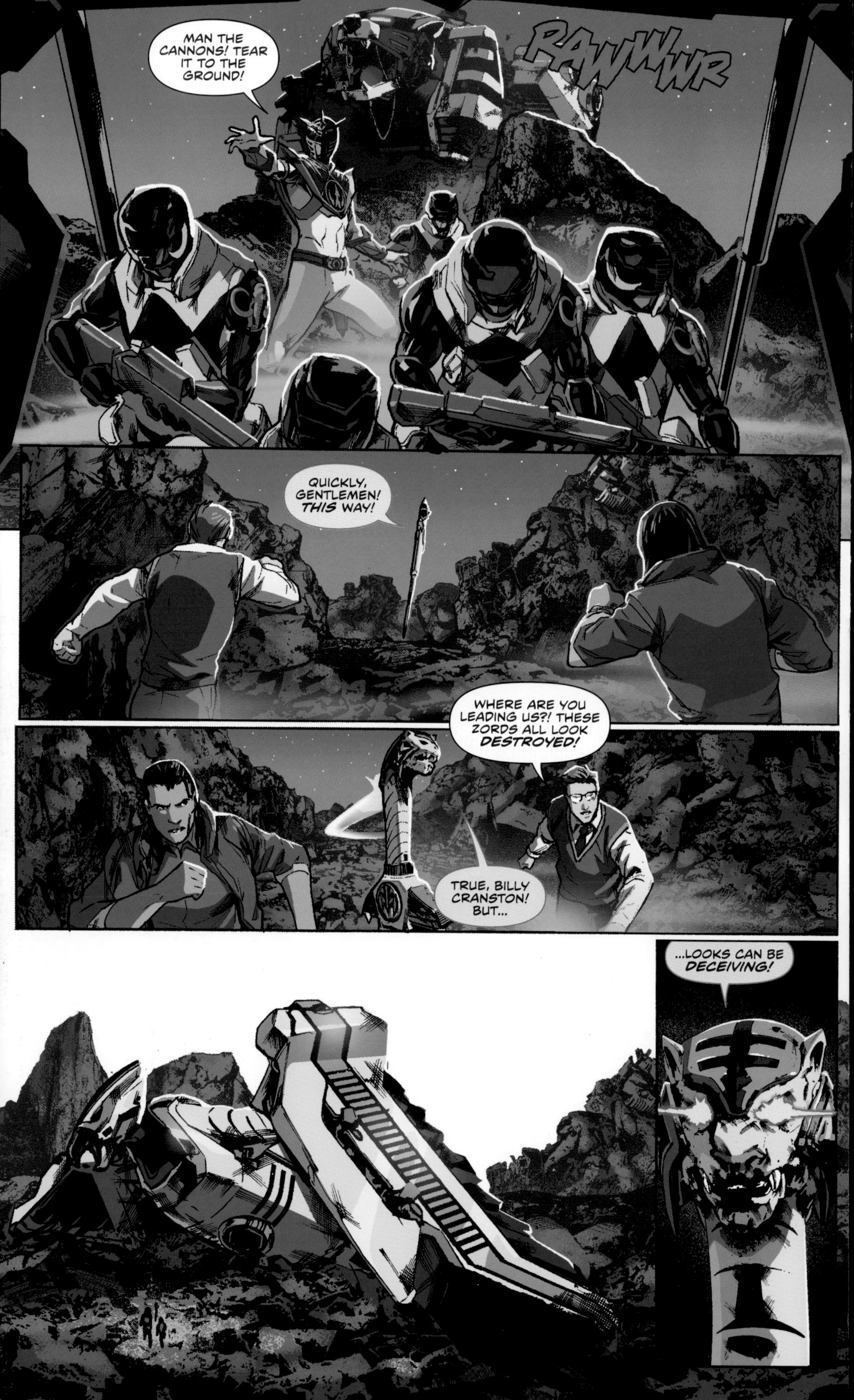
MAN THE CANNONS! TEAR IT TO THE GROUND!
RAWWWR
QUICKLY, GENTLEMEN! THIS WAY!
WHERE ARE YOU LEADING US?! THESE ZORDS ALL LOOK DESTROYED!
TRUE, BILLY CRANSTON! BUT...
...LOOKS CAN BE DECEIVING!

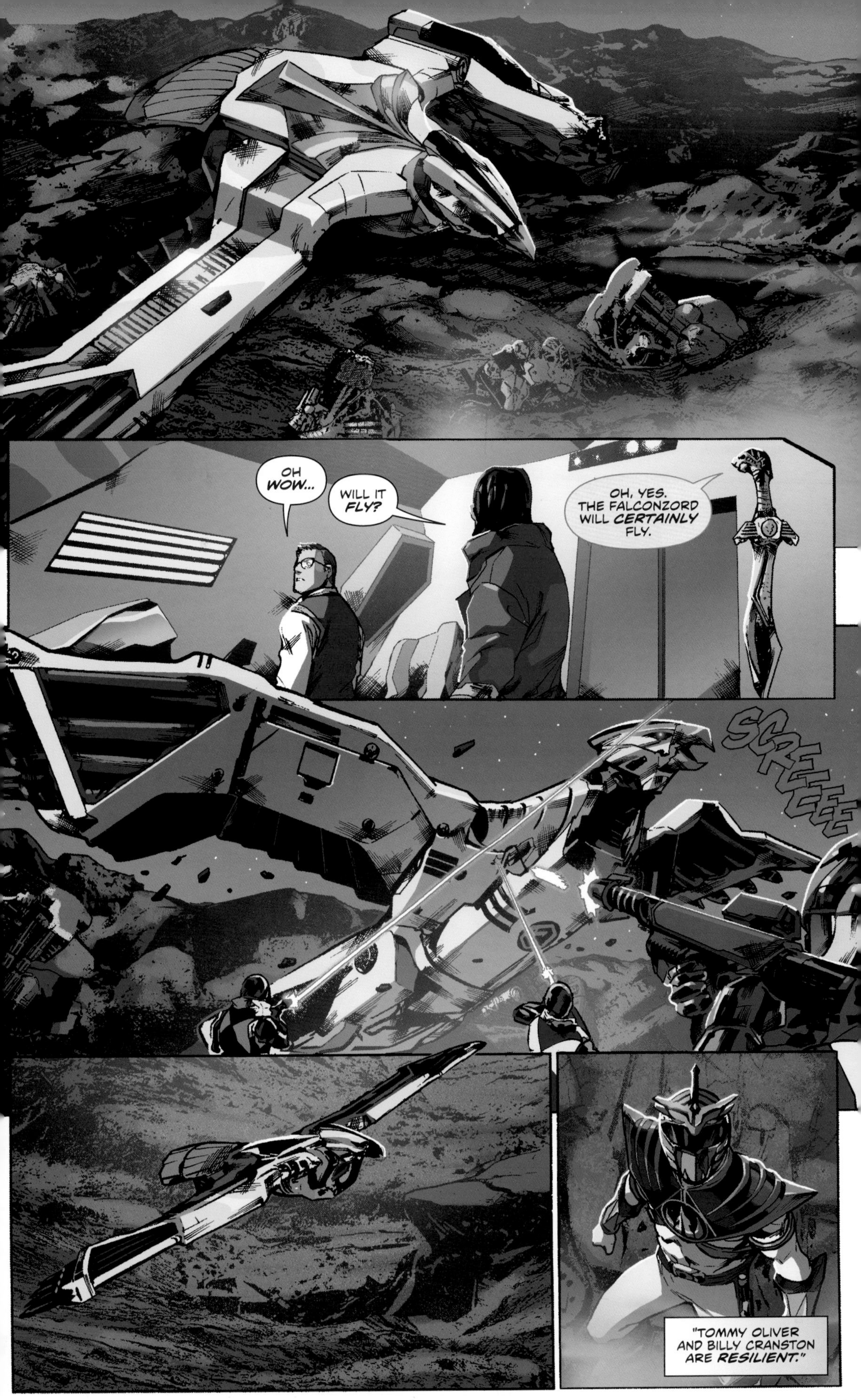
OH WOW...
WILL IT FLY?
OH, YES. THE FALCONZORD WILL CERTAINLY FLY.
SCREEEEE
"TOMMY OLIVER AND BILLY CRANSTON ARE RESILIENT."

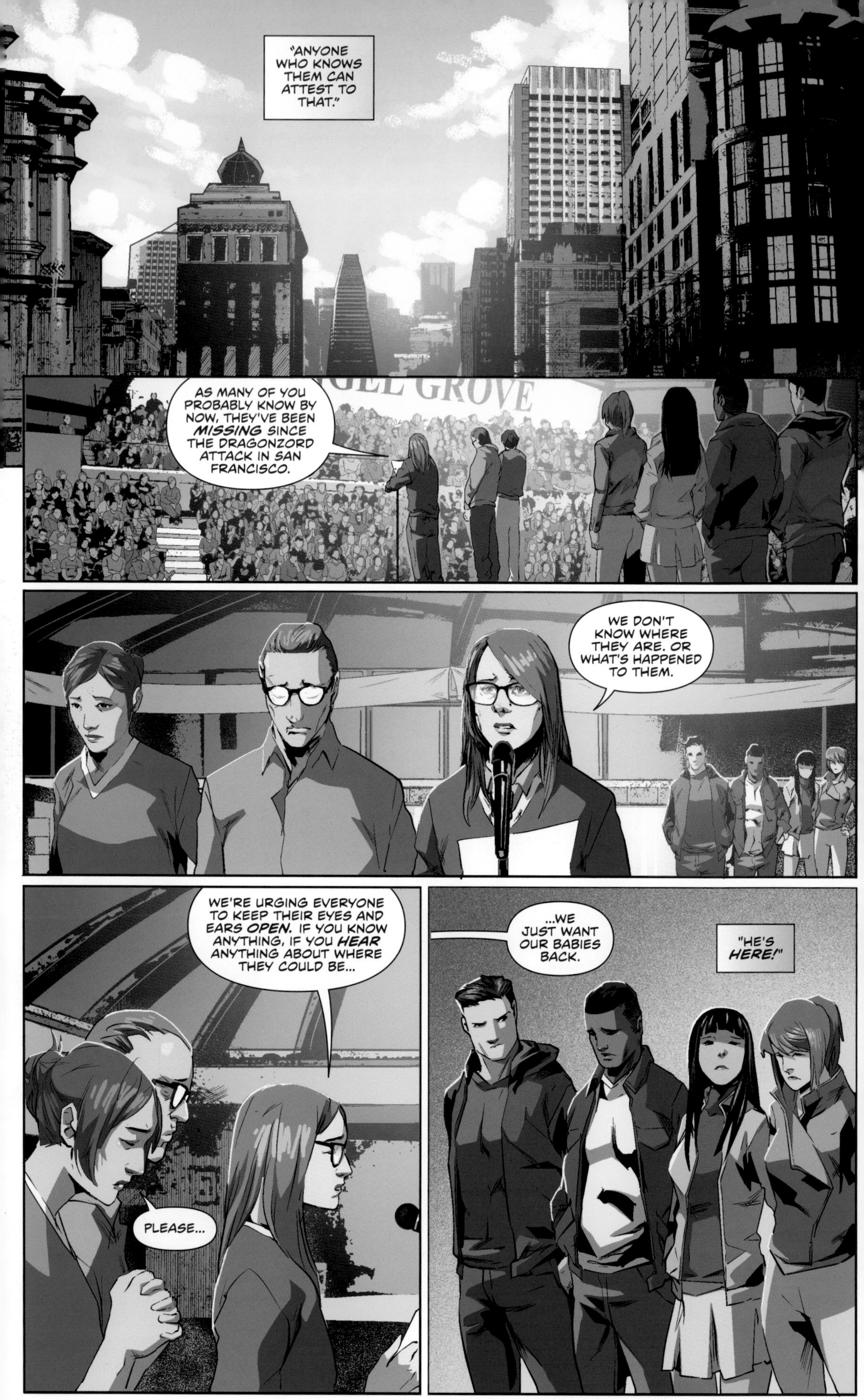
"ANYONE WHO KNOWS THEM CAN ATTEST TO THAT."
AS MANY OF YOU PROBABLY KNOW BY NOW, THEY'VE BEEN *MISSING* SINCE THE DRAGONZORD ATTACK IN SAN FRANCISCO.
WE DON'T KNOW WHERE THEY ARE. OR WHAT'S HAPPENED TO THEM.
WE'RE URGING EVERYONE TO KEEP THEIR EYES AND EARS *OPEN.* IF YOU KNOW ANYTHING, IF YOU *HEAR* ANYTHING ABOUT WHERE THEY COULD BE...
PLEASE...
...WE JUST WANT OUR BABIES BACK.
"HE'S *HERE!*"

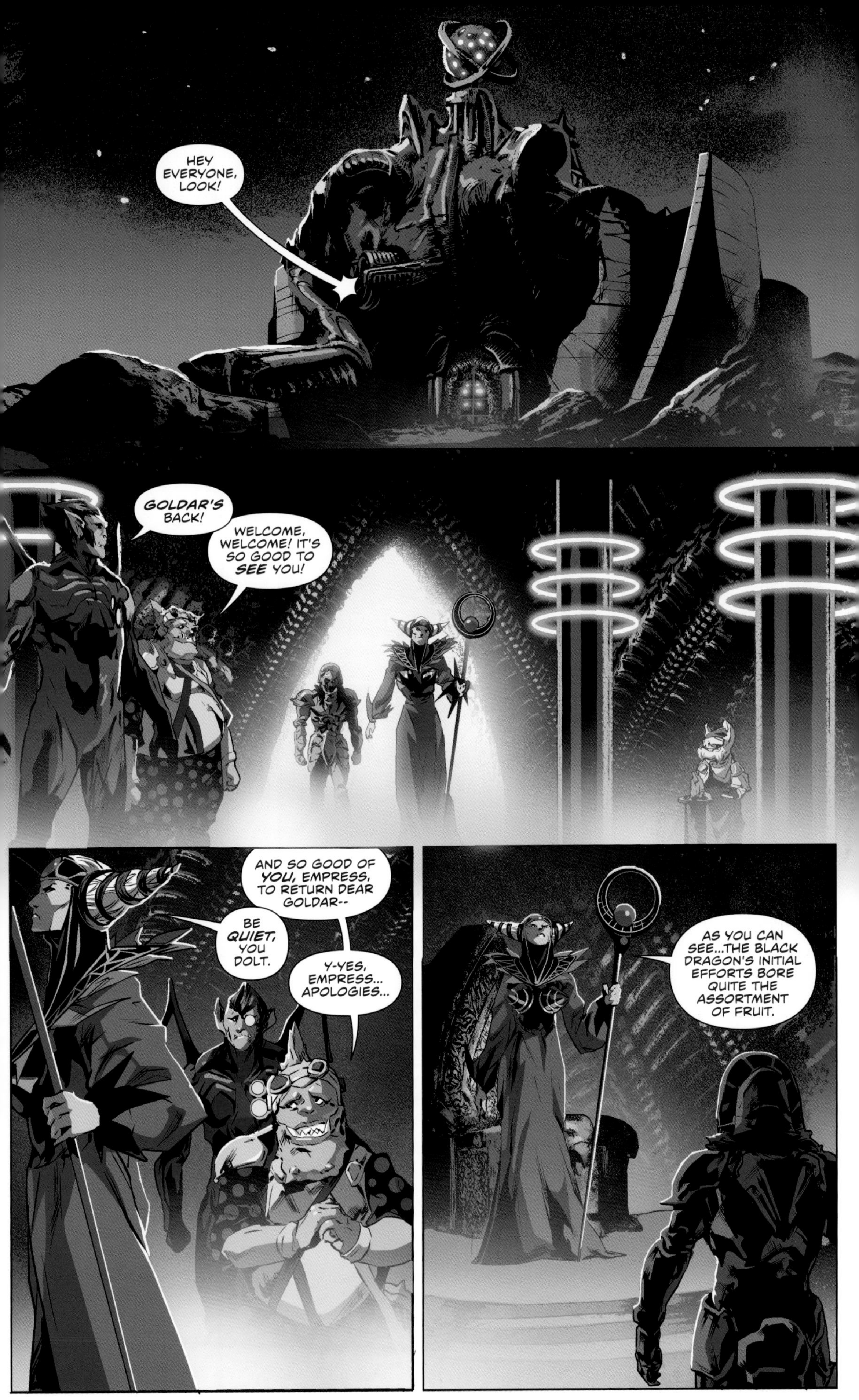
HEY EVERYONE, LOOK!
GOLDAR'S BACK!
WELCOME, WELCOME! IT'S SO GOOD TO SEE YOU!
AND SO GOOD OF YOU, EMPRESS, TO RETURN DEAR GOLDAR--
BE QUIET, YOU DOLT.
Y-YES, EMPRESS... APOLOGIES...
AS YOU CAN SEE...THE BLACK DRAGON'S INITIAL EFFORTS BORE QUITE THE ASSORTMENT OF FRUIT.

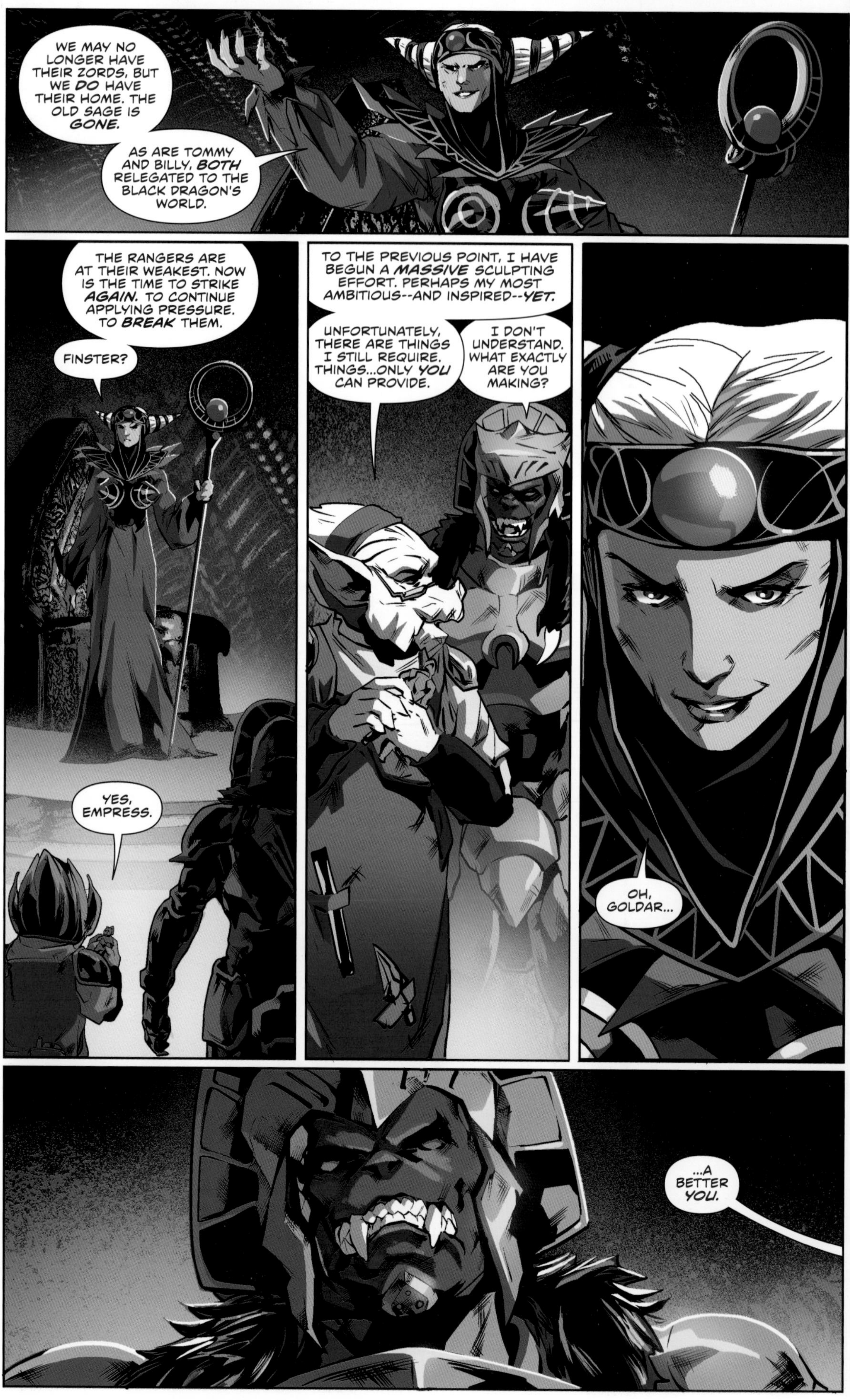
WE MAY NO LONGER HAVE THEIR ZORDS, BUT WE DO HAVE THEIR HOME. THE OLD SAGE IS GONE.
AS ARE TOMMY AND BILLY, BOTH RELEGATED TO THE BLACK DRAGON'S WORLD.
THE RANGERS ARE AT THEIR WEAKEST. NOW IS THE TIME TO STRIKE AGAIN. TO CONTINUE APPLYING PRESSURE. TO BREAK THEM.
FINSTER?
YES, EMPRESS.
TO THE PREVIOUS POINT, I HAVE BEGUN A MASSIVE SCULPTING EFFORT. PERHAPS MY MOST AMBITIOUS--AND INSPIRED--YET.
UNFORTUNATELY, THERE ARE THINGS I STILL REQUIRE. THINGS...ONLY YOU CAN PROVIDE.
I DON'T UNDERSTAND. WHAT EXACTLY ARE YOU MAKING?
OH, GOLDAR...
...A BETTER YOU.

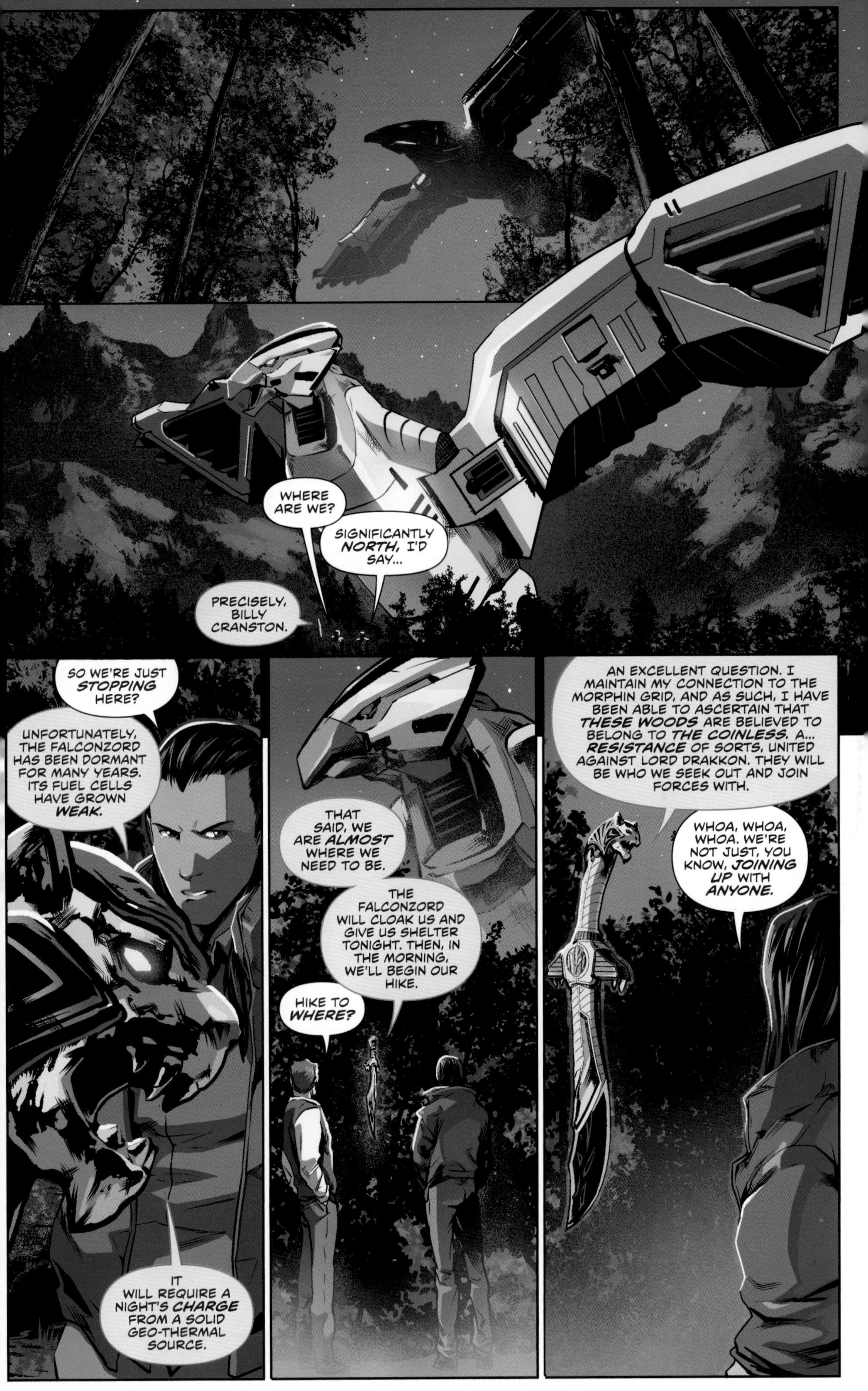

WHERE ARE WE?
SIGNIFICANTLY NORTH, I'D SAY...
PRECISELY, BILLY CRANSTON.
SO WE'RE JUST STOPPING HERE?
UNFORTUNATELY, THE FALCONZORD HAS BEEN DORMANT FOR MANY YEARS. ITS FUEL CELLS HAVE GROWN WEAK.
IT WILL REQUIRE A NIGHT'S CHARGE FROM A SOLID GEO-THERMAL SOURCE.
THAT SAID, WE ARE ALMOST WHERE WE NEED TO BE.
THE FALCONZORD WILL CLOAK US AND GIVE US SHELTER TONIGHT. THEN, IN THE MORNING, WE'LL BEGIN OUR HIKE.
HIKE TO WHERE?
AN EXCELLENT QUESTION. I MAINTAIN MY CONNECTION TO THE MORPHIN GRID, AND AS SUCH, I HAVE BEEN ABLE TO ASCERTAIN THAT THESE WOODS ARE BELIEVED TO BELONG TO THE COINLESS. A... RESISTANCE OF SORTS, UNITED AGAINST LORD DRAKKON. THEY WILL BE WHO WE SEEK OUT AND JOIN FORCES WITH.
WHOA, WHOA, WHOA. WE'RE NOT JUST, YOU KNOW, JOINING UP WITH ANYONE.

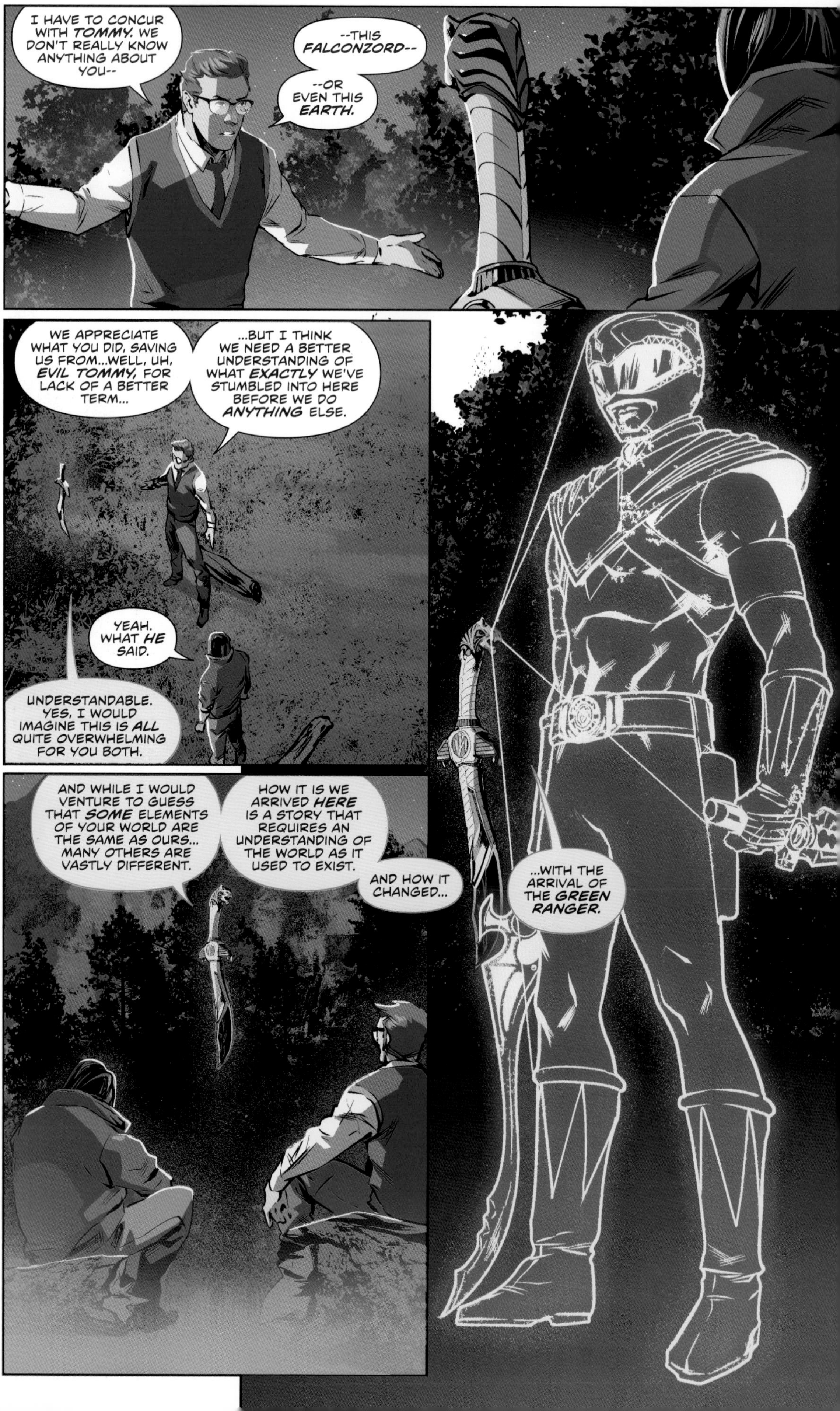

I HAVE TO CONCUR WITH TOMMY. WE DON'T REALLY KNOW ANYTHING ABOUT YOU--
--THIS FALCONZORD--
--OR EVEN THIS EARTH.
WE APPRECIATE WHAT YOU DID, SAVING US FROM...WELL, UH, EVIL TOMMY, FOR LACK OF A BETTER TERM...
...BUT I THINK WE NEED A BETTER UNDERSTANDING OF WHAT EXACTLY WE'VE STUMBLED INTO HERE BEFORE WE DO ANYTHING ELSE.
YEAH. WHAT HE SAID.
UNDERSTANDABLE. YES, I WOULD IMAGINE THIS IS ALL QUITE OVERWHELMING FOR YOU BOTH.
AND WHILE I WOULD VENTURE TO GUESS THAT SOME ELEMENTS OF YOUR WORLD ARE THE SAME AS OURS... MANY OTHERS ARE VASTLY DIFFERENT.
HOW IT IS WE ARRIVED HERE IS A STORY THAT REQUIRES AN UNDERSTANDING OF THE WORLD AS IT USED TO EXIST.
AND HOW IT CHANGED...
...WITH THE ARRIVAL OF THE GREEN RANGER.

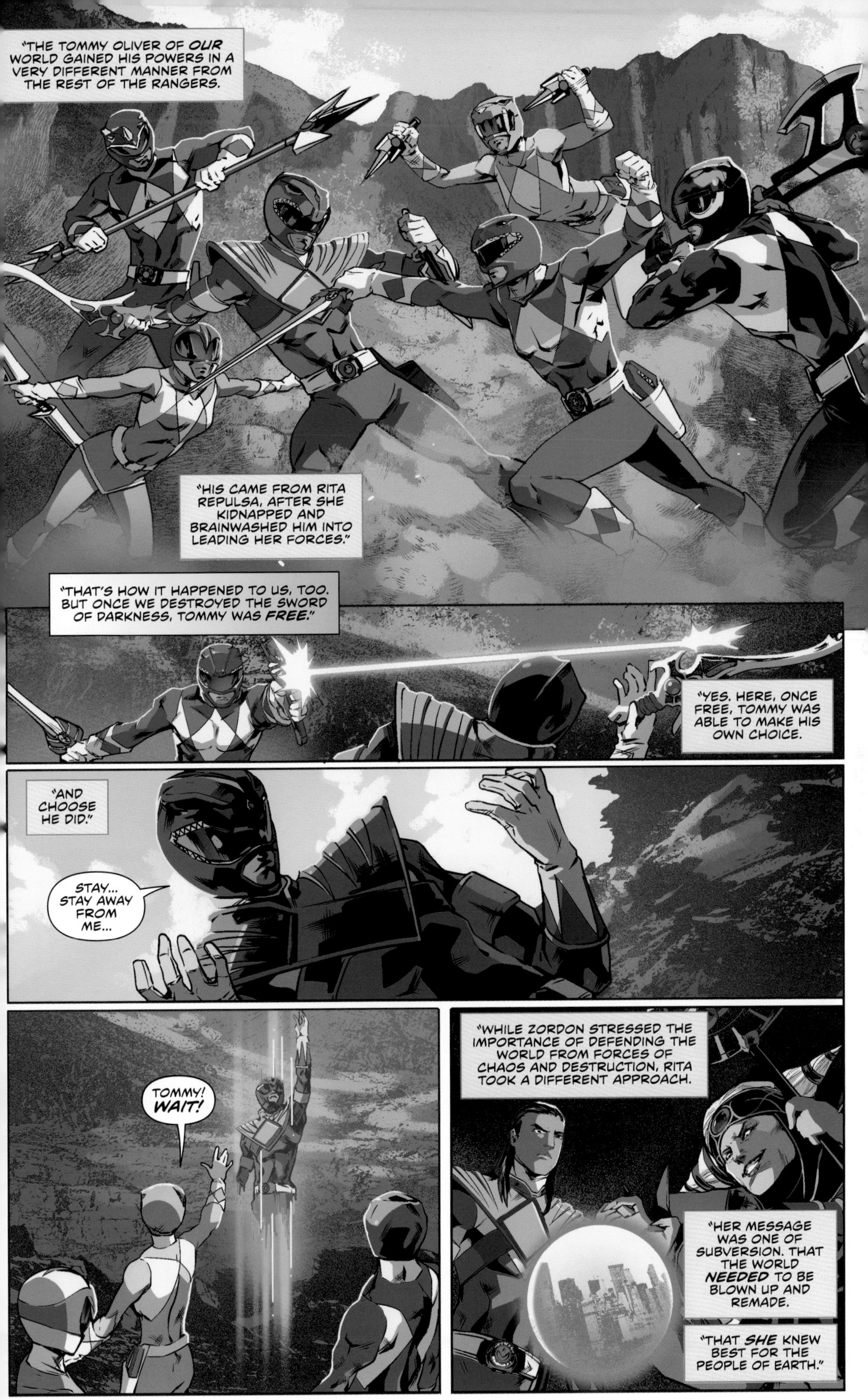
"THE TOMMY OLIVER OF *OUR* WORLD GAINED HIS POWERS IN A VERY DIFFERENT MANNER FROM THE REST OF THE RANGERS.
"HIS CAME FROM RITA REPULSA, AFTER SHE KIDNAPPED AND BRAINWASHED HIM INTO LEADING HER FORCES."
"THAT'S HOW IT HAPPENED TO US, TOO. BUT ONCE WE DESTROYED THE SWORD OF DARKNESS, TOMMY WAS *FREE*."
"YES. HERE, ONCE FREE, TOMMY WAS ABLE TO MAKE HIS OWN CHOICE.
"AND CHOOSE HE DID."
STAY... STAY AWAY FROM ME...
TOMMY! *WAIT!*
"WHILE ZORDON STRESSED THE IMPORTANCE OF DEFENDING THE WORLD FROM FORCES OF CHAOS AND DESTRUCTION, RITA TOOK A DIFFERENT APPROACH.
"HER MESSAGE WAS ONE OF SUBVERSION. THAT THE WORLD *NEEDED* TO BE BLOWN UP AND REMADE.
"THAT *SHE* KNEW BEST FOR THE PEOPLE OF EARTH."

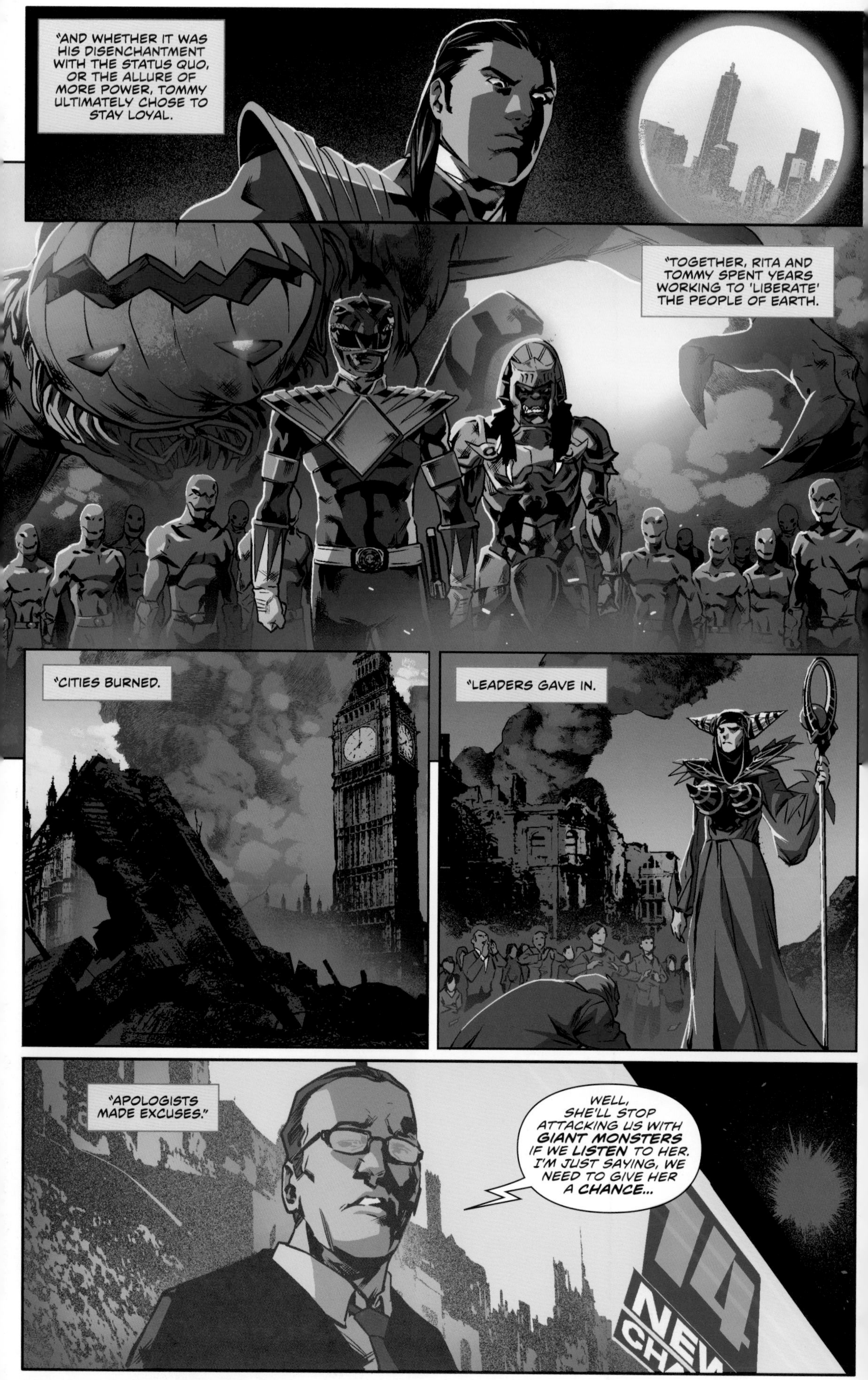
"AND WHETHER IT WAS HIS DISENCHANTMENT WITH THE STATUS QUO, OR THE ALLURE OF MORE POWER, TOMMY ULTIMATELY CHOSE TO STAY LOYAL.
"TOGETHER, RITA AND TOMMY SPENT YEARS WORKING TO 'LIBERATE' THE PEOPLE OF EARTH.
"CITIES BURNED.
"LEADERS GAVE IN.
"APOLOGISTS MADE EXCUSES."
WELL, SHE'LL STOP ATTACKING US WITH GIANT MONSTERS IF WE LISTEN TO HER. I'M JUST SAYING, WE NEED TO GIVE HER A CHANCE...
NEW

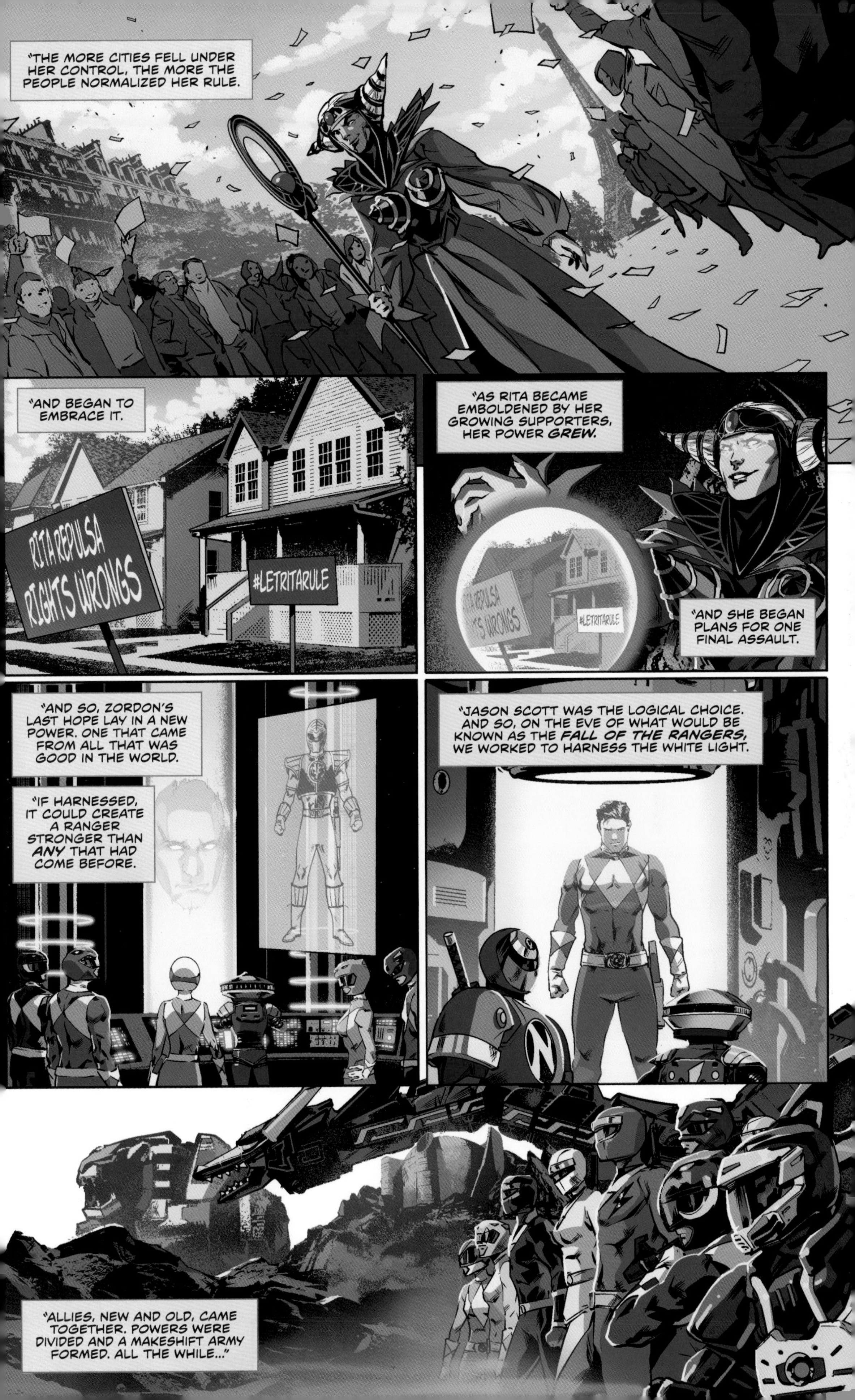
"THE MORE CITIES FELL UNDER HER CONTROL, THE MORE THE PEOPLE NORMALIZED HER RULE.
"AND BEGAN TO EMBRACE IT.
RITA REPULSA RIGHTS WRONGS
#LETRITARULE
"AS RITA BECAME EMBOLDENED BY HER GROWING SUPPORTERS, HER POWER *GREW.*
RITA REPULSA RIGHTS WRONGS
#LETRITARULE
"AND SHE BEGAN PLANS FOR ONE FINAL ASSAULT.
"AND SO, ZORDON'S LAST HOPE LAY IN A NEW POWER. ONE THAT CAME FROM ALL THAT WAS GOOD IN THE WORLD.
"IF HARNESSED, IT COULD CREATE A RANGER STRONGER THAN *ANY* THAT HAD COME BEFORE.
"JASON SCOTT WAS THE LOGICAL CHOICE. AND SO, ON THE EVE OF WHAT WOULD BE KNOWN AS THE *FALL OF THE RANGERS,* WE WORKED TO HARNESS THE WHITE LIGHT.
"ALLIES, NEW AND OLD, CAME TOGETHER. POWERS WERE DIVIDED AND A MAKESHIFT ARMY FORMED. ALL THE WHILE..."

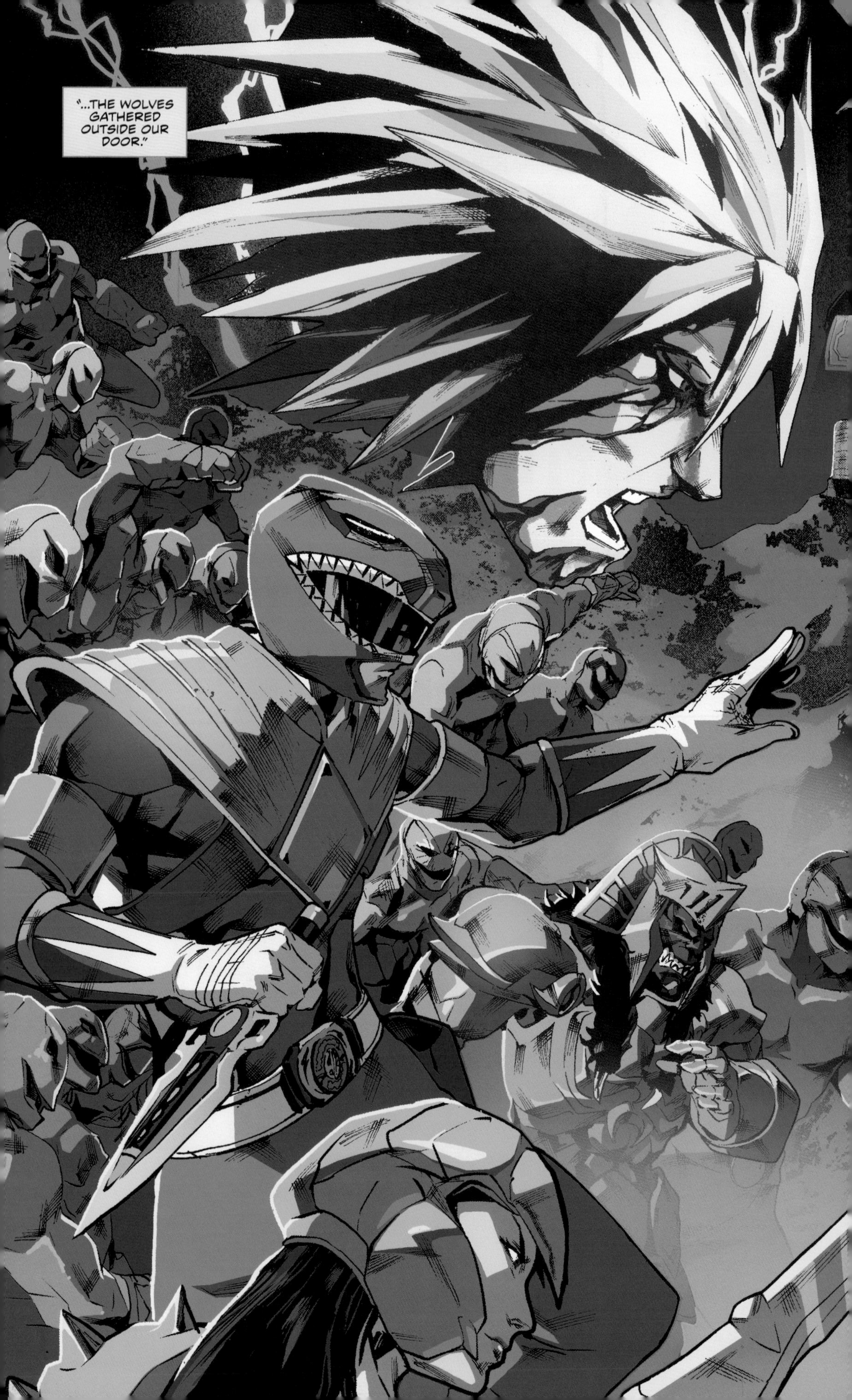
"...THE WOLVES GATHERED OUTSIDE OUR DOOR."

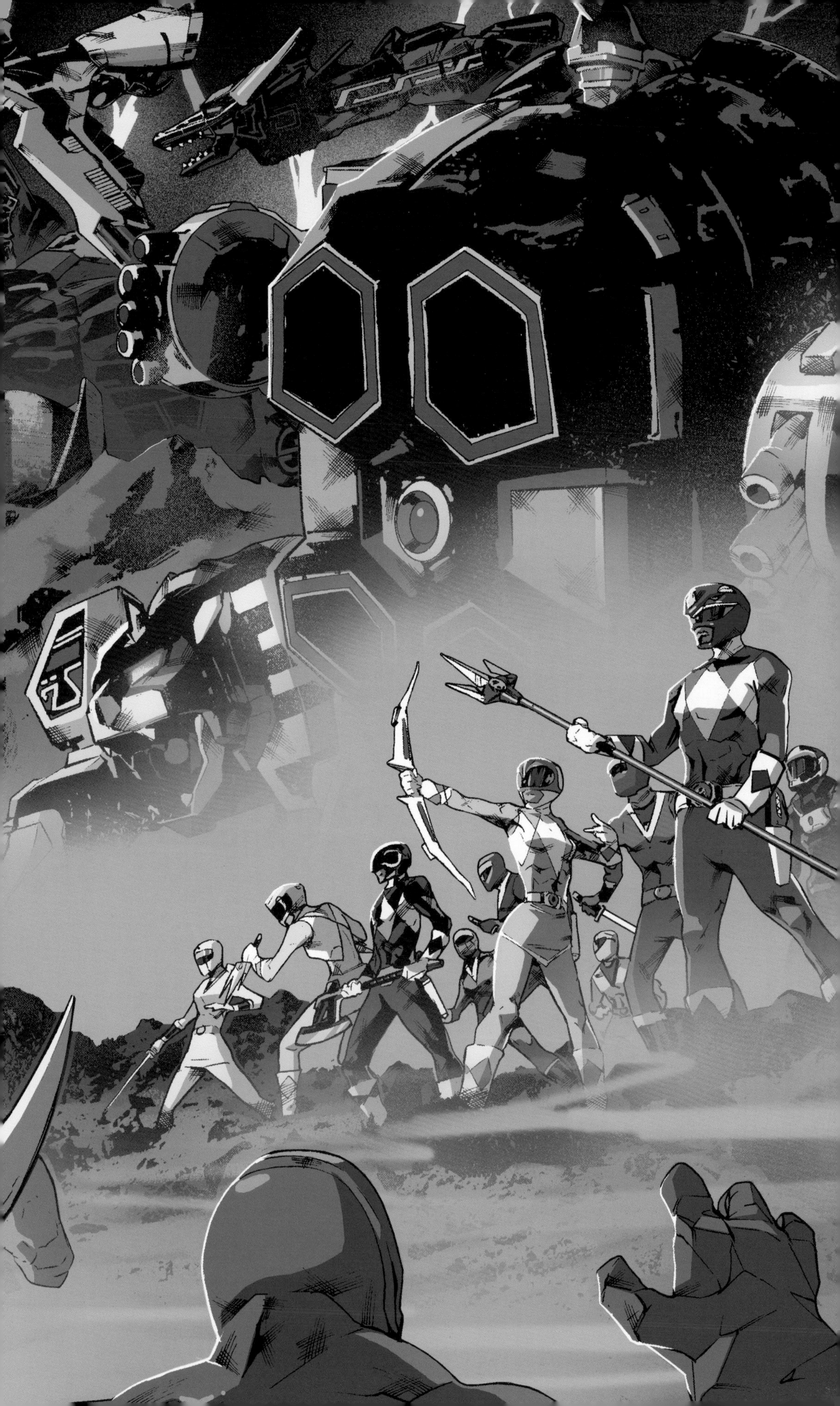

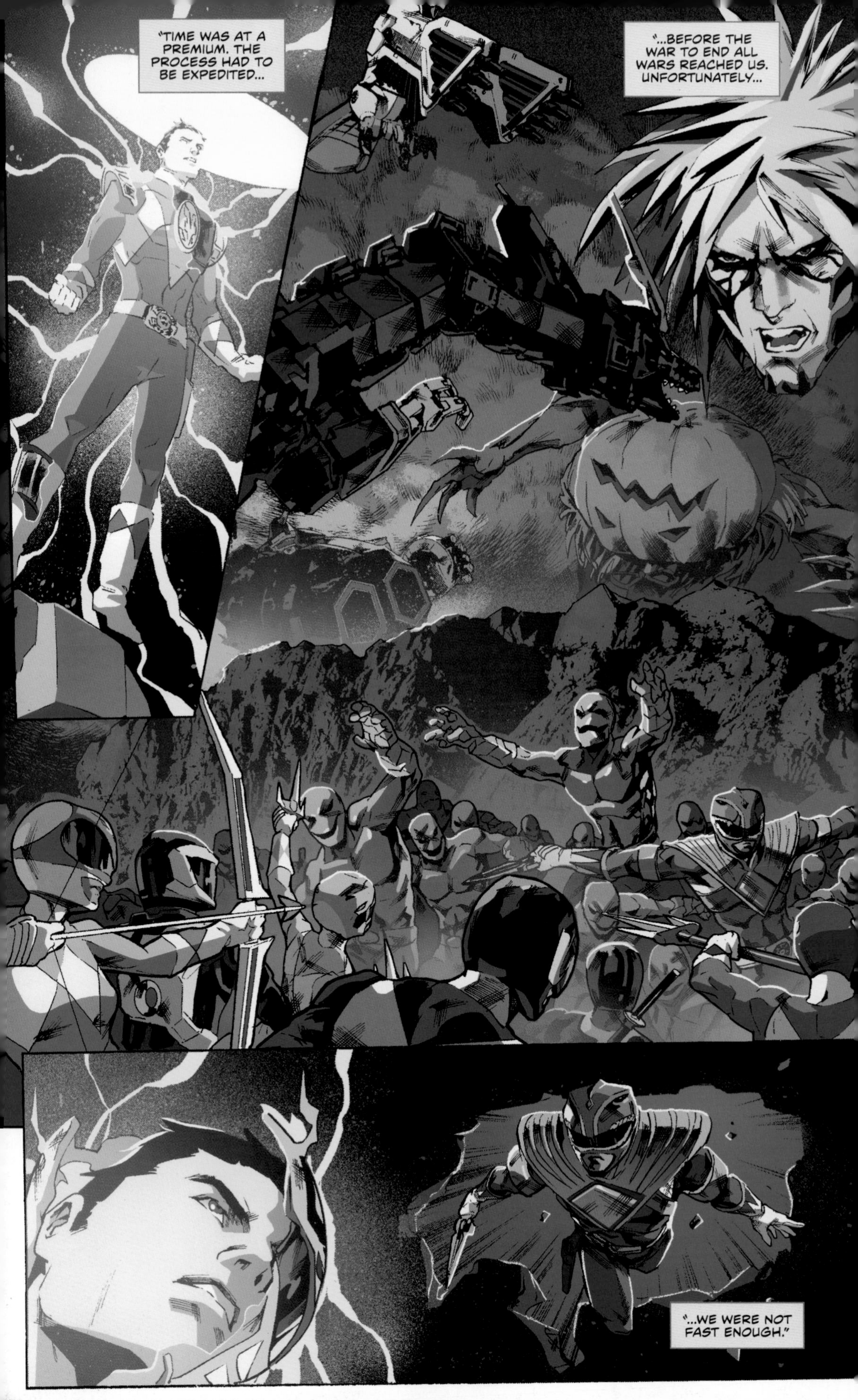
"TIME WAS AT A PREMIUM. THE PROCESS HAD TO BE EXPEDITED...
"...BEFORE THE WAR TO END ALL WARS REACHED US. UNFORTUNATELY...
"...WE WERE NOT FAST ENOUGH."

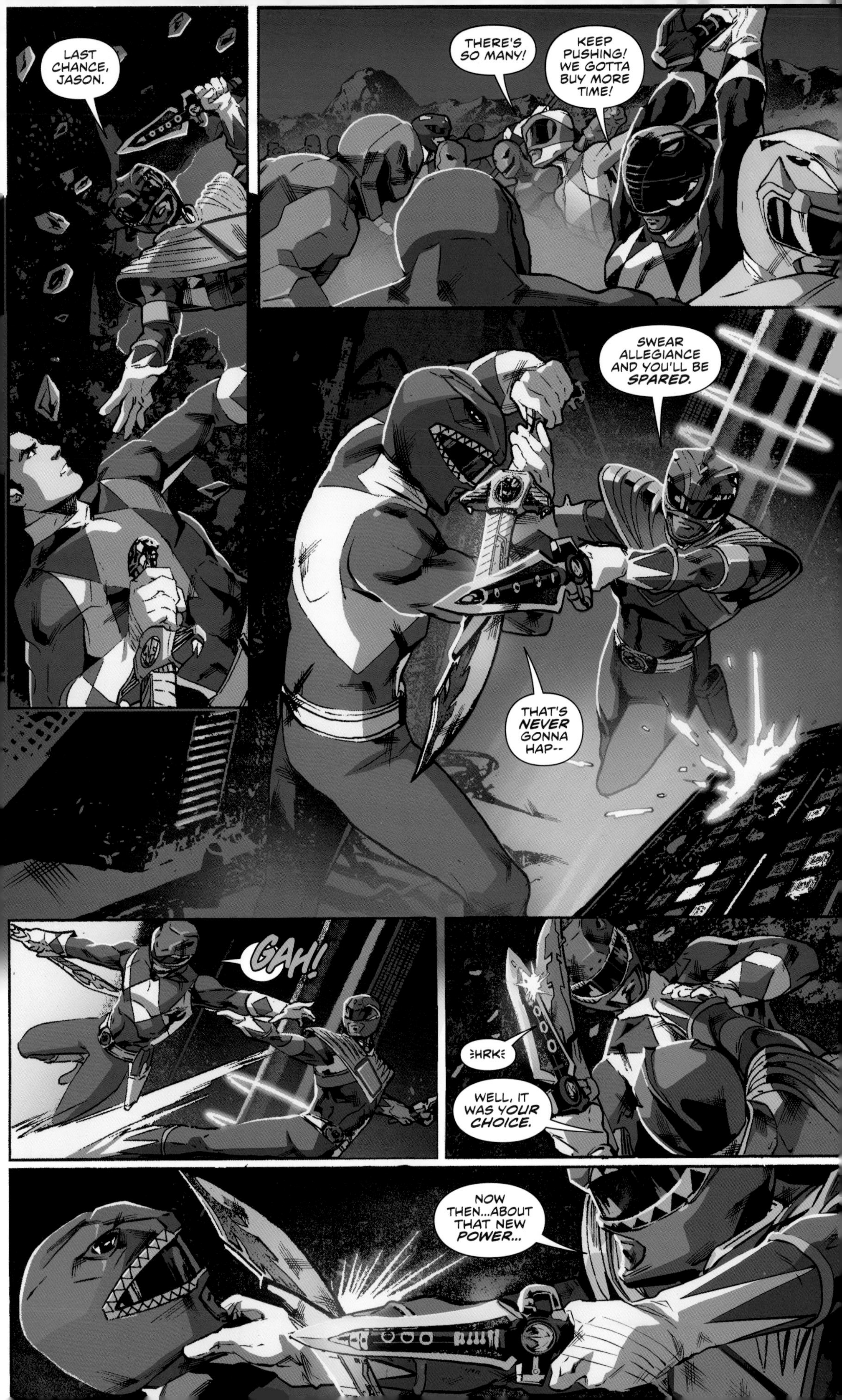
LAST CHANCE, JASON.
THERE'S SO MANY!
KEEP PUSHING! WE GOTTA BUY MORE TIME!
SWEAR ALLEGIANCE AND YOU'LL BE SPARED.
THAT'S NEVER GONNA HAP--
GAH!
HRK
WELL, IT WAS YOUR CHOICE.
NOW THEN...ABOUT THAT NEW POWER...

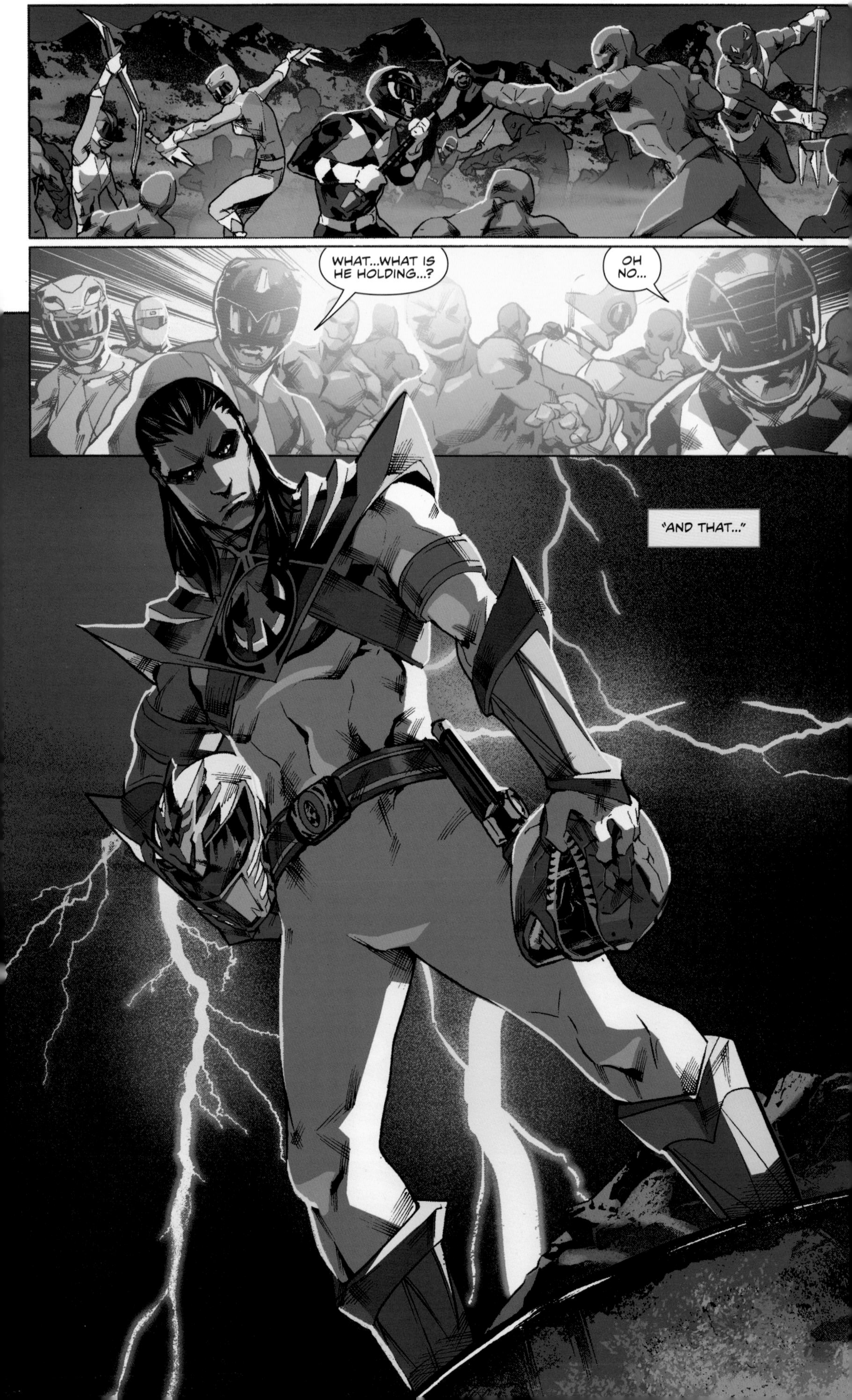
WHAT...WHAT IS HE HOLDING...?
OH NO...
"AND THAT..."

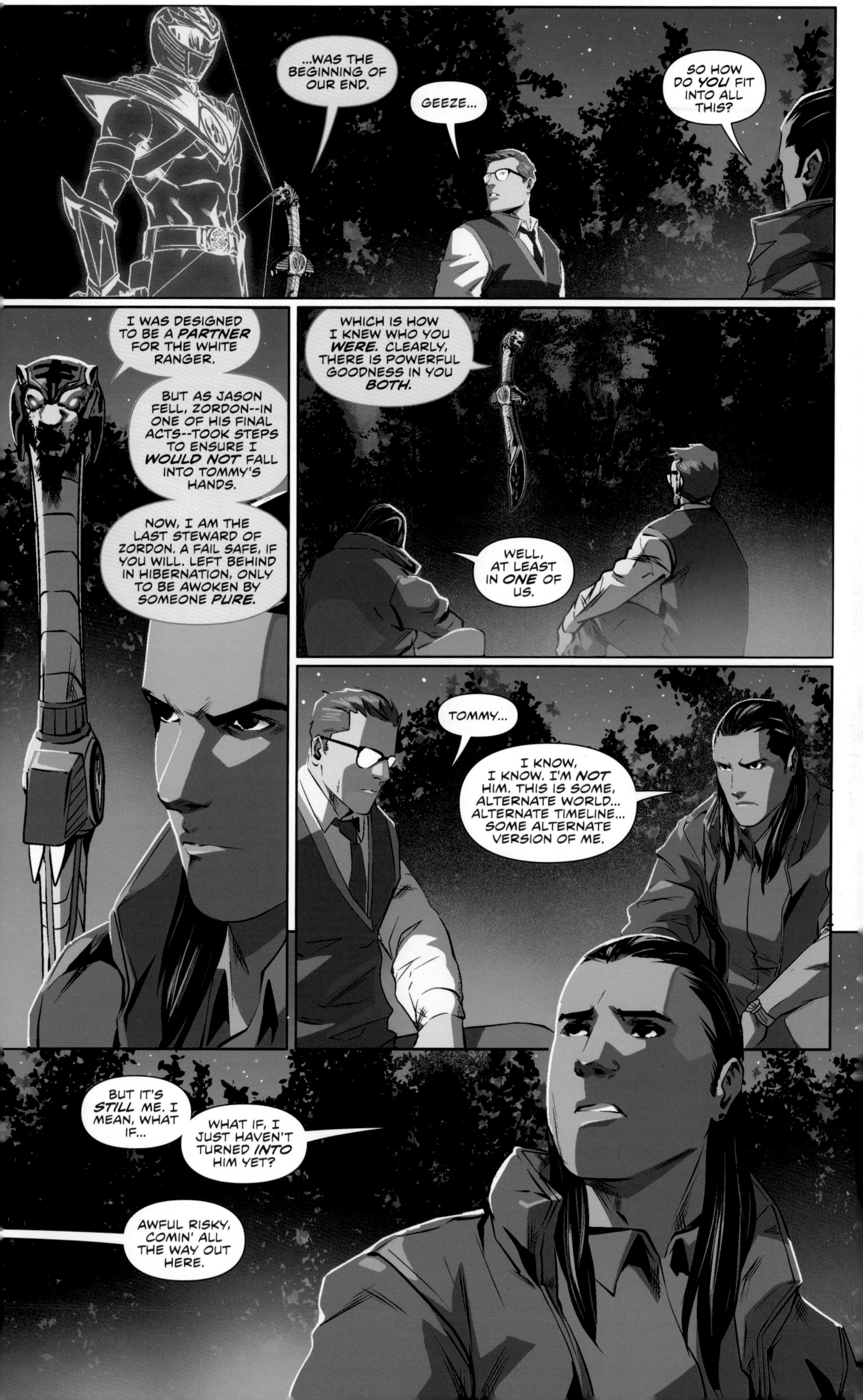
...WAS THE BEGINNING OF OUR END.
GEEZE...
SO HOW DO *YOU* FIT INTO ALL THIS?
I WAS DESIGNED TO BE A *PARTNER* FOR THE WHITE RANGER.
BUT AS JASON FELL, ZORDON--IN ONE OF HIS FINAL ACTS--TOOK STEPS TO ENSURE I *WOULD NOT* FALL INTO TOMMY'S HANDS.
NOW, I AM THE LAST STEWARD OF ZORDON. A FAIL SAFE, IF YOU WILL. LEFT BEHIND IN HIBERNATION, ONLY TO BE AWOKEN BY SOMEONE *PURE.*
WHICH IS HOW I KNEW WHO YOU *WERE.* CLEARLY, THERE IS POWERFUL GOODNESS IN YOU *BOTH.*
WELL, AT LEAST IN *ONE* OF US.
TOMMY...
I KNOW, I KNOW. I'M *NOT* HIM. THIS IS SOME, ALTERNATE WORLD... ALTERNATE TIMELINE... SOME ALTERNATE VERSION OF ME.
BUT IT'S *STILL* ME. I MEAN, WHAT IF...
WHAT IF, I JUST HAVEN'T TURNED *INTO* HIM YET?
AWFUL RISKY, COMIN' ALL THE WAY OUT HERE.

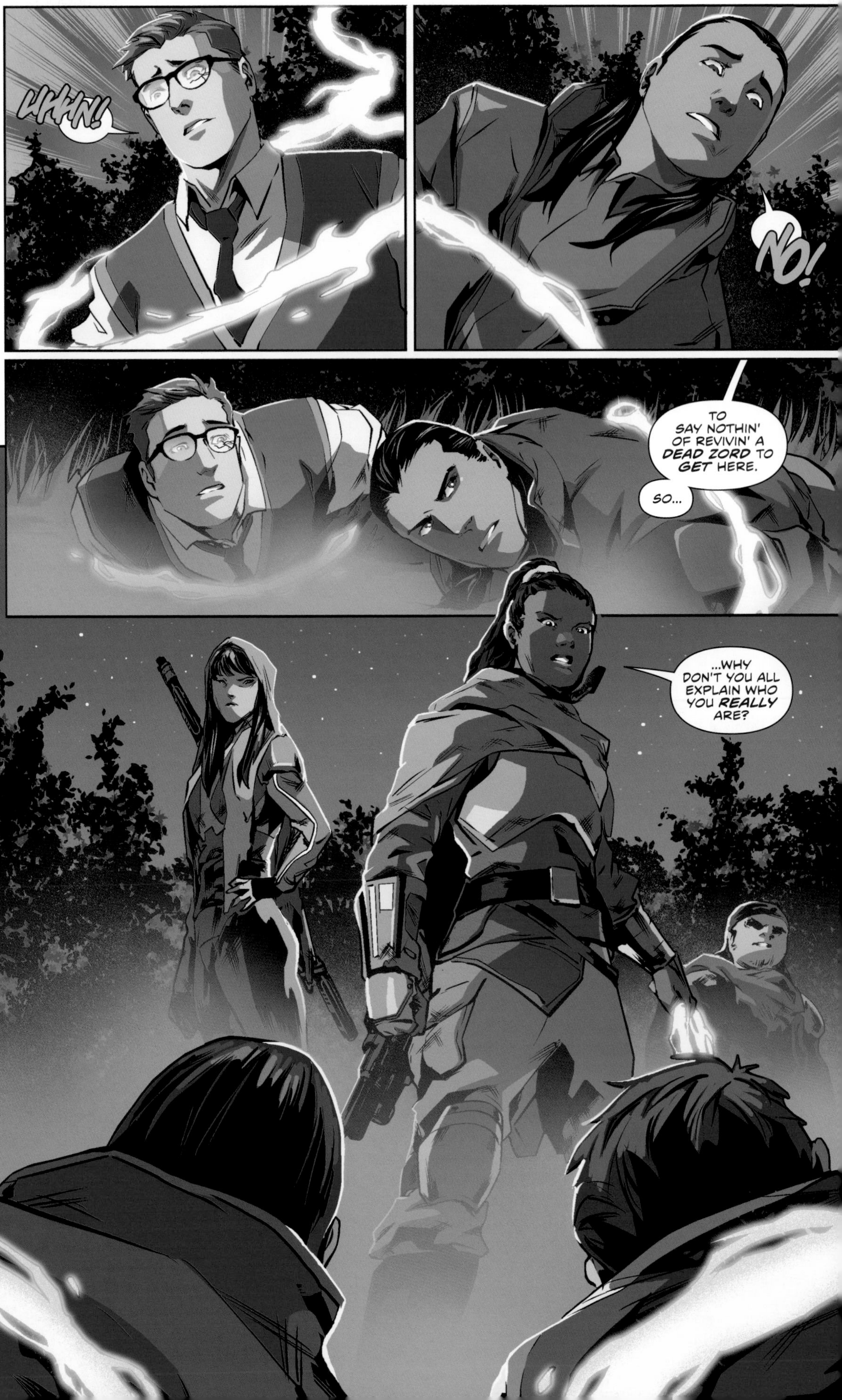
UHHN!
NO!
TO SAY NOTHIN' OF REVIVIN' A DEAD ZORD TO GET HERE.
SO...
...WHY DON'T YOU ALL EXPLAIN WHO YOU REALLY ARE?

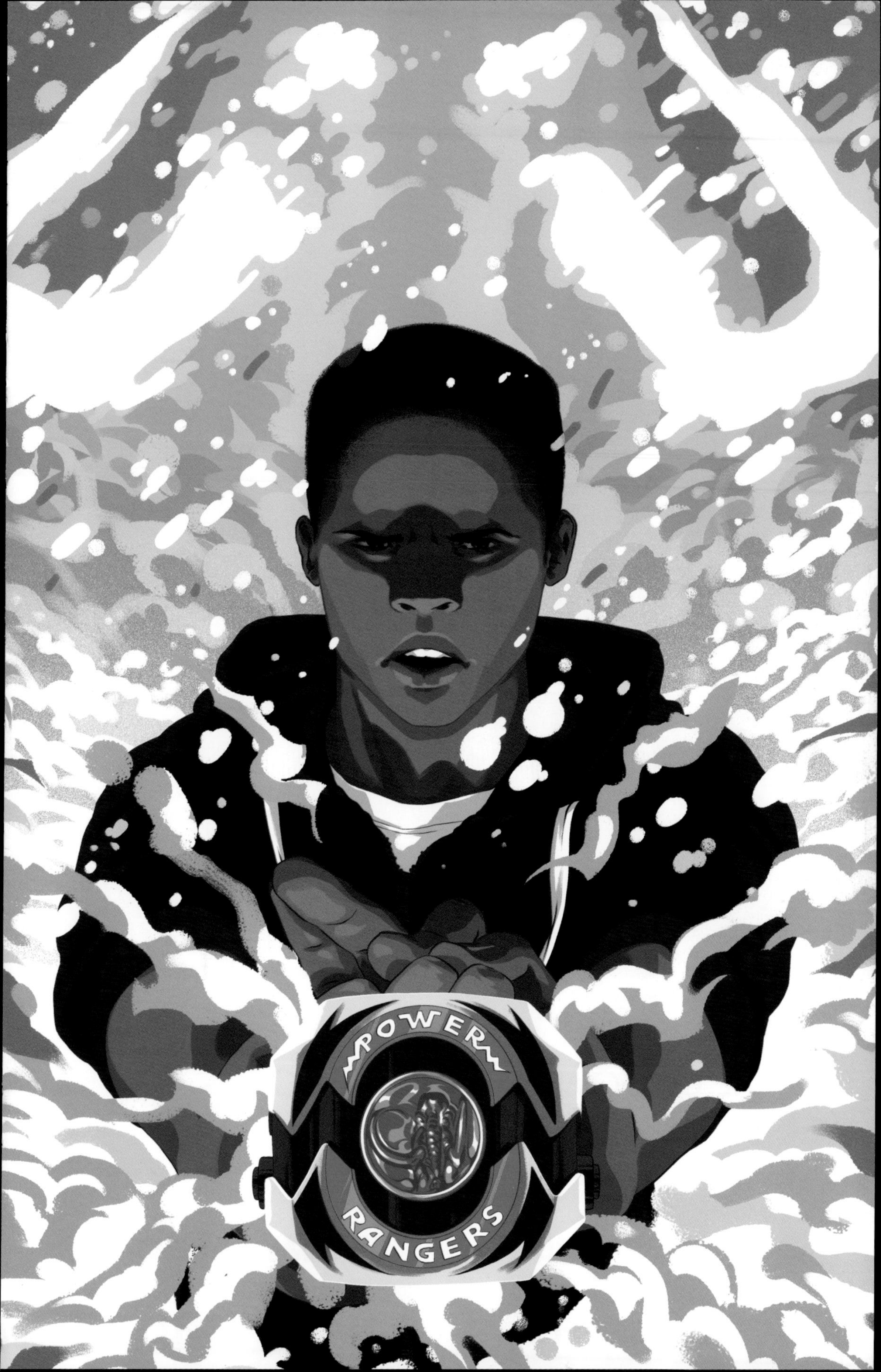
POWER
RANGERS

GOÑI MONTES ISSUE TWELVE MORPHIN VARIANT COVER

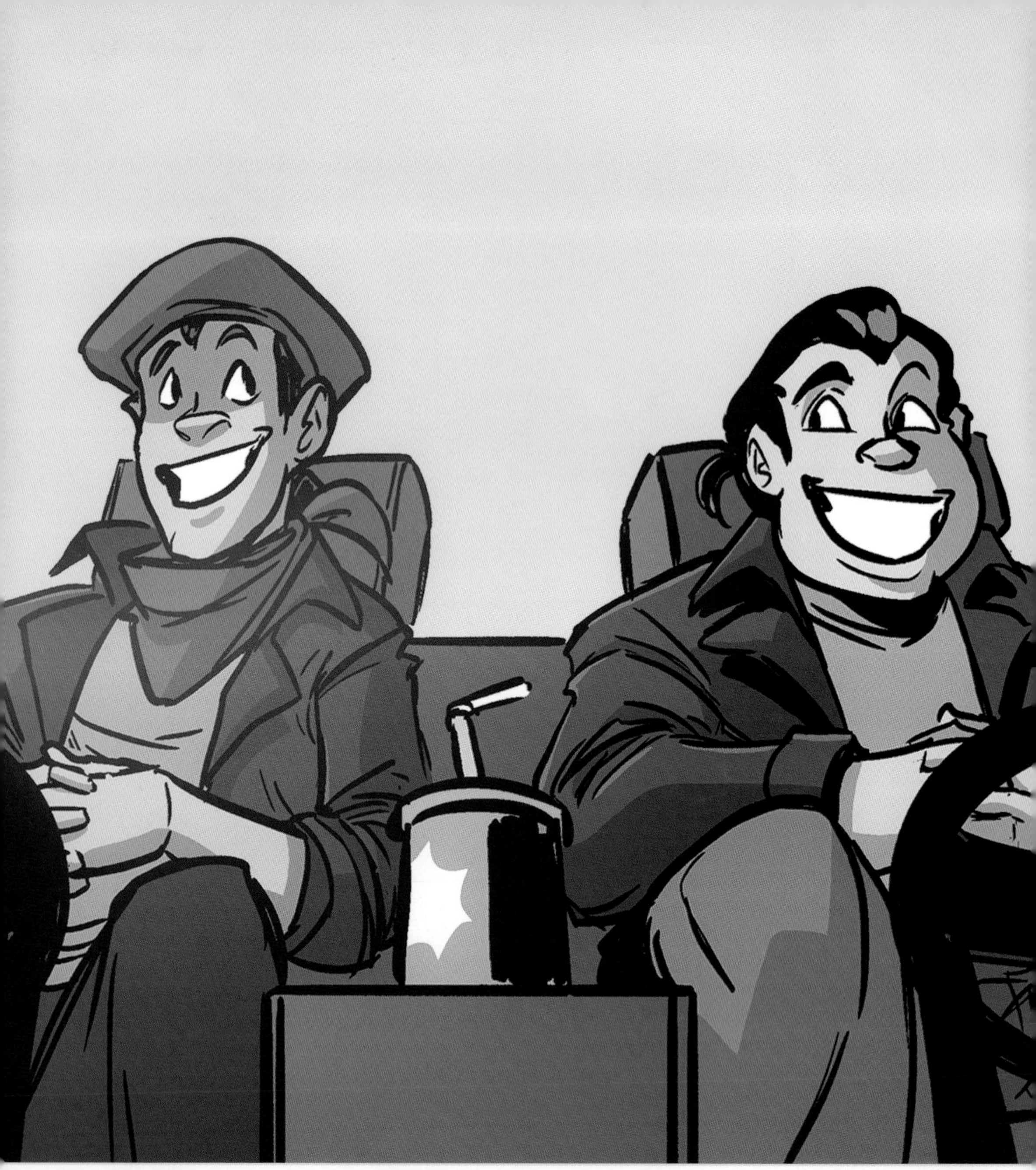

THE ONGOING ADVENTURES OF
BULK & SKULL

WRITTEN BY
STEVE ORLANDO

ILLUSTRATED BY
CORIN HOWELL

COLORS BY
JEREMY LAWSON

LETTERS BY
JIM CAMPBELL

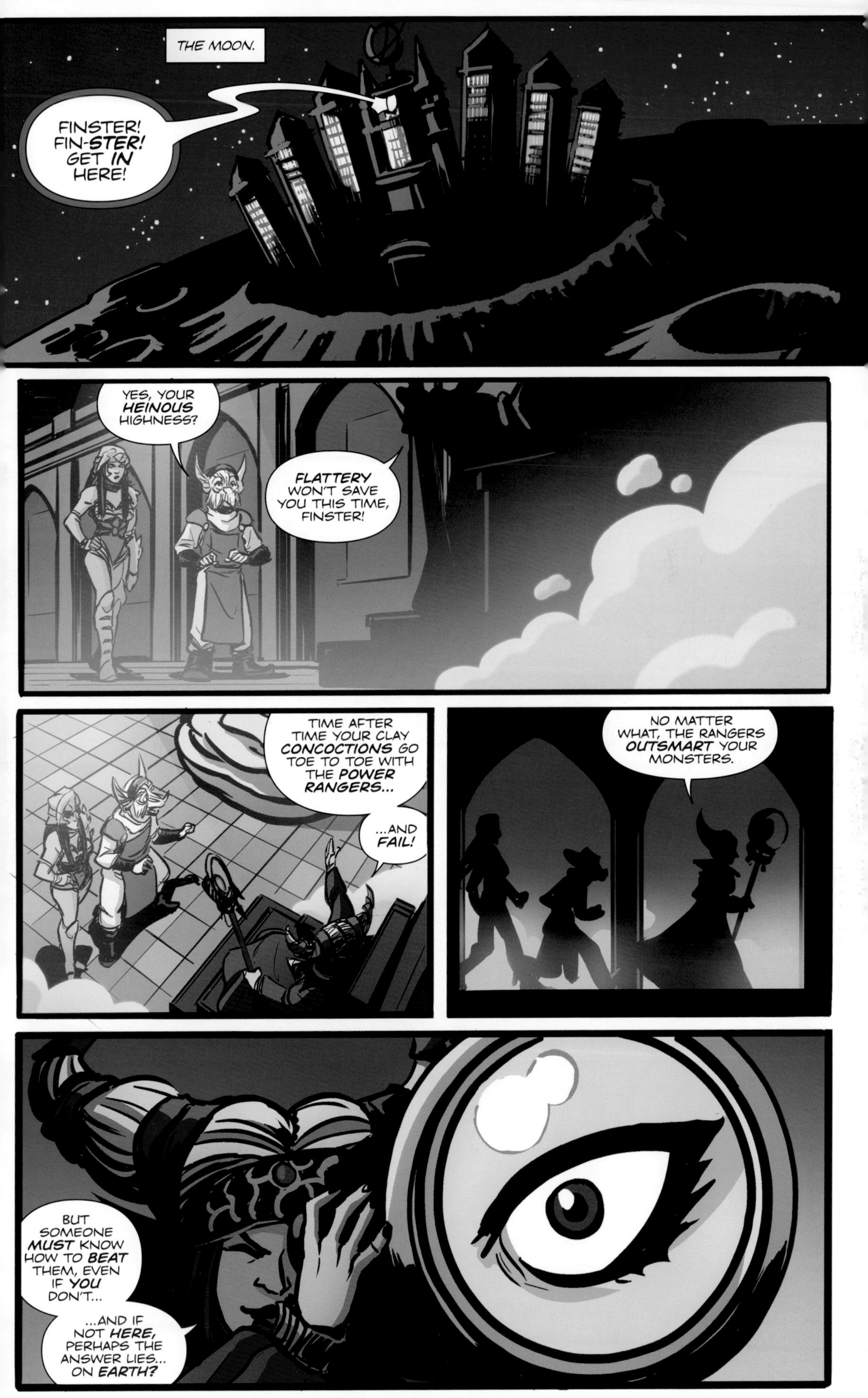
THE MOON.
FINSTER! FIN-STER! GET IN HERE!
YES, YOUR HEINOUS HIGHNESS?
FLATTERY WON'T SAVE YOU THIS TIME, FINSTER!
TIME AFTER TIME YOUR CLAY CONCOCTIONS GO TOE TO TOE WITH THE POWER RANGERS...
...AND FAIL!
NO MATTER WHAT, THE RANGERS OUTSMART YOUR MONSTERS.
BUT SOMEONE MUST KNOW HOW TO BEAT THEM, EVEN IF YOU DON'T...
...AND IF NOT HERE, PERHAPS THE ANSWER LIES... ON EARTH?

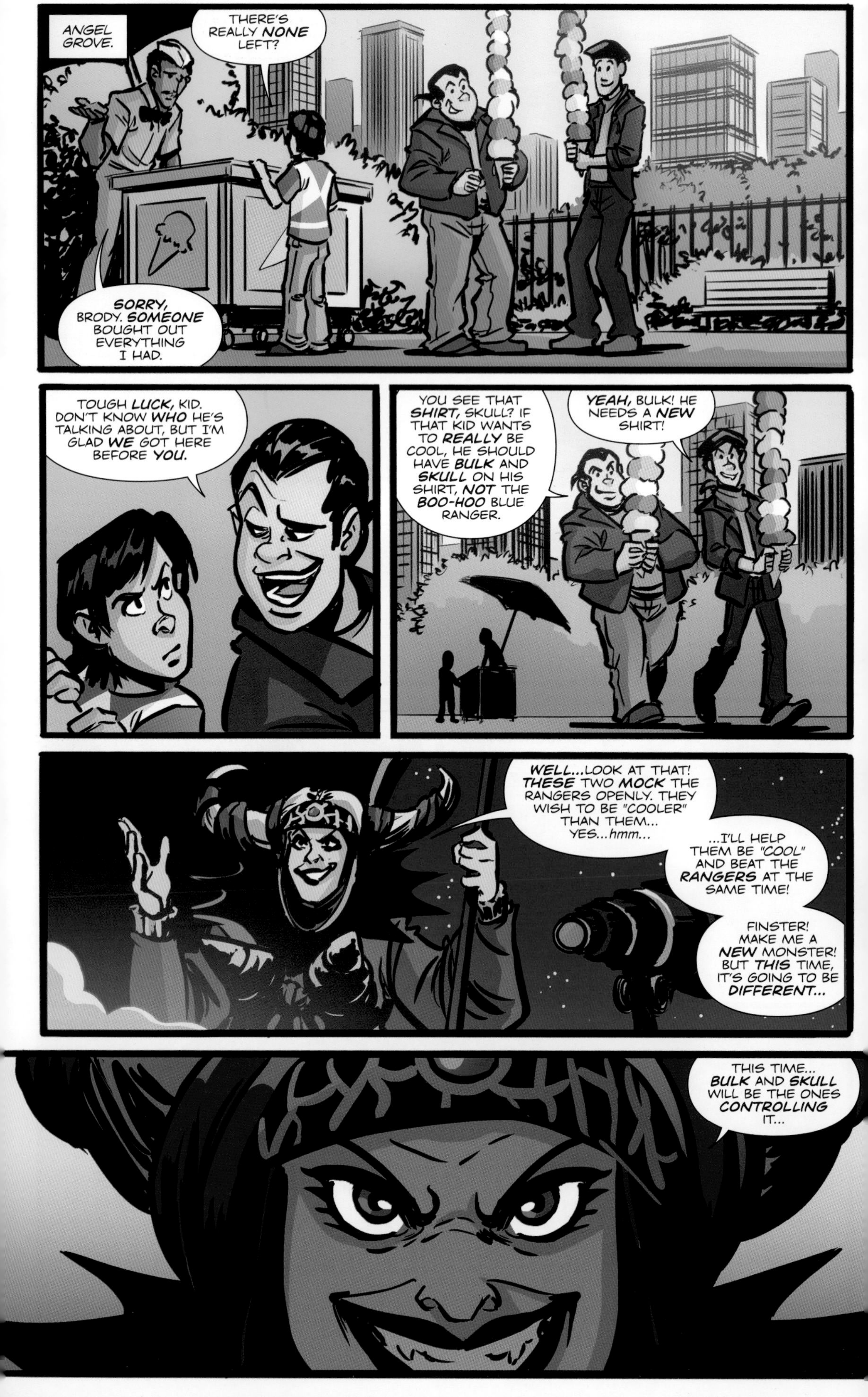

ANGEL GROVE.
THERE'S REALLY NONE LEFT?
SORRY, BRODY. SOMEONE BOUGHT OUT EVERYTHING I HAD.
TOUGH LUCK, KID. DON'T KNOW WHO HE'S TALKING ABOUT, BUT I'M GLAD WE GOT HERE BEFORE YOU.
YOU SEE THAT SHIRT, SKULL? IF THAT KID WANTS TO REALLY BE COOL, HE SHOULD HAVE BULK AND SKULL ON HIS SHIRT, NOT THE BOO-HOO BLUE RANGER.
YEAH, BULK! HE NEEDS A NEW SHIRT!
WELL...LOOK AT THAT! THESE TWO MOCK THE RANGERS OPENLY. THEY WISH TO BE "COOLER" THAN THEM... YES...hmm...
...I'LL HELP THEM BE "COOL" AND BEAT THE RANGERS AT THE SAME TIME!
FINSTER! MAKE ME A NEW MONSTER! BUT THIS TIME, IT'S GOING TO BE DIFFERENT...
THIS TIME... BULK AND SKULL WILL BE THE ONES CONTROLLING IT...

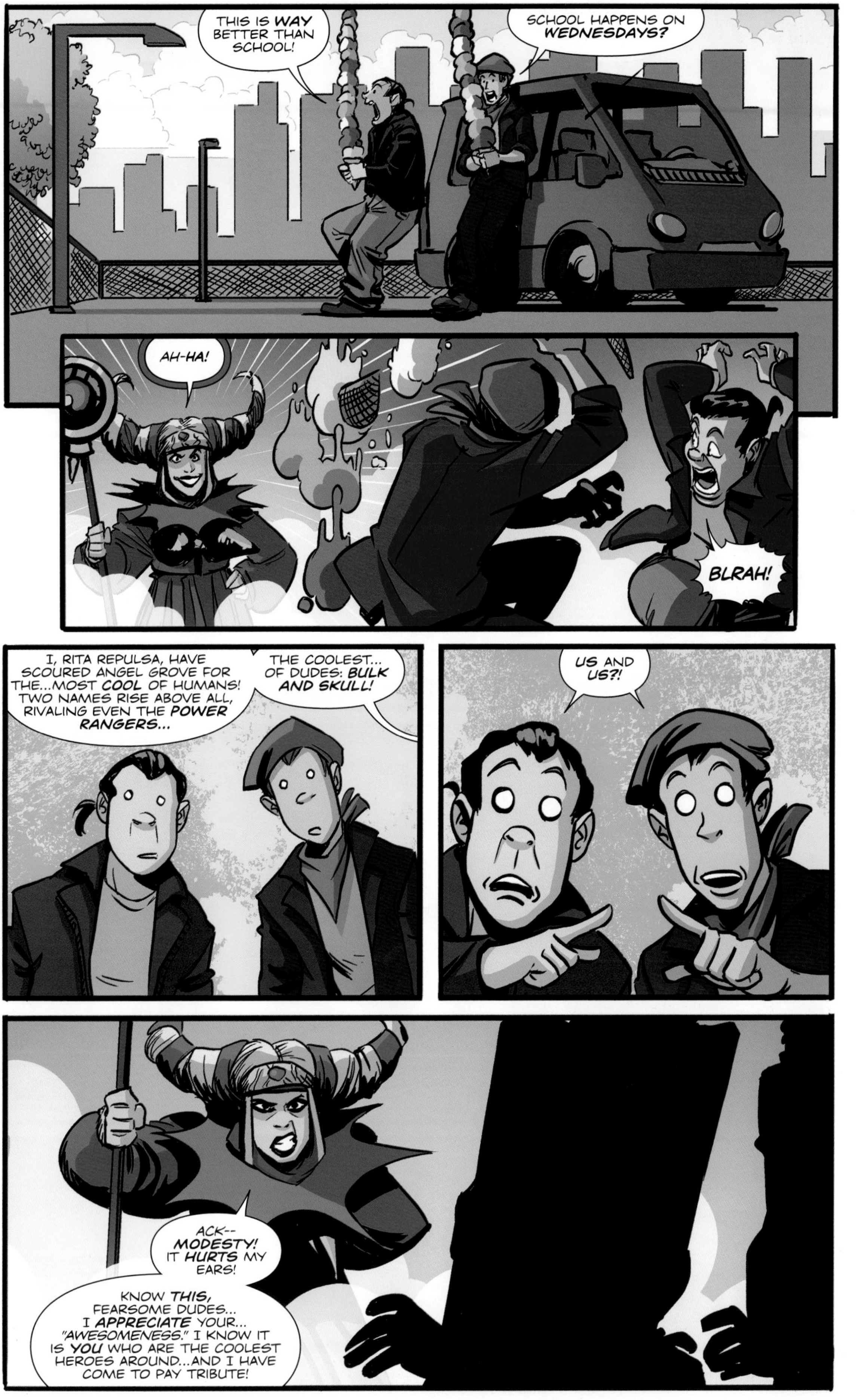
THIS IS WAY BETTER THAN SCHOOL!
SCHOOL HAPPENS ON WEDNESDAYS?
AH-HA!
BLRAH!
I, RITA REPULSA, HAVE SCOURED ANGEL GROVE FOR THE...MOST COOL OF HUMANS! TWO NAMES RISE ABOVE ALL, RIVALING EVEN THE POWER RANGERS...
THE COOLEST... OF DUDES: BULK AND SKULL!
US AND US?!
ACK-- MODESTY! IT HURTS MY EARS!
KNOW THIS, FEARSOME DUDES... I APPRECIATE YOUR... "AWESOMENESS." I KNOW IT IS YOU WHO ARE THE COOLEST HEROES AROUND...AND I HAVE COME TO PAY TRIBUTE!

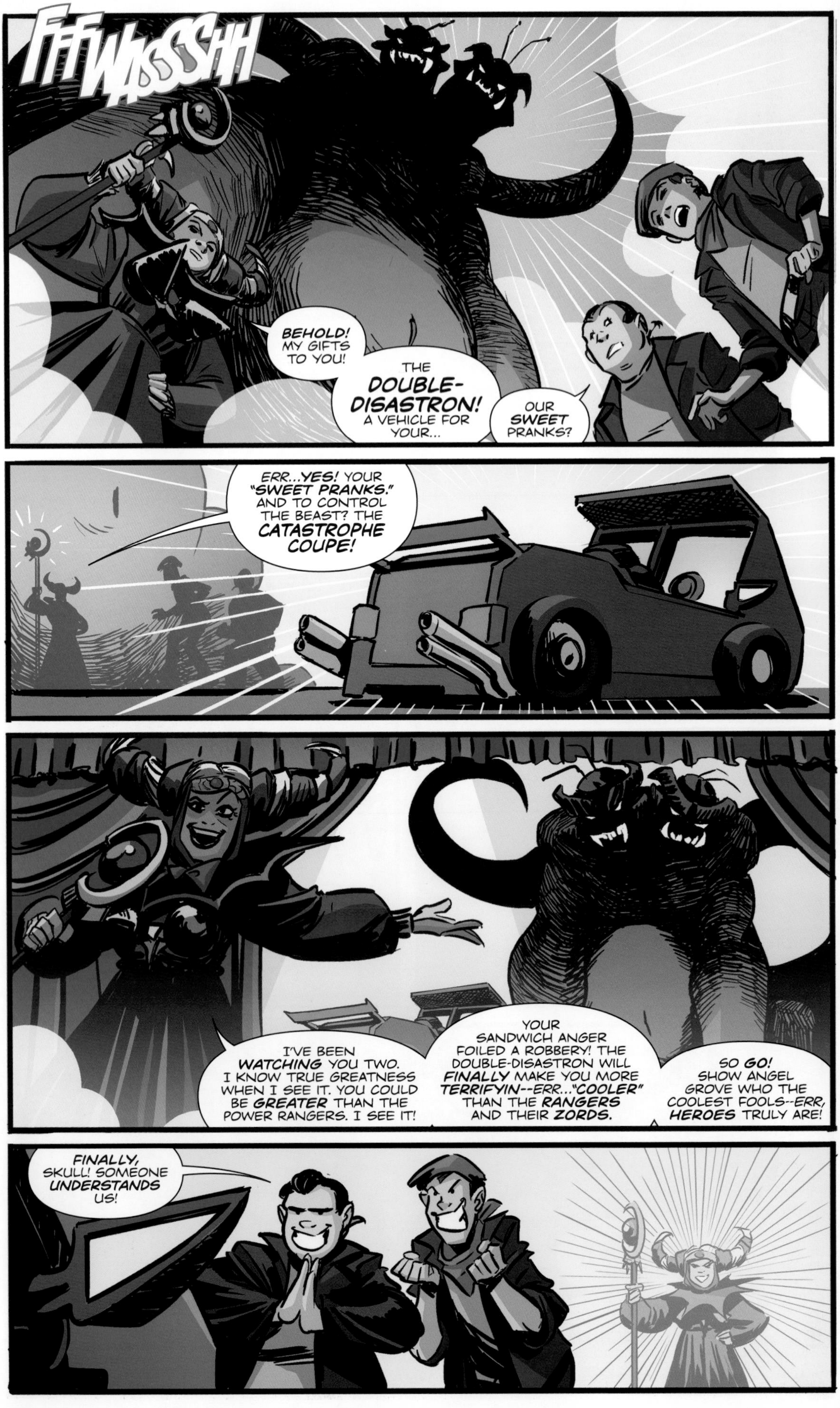
FFFWASSSHH
BEHOLD! MY GIFTS TO YOU!
THE DOUBLE-DISASTRON! A VEHICLE FOR YOUR...
OUR SWEET PRANKS?
ERR...YES! YOUR "SWEET PRANKS." AND TO CONTROL THE BEAST? THE CATASTROPHE COUPE!
I'VE BEEN WATCHING YOU TWO. I KNOW TRUE GREATNESS WHEN I SEE IT. YOU COULD BE GREATER THAN THE POWER RANGERS. I SEE IT!
YOUR SANDWICH ANGER FOILED A ROBBERY! THE DOUBLE-DISASTRON WILL FINALLY MAKE YOU MORE TERRIFYIN--ERR..."COOLER" THAN THE RANGERS AND THEIR ZORDS.
SO GO! SHOW ANGEL GROVE WHO THE COOLEST FOOLS--ERR, HEROES TRULY ARE!
FINALLY, SKULL! SOMEONE UNDERSTANDS US!

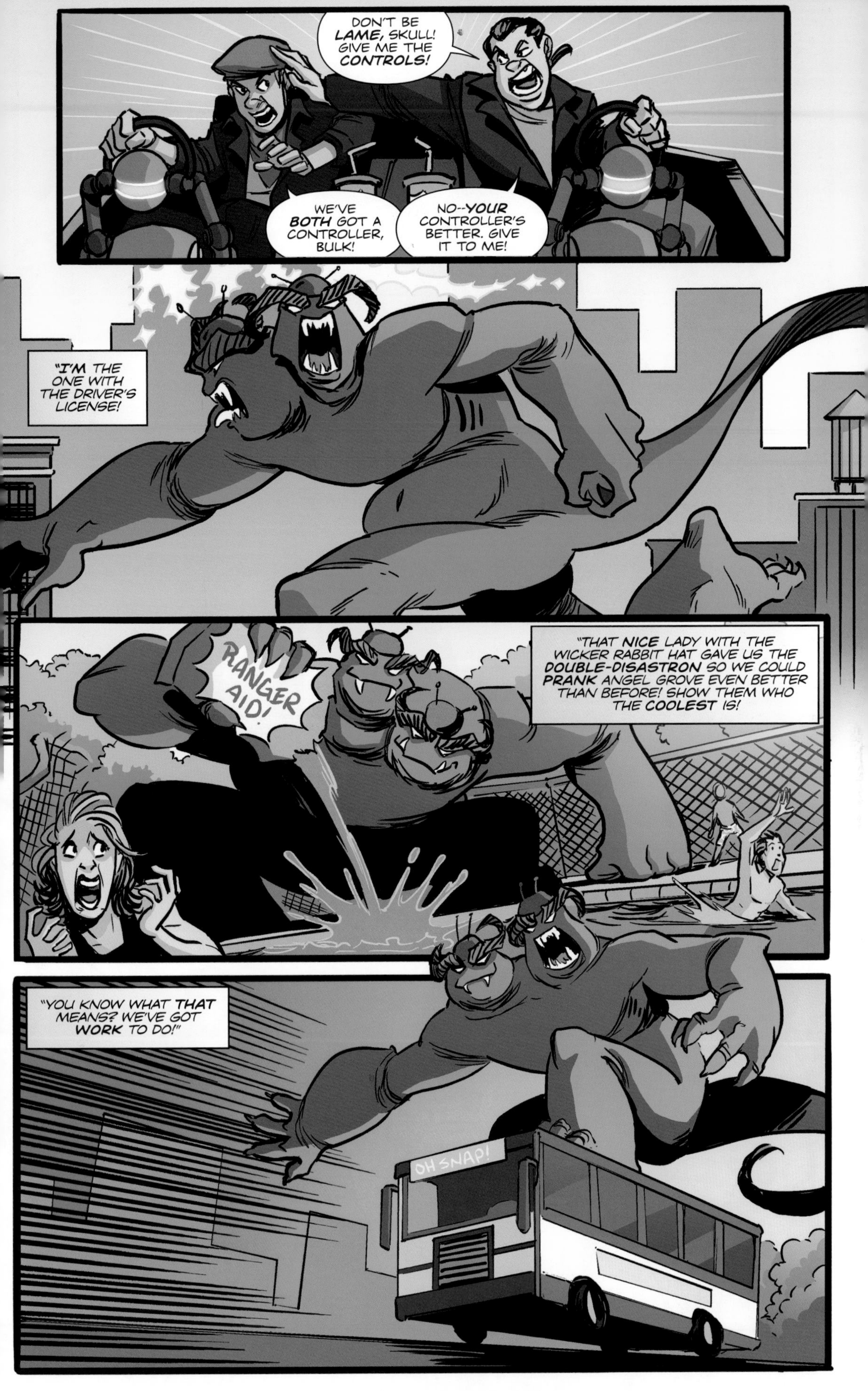
DON'T BE LAME, SKULL! GIVE ME THE CONTROLS!
WE'VE BOTH GOT A CONTROLLER, BULK!
NO--YOUR CONTROLLER'S BETTER. GIVE IT TO ME!
"I'M THE ONE WITH THE DRIVER'S LICENSE!
RANGER AID!
"THAT NICE LADY WITH THE WICKER RABBIT HAT GAVE US THE DOUBLE-DISASTRON SO WE COULD PRANK ANGEL GROVE EVEN BETTER THAN BEFORE! SHOW THEM WHO THE COOLEST IS!
"YOU KNOW WHAT THAT MEANS? WE'VE GOT WORK TO DO!"
OH SNAP!

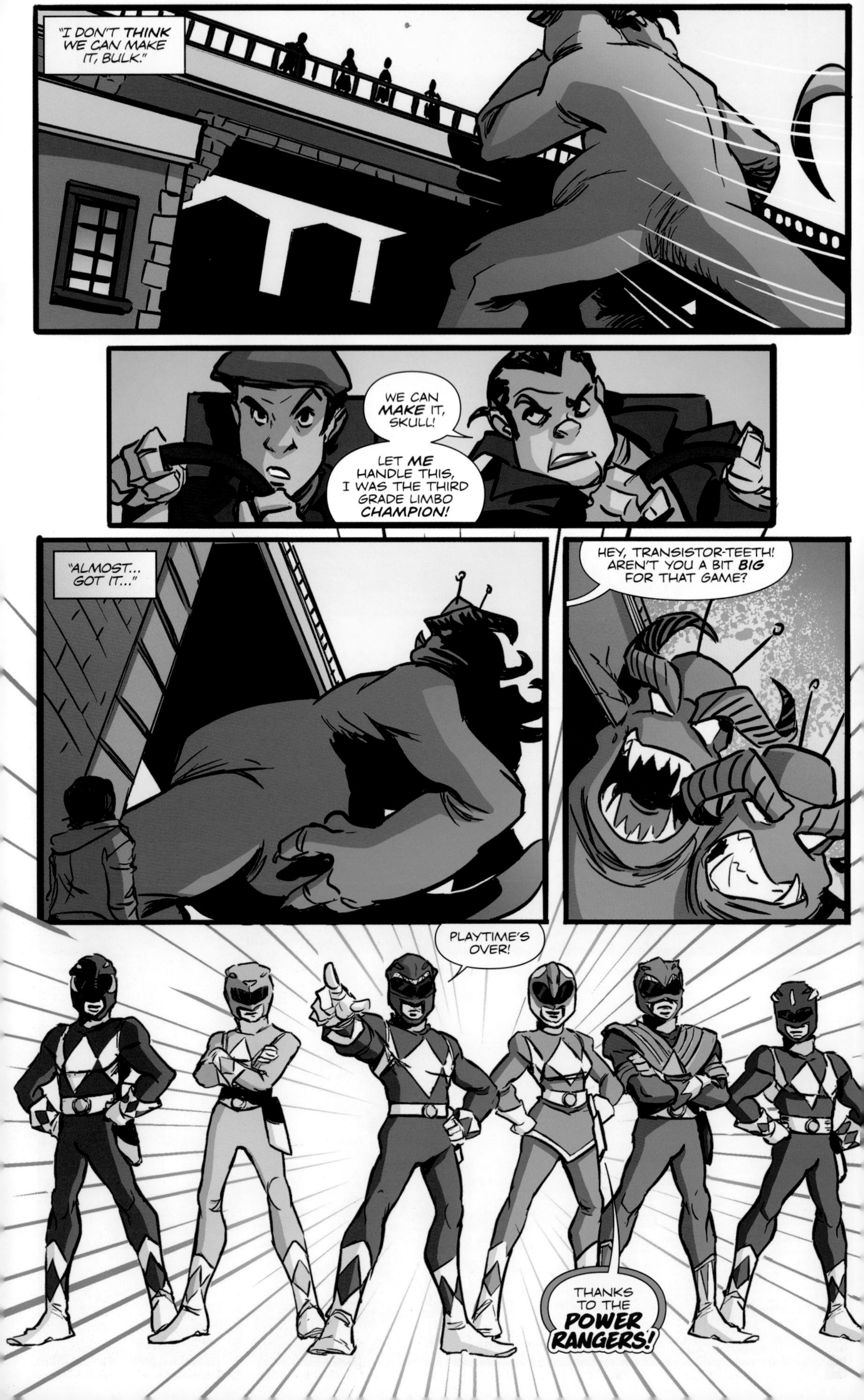
"I DON'T THINK WE CAN MAKE IT, BULK."
WE CAN MAKE IT, SKULL!
LET ME HANDLE THIS, I WAS THE THIRD GRADE LIMBO CHAMPION!
"ALMOST... GOT IT..."
HEY, TRANSISTOR-TEETH! AREN'T YOU A BIT BIG FOR THAT GAME?
PLAYTIME'S OVER!
THANKS TO THE POWER RANGERS!

HEY! LOOK WHO IT IS! AND THEY DON'T LOOK HAPPY!
I KNOW WHO IT IS! I GUESS THE RANGERS STILL CAN'T TELL WHEN THE REAL HEROES HAVE ARRIVED.
WHAT DO WE DO?
I'LL THINK OF SOMETHING!
...DID THAT THING JUST SAY "THE REAL HEROES HAVE ARRIVED?" THAT SOUNDS FAMILIAR...
GIVE IT HERE! I KNOW WHAT TO DO!
YOU HAD A TURN! LET ME TRY!
NO WAY! IF ANYONE'S GOING TO GET US OUT OF THIS IT'S ME!
BONK!
IT'S MY TURN!
IT'S MINE!
LET ME TRY FOR ONCE!
YOU ALREADY TRIED!
BUT IT'S MY TURN!
MINE!

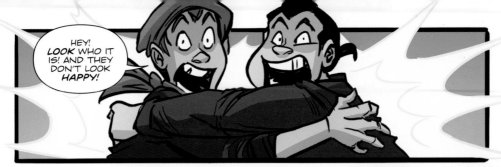

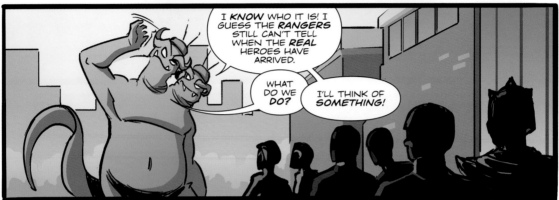

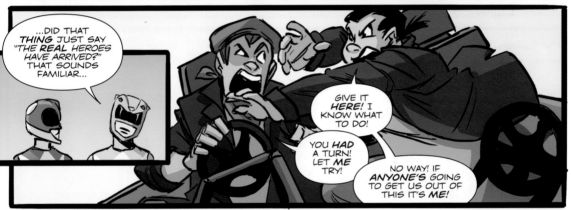

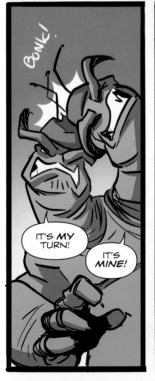

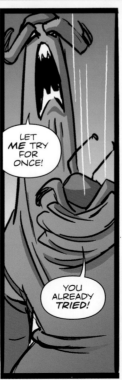

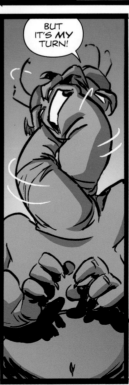

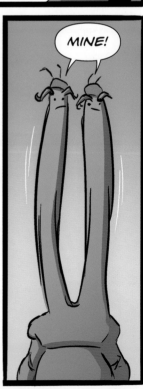

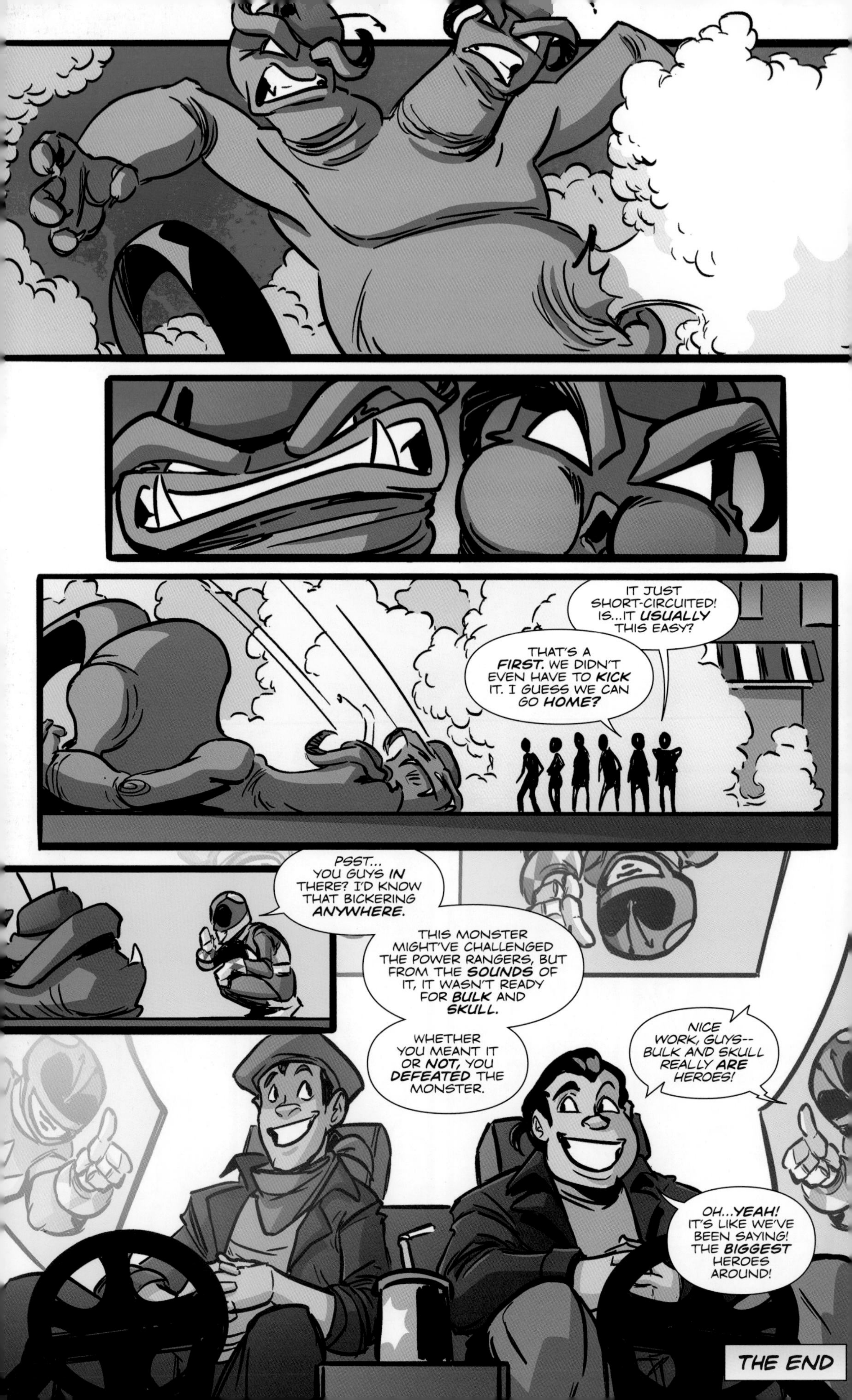

IT JUST SHORT-CIRCUITED! IS...IT USUALLY THIS EASY?
THAT'S A FIRST. WE DIDN'T EVEN HAVE TO KICK IT. I GUESS WE CAN GO HOME?
PSST... YOU GUYS IN THERE? I'D KNOW THAT BICKERING ANYWHERE.
THIS MONSTER MIGHT'VE CHALLENGED THE POWER RANGERS, BUT FROM THE SOUNDS OF IT, IT WASN'T READY FOR BULK AND SKULL.
WHETHER YOU MEANT IT OR NOT, YOU DEFEATED THE MONSTER.
NICE WORK, GUYS-- BULK AND SKULL REALLY ARE HEROES!
OH...YEAH! IT'S LIKE WE'VE BEEN SAYING! THE BIGGEST HEROES AROUND!
THE END

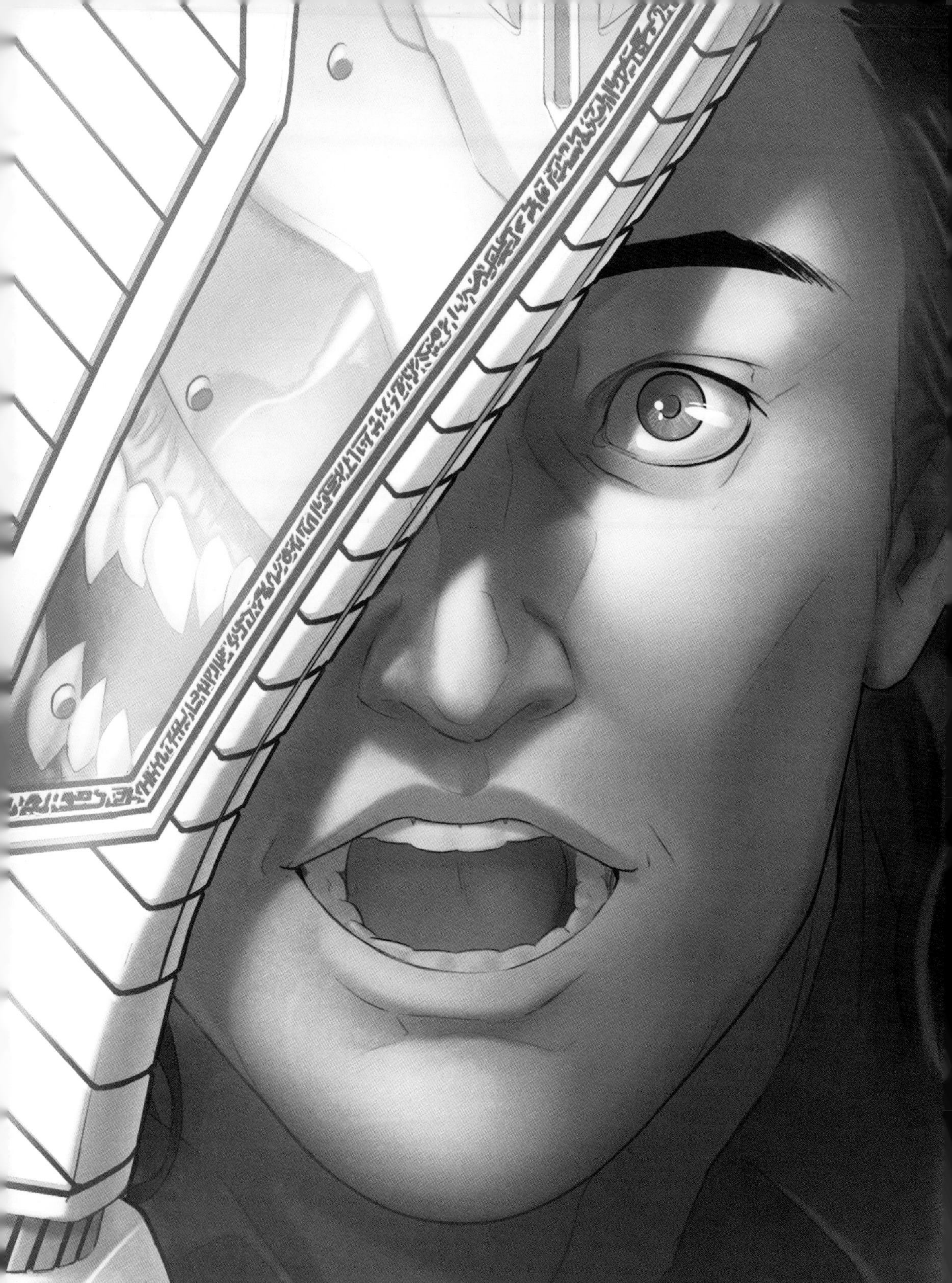

COVER GALLERY

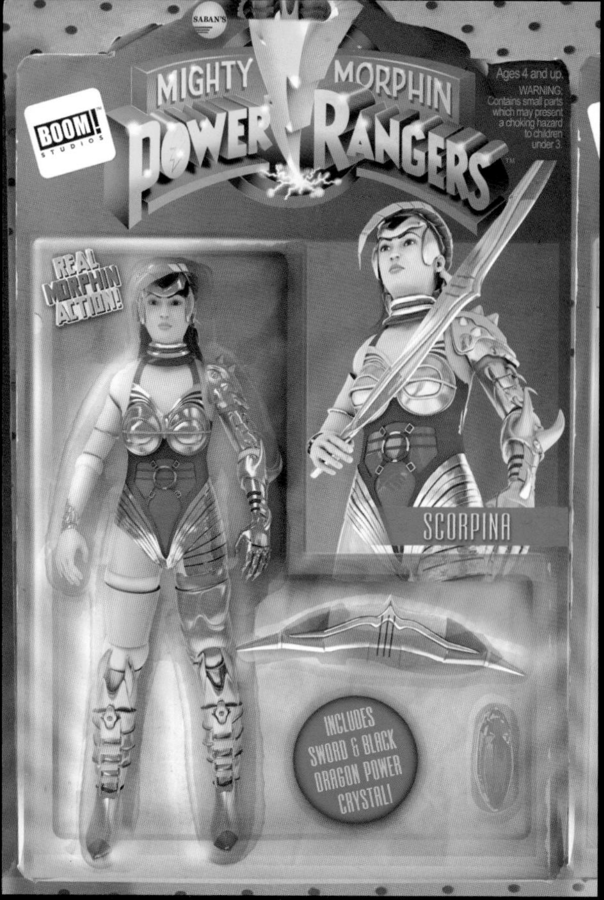
SABAN'S
MIGHTY MORPHIN
POWER RANGERS
BOOM! STUDIOS
Ages 4 and up.
WARNING:
Contains small parts
which may present
a choking hazard
to children
under 3.
REAL MORPHIN ACTION!
SCORPINA
INCLUDES SWORD & BLACK DRAGON POWER CRYSTAL!

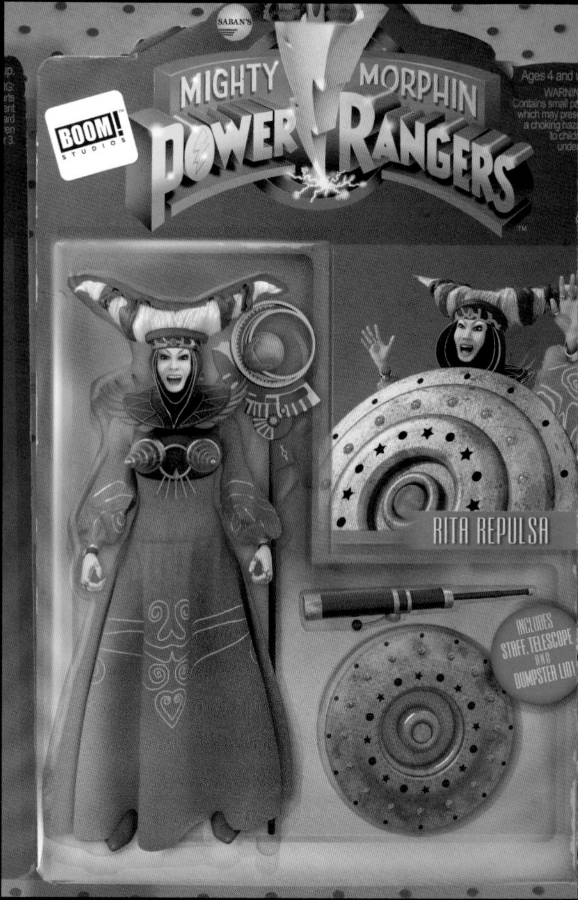
SABAN'S
MIGHTY MORPHIN
POWER RANGERS
BOOM! STUDIOS
RITA REPULSA
INCLUDES STAFF, TELESCOPE AND DUMPSTER LID!

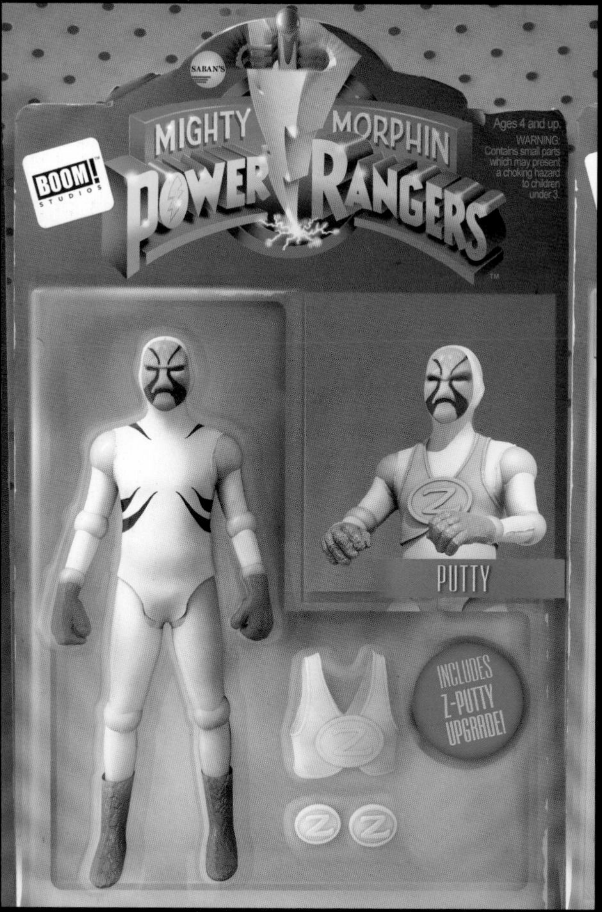
SABAN'S
MIGHTY MORPHIN
POWER RANGERS
BOOM! STUDIOS
Ages 4 and up.
WARNING:
Contains small parts
which may present
a choking hazard
to children
under 3.
PUTTY
INCLUDES Z-PUTTY UPGRADE!

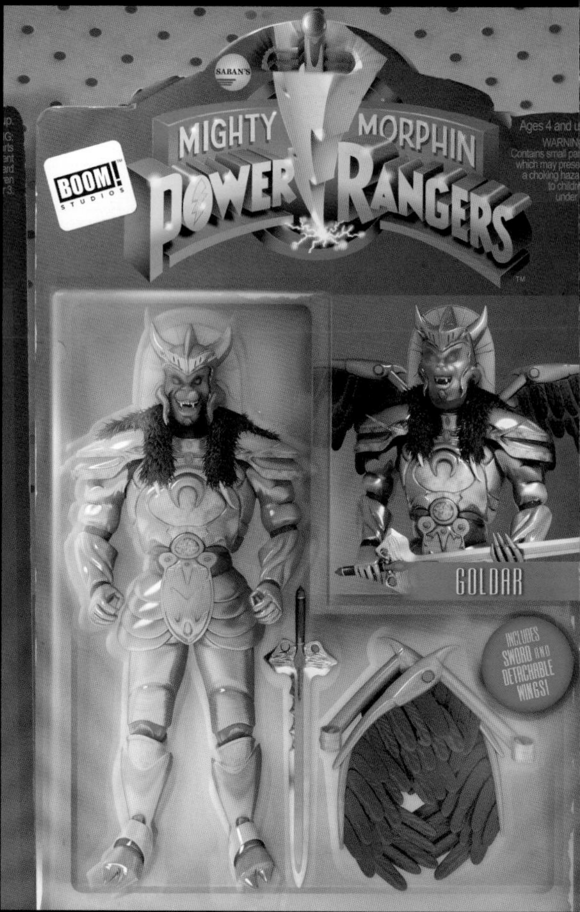
SABAN'S
MIGHTY MORPHIN
POWER RANGERS
BOOM! STUDIOS
GOLDAR
INCLUDES SWORD AND DETACHABLE WINGS!

TELMOS SANTOS WITH PACKAGING DESIGN BY **DAVID RYAN ROBINSON**
ISSUES NINE-TWELVE ACTION FIGURE VARIANT COVERS

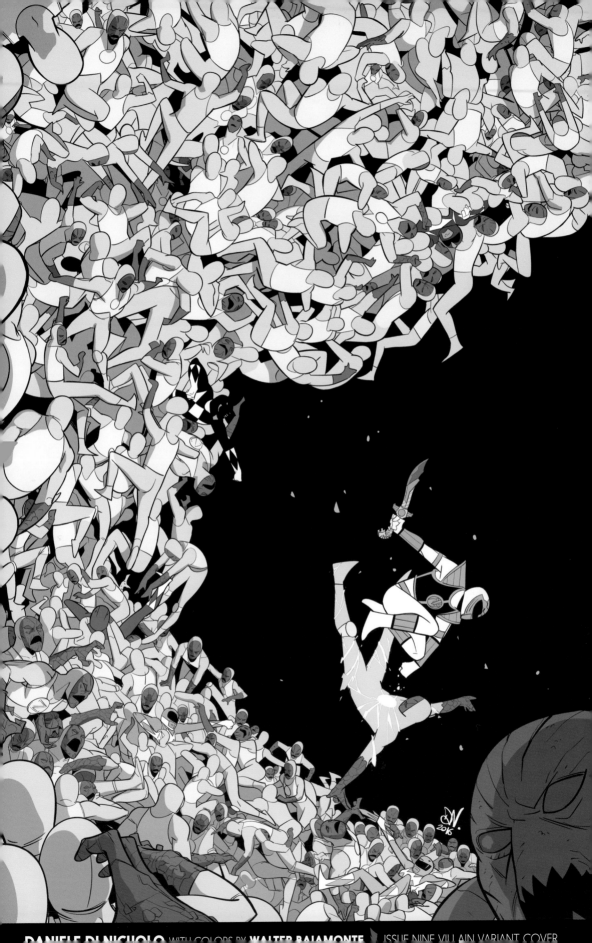

DANIELE DI NICUOLO WITH COLORS BY **WALTER BAIAMONTE** ISSUE NINE VILLAIN VARIANT COVER

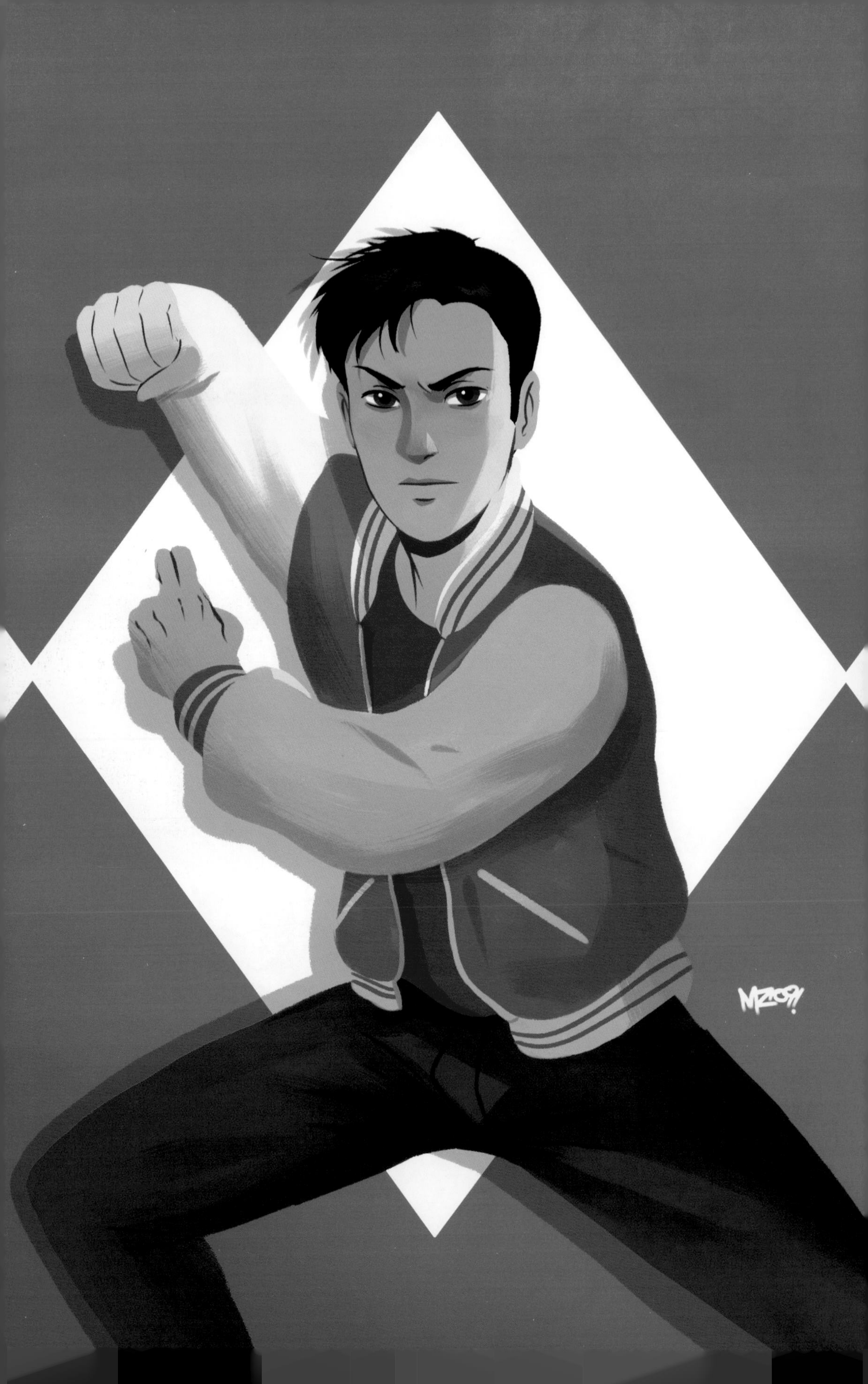

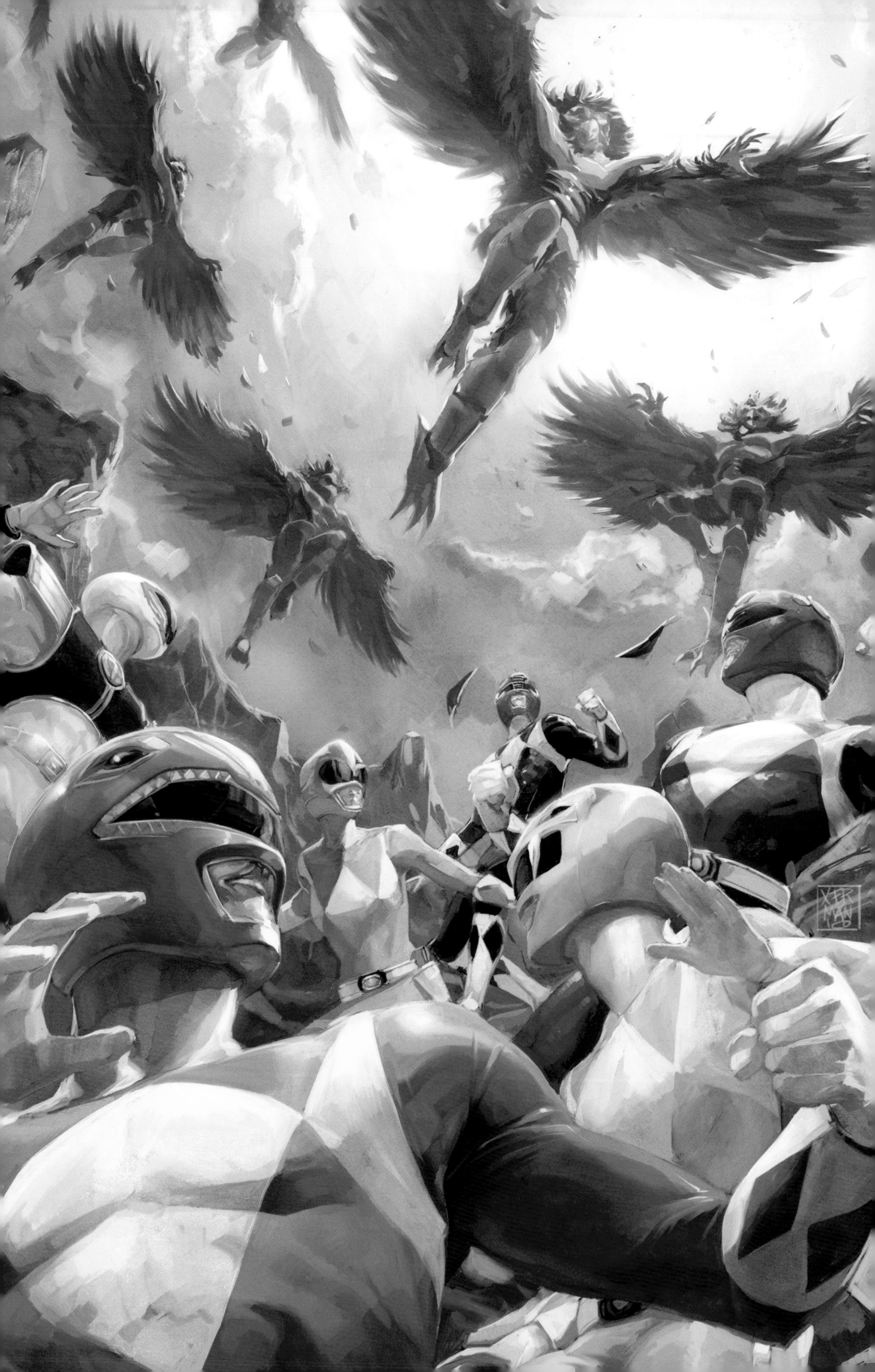

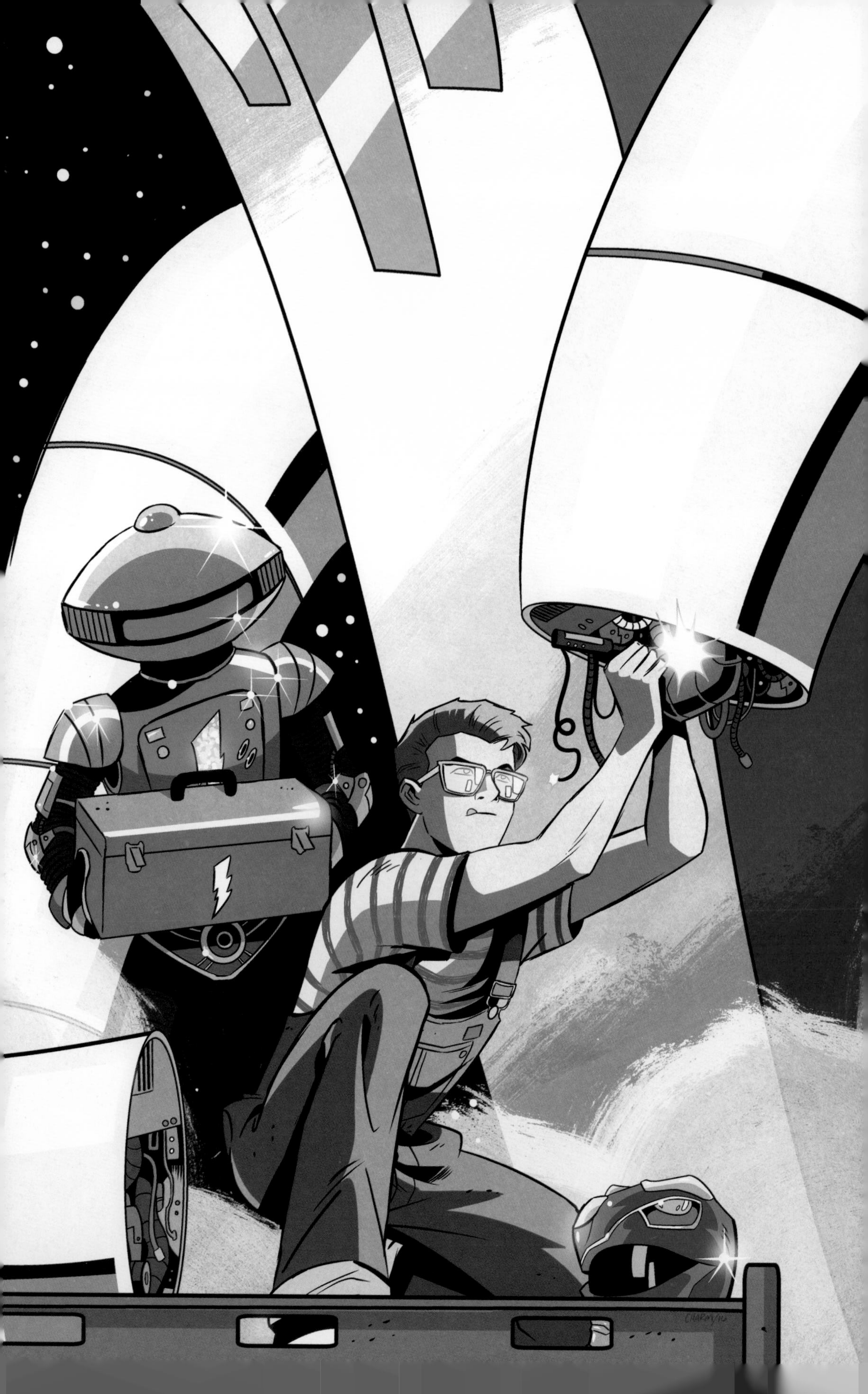

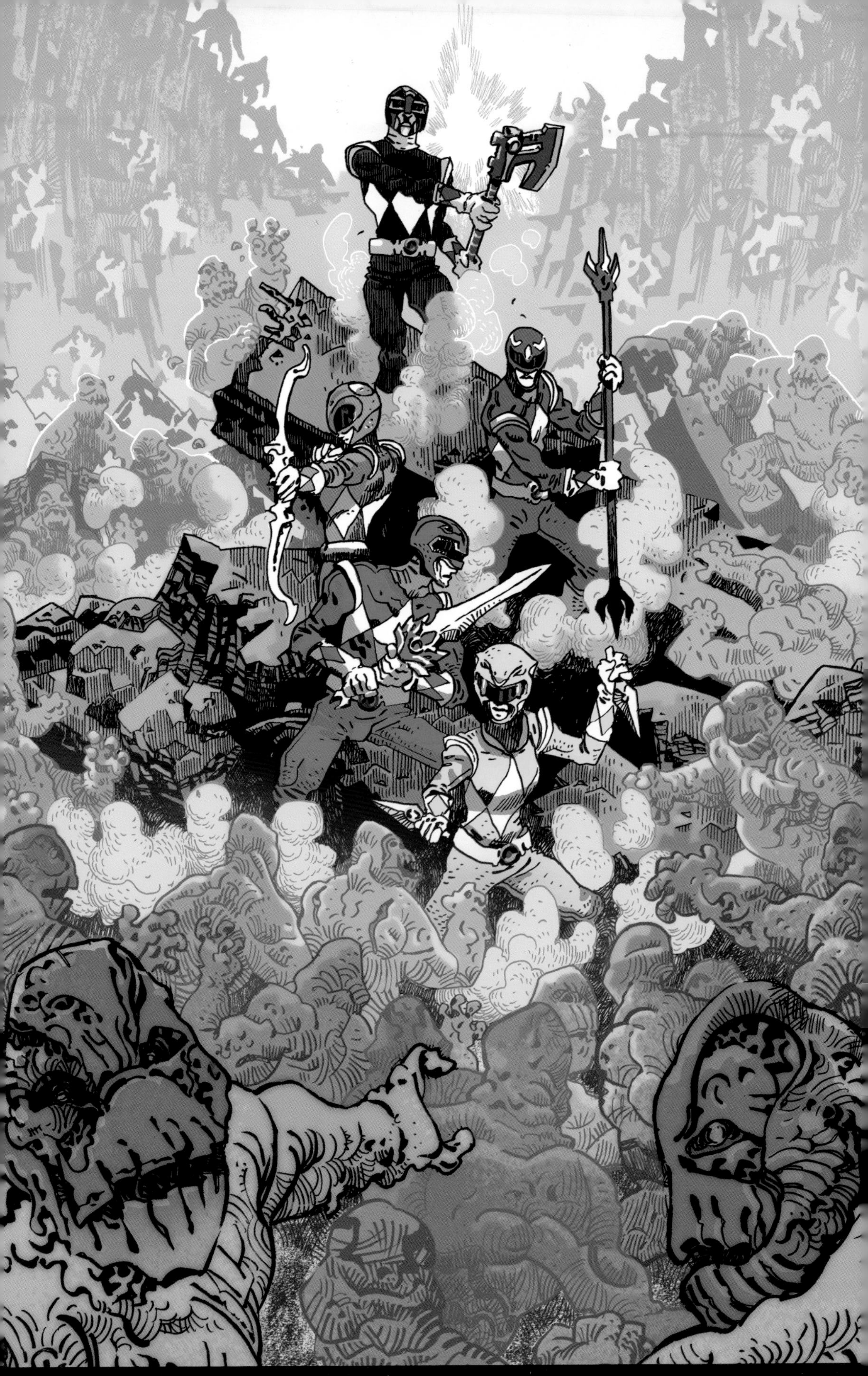

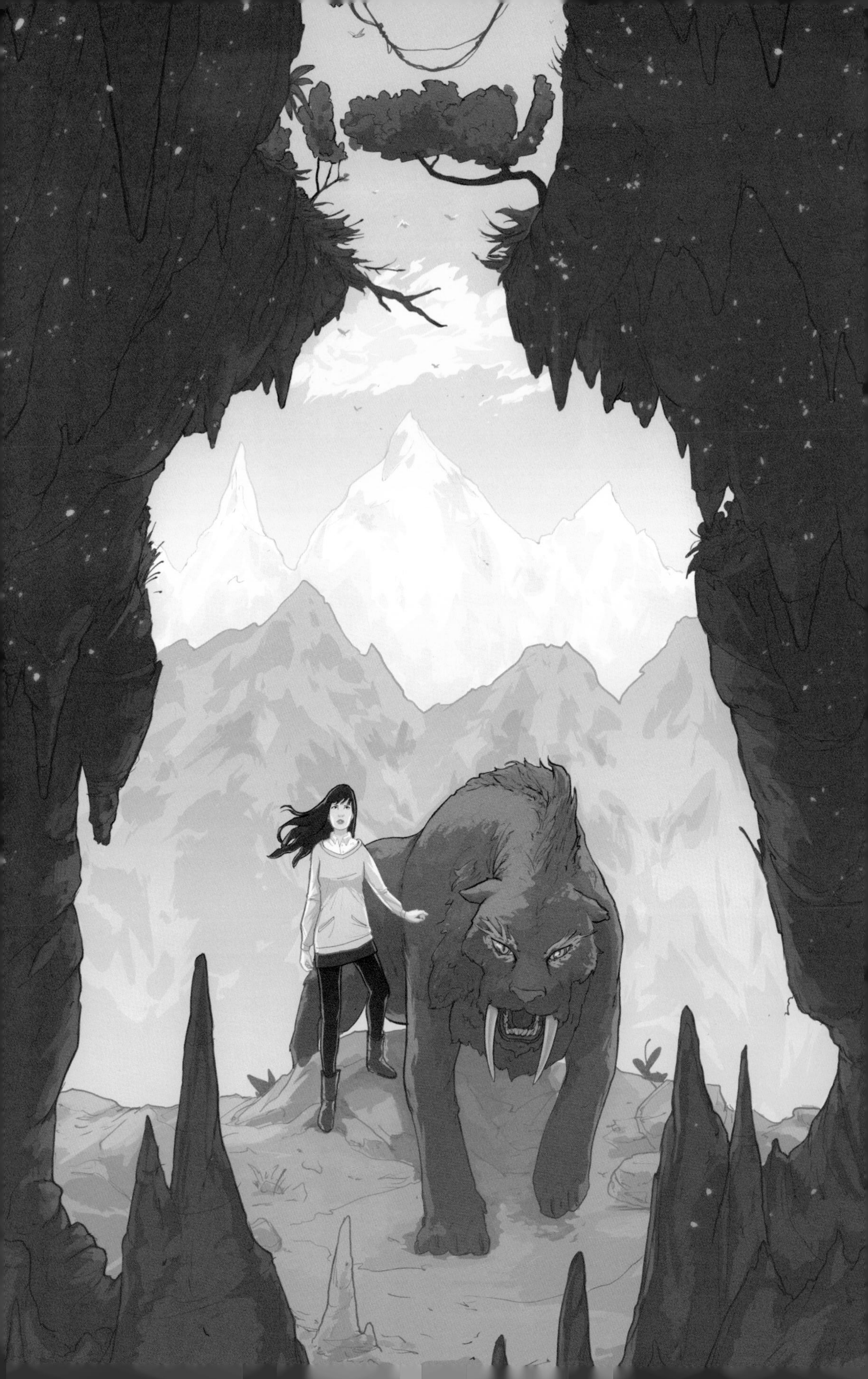

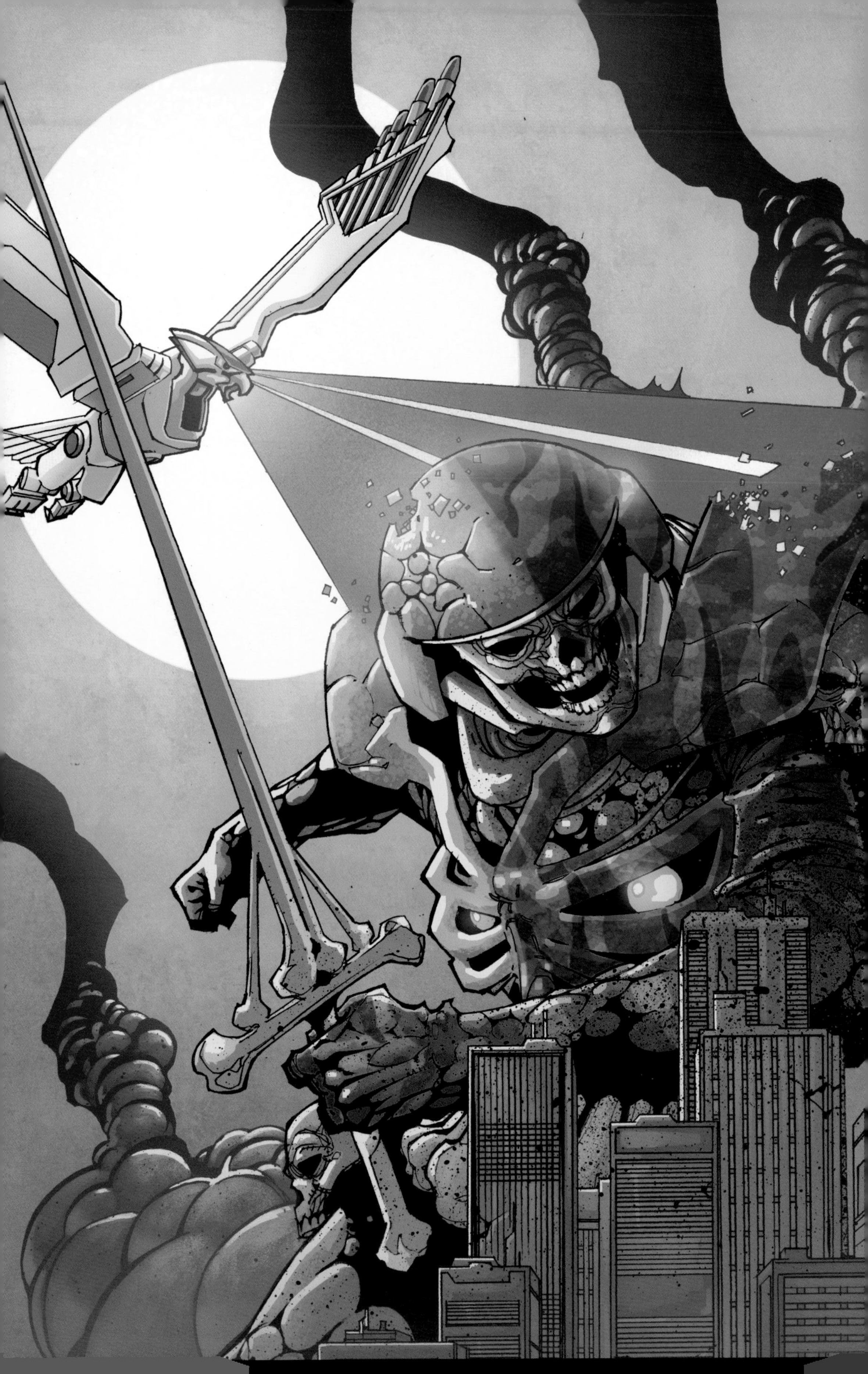

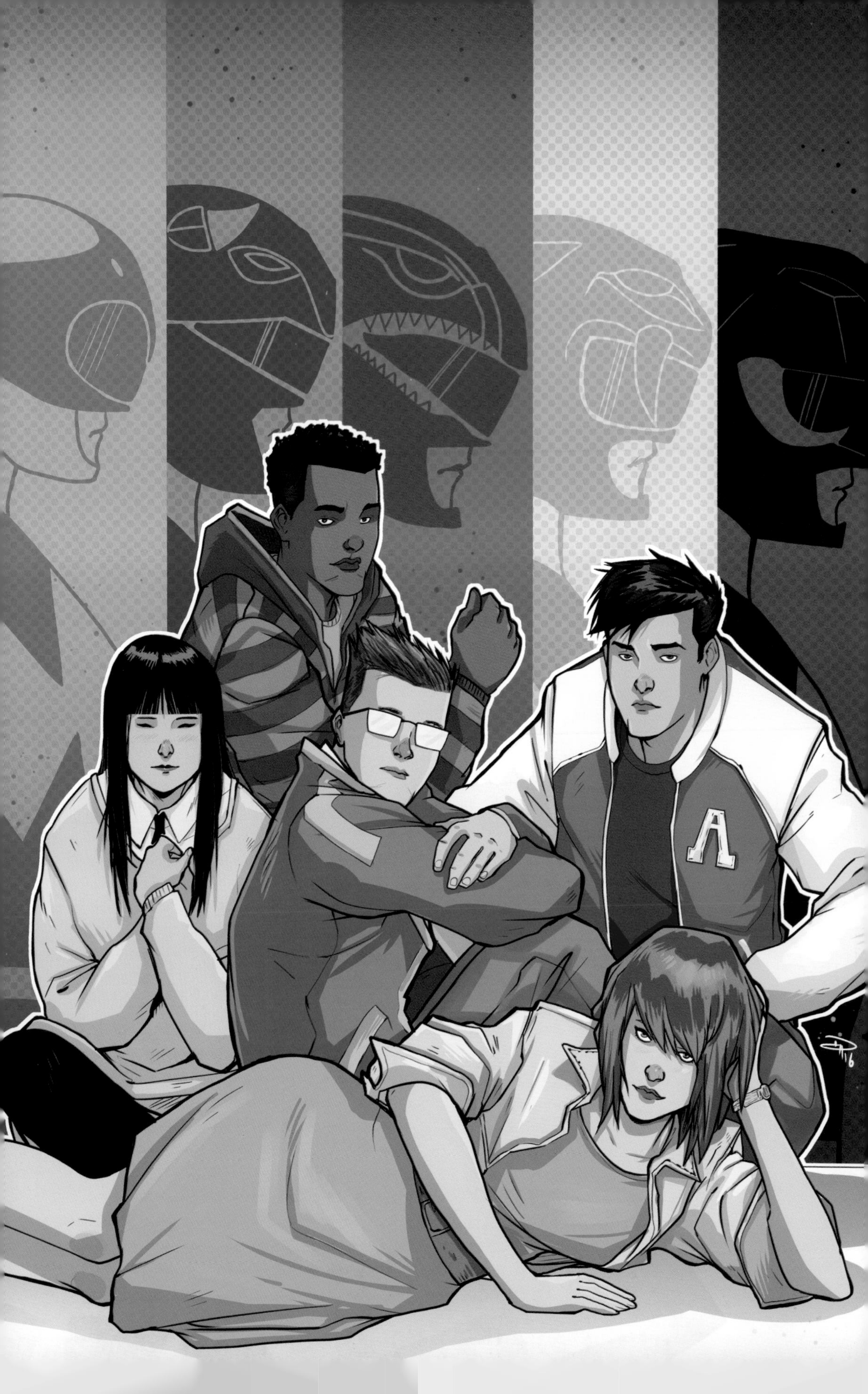

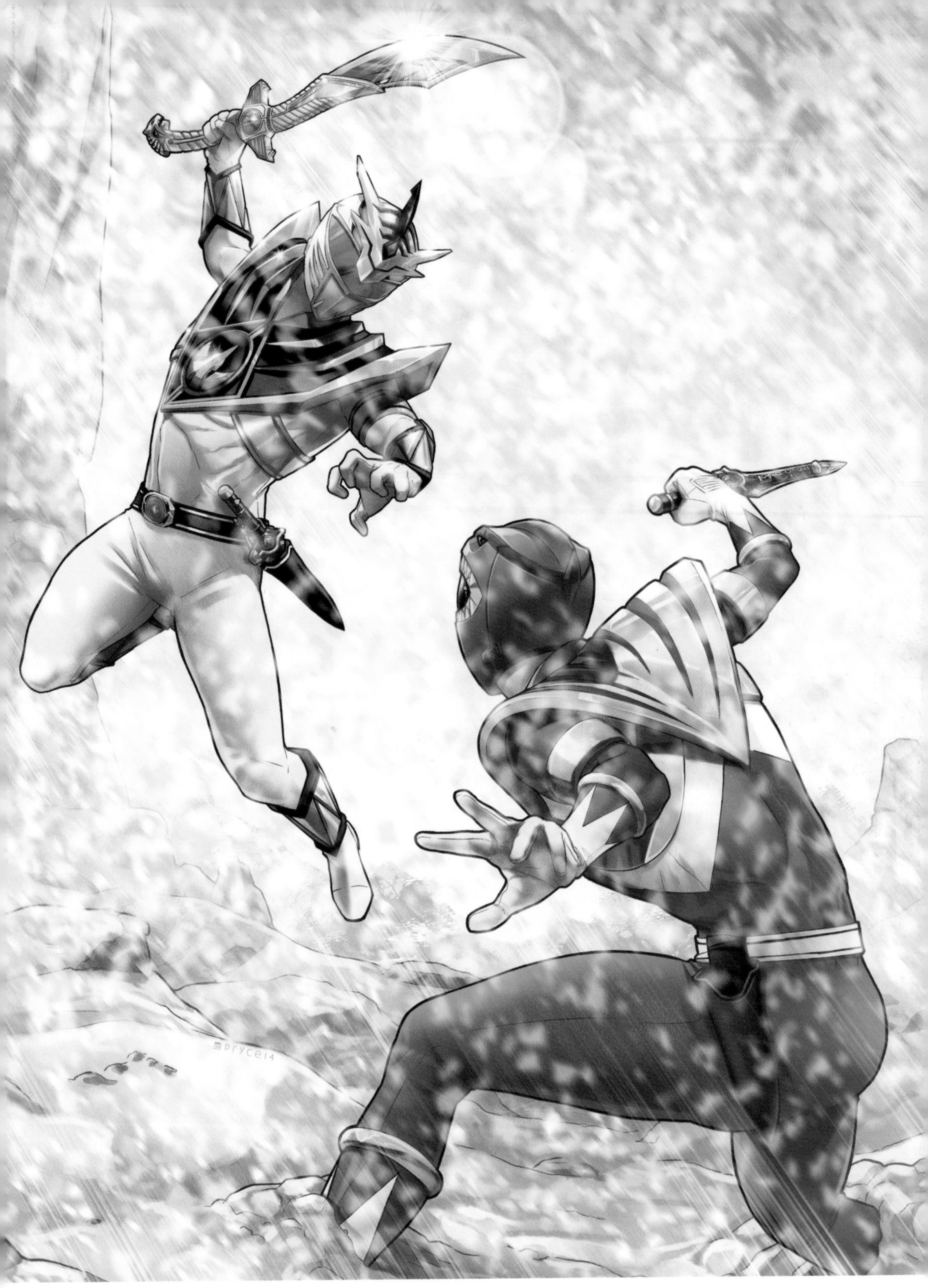
pryce14

VOLUME FOUR
COMING IN 2017

DISCOVER
VISIONARY CREATORS

THE
WOODS
JAMES TYNION IV • MICHAEL DIALYNAS
VOL. 1
THE ARROW

"The Spire is fantastic! My kind of genre free-for-all."
—BRIAN K. VAUGHAN (Saga)
THE
SPIRE
SIMON SPURRIER
JEFF STOKELY
ANDRÉ MAY
NOMINEE

MARK WAID • PETER KRAUSE
IRREDEEMABLE
AFTERWORD BY
GRANT MORRISON

J.G.
JONES
MARK
WAID
STRANGE
FRUIT
Foreword by
ELVIS MITCHELL

MICHAEL ALAN NELSON
DAN MORA
GABRIEL CASSATA
HEXED
THE HARLOT & THE THIEF VOLUME ONE

ABNETT & CULBARD
WILD'S
END
FIRST LIGHT
"IT'S REALLY GREAT!"
JEFF LEMIRE

AVAILABLE AT YOUR LOCAL COMICS SHOP AND BOOKSTORE

To find a comics shop in your area, call 1-888-266-4226

WWW.**BOOM-STUDIOS**.COM

James Tynion IV

The Woods

Volume 1
ISBN: 978-1-60886-454-6 | $9.99
Volume 2
ISBN: 978-1-60886-495-9 | $14.99
Volume 3
ISBN: 978-1-60886-773-8 | $14.99

The Backstagers
ISBN: 978-1-60886-993-0 | $29.99

Simon Spurrier

Six-Gun Gorilla
ISBN: 978-1-60886-390-7 | $19.99

The Spire
ISBN: 978-1-60886-913-8 | $29.99

Weavers
ISBN: 978-1-60886-963-3 | $19.99

Mark Waid

Irredeemable

Volume 1
ISBN: 978-1-93450-690-5 | $16.99
Volume 2
ISBN: 978-1-60886-000-5 | $16.99

Incorruptible

Volume 1
ISBN: 978-1-60886-015-9 | $16.99
Volume 2
ISBN: 978-1-60886-028-9 | $16.99

Strange Fruit
ISBN: 978-1-60886-872-8 | $24.99

Michael Alan Nelson

Hexed The Harlot & The Thief

Volume 1
ISBN: 978-1-60886-718-9 | $14.99
Volume 2
ISBN: 978-1-60886-816-2 | $14.99

Day Men

Volume 1
ISBN: 978-1-60886-393-8 | $9.99
Volume 2
ISBN: 978-1-60886-852-0 | $9.99

Dan Abnett

Wild's End

Volume 1: First Light
ISBN: 978-1-60886-735-6 | $19.99
Volume 2: The Enemy Within
ISBN: 978-1-60886-877-3 | $19.99

Hypernaturals

Volume 1
ISBN: 978-1-60886-298-6 | $16.99
Volume 2
ISBN: 978-1-60886-319-8 | $19.99

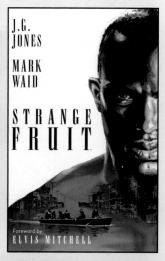